DATE DUE

NO 16 00			
OC 29 00			

DEMCO 38-296

THE PACIFIC ISLAND STATES

Also by Stephen Henningham

FRANCE AND THE SOUTH PACIFIC
A Contemporary History

A GREAT ESTATE AND ITS LANDLORDS IN COLONIAL INDIA
Darbhanga, 1860–1942

PEASANT MOVEMENTS IN COLONIAL INDIA
North Bihar, 1917–1942

RESOURCES, DEVELOPMENT AND POLITICS IN THE PACIFIC
ISLANDS (*edited with R. J. May and Lulu Turner*)

SOUTH PACIFIC SECURITY
Issues and Perspectives (*edited with Desmond Ball*)

The Pacific Island States

Security and Sovereignty in the Post-Cold War World

Stephen Henningham
Senior Research Fellow
Pacific and Asian History Division
Australian National University

321 6XS
and London
Companies and representatives
throughout the world

A catalogue record for this book is available
from the British Library.

ISBN 0-333-63311-3

 First published in the United States of America 1995 by
ST. MARTIN'S PRESS, INC.,
Scholarly and Reference Division,
175 Fifth Avenue,
New York, N.Y. 10010

ISBN 0-312-12513-5

Library of Congress Cataloging-in-Publication Data
Henningham, Stephen, 1950–
The Pacific island states : security and sovereignty in the post
–Cold War world / Stephen Henningham.
p. cm.
Includes bibliographical references and index.
ISBN 0-312-12513-5
1. Oceania. II. Title.
DU17H46   1995
995—dc20   95-14906
                                            CIP

10   9   8   7   6   5   4   3   2   1
04   03   02   01   00   99   98   97   96   95

Printed and bound in Great Britain by
Antony Rowe Ltd, Chippenham, Wiltshire

For Kate, Elizabeth, Patrick, David, Minou and H. Paul

Contents

List of Tables and Maps   viii

Preface   ix

Acknowledgements   xvi

Maps   xvii

1   Introduction: Diversity but Common Interests   1

2   Pacific in Nature as well as Name?   16

3   Beyond 'Whose Sail...on the Horizon':
    Island State Security Perspectives   29

4   Decolonisation, Indigenous Rights and Internal Conflicts   52

5   Environmental, Resource and Nuclear Issues   71

6   External Actors: The Trend to Diversification   91

7   The Limits on Power: Australia and New Zealand
    and the Region   114

8   Intervention Contingencies: A Gap between
    Ends and Means?   137

9   Conclusion: An Uncertain Future   148

Notes and References   152

Select Bibliography   163

Index   168

List of Tables and Maps

Table

1.1	Member states of the South Pacific Forum – basic data	2
1.2	Decolonisation in the Pacific islands region	3
1.3	Entities of 'American' Micronesia – basic data	11
1.4	Entities of Melanesia and Fiji – basic data	12
1.5	Entities of Polynesia and 'Commonwealth' Micronesia – basic data	13
6.1	Pacific islands region – external connections, 1994	92

Maps

1	The Pacific islands in their Asia–Pacific setting	xvii
2	The Pacific islands: Micronesia, Polynesia and Melanesia	xviii
3	The Pacific islands – Exclusive Economic Zones	xix
4	Three security and defence sub-regions: 'American' Micronesia, Melanesia and Fiji, and Polynesia and 'Commonwealth' Micronesia	xx
5	The Pacific island states – troubled border zones and disputed maritime areas	xxi
6	French Polynesia – the French nuclear testing sites	xxii
7	The treaty area of the South Pacific Nuclear Free Zone	xxiii

Preface

The Pacific islands region was one of the last parts of the world to be decolonised. From 1962 however, beginning with Western Samoa, fourteen small states emerged. These new states maintained close connections with the Western nations. In contrast to some other regions of the developing world, constitutional and more or less democratic forms of government have mostly been present. During the Cold War era, tendencies to 'non-alignment' were muted. Soviet overtures to the island states were in most instances rebuffed, especially following the invasion of Afghanistan in December 1979.

But in the mid- and late 1980s, the region became more unsettled. The key developments included the following. The conflict in New Caledonia between the Kanak nationalist movement and its opponents erupted in violence; the United States/New Zealand leg of the ANZUS (Australia–New Zealand–United States) treaty relationship ceased to operate; two coups took place in Fiji in 1987, ending what had been presented as an example of multiracial and democratic harmony; the constitutional arrangements established at the time of independence came under question in several other states; French agents blew up the Greenpeace vessel *Rainbow Warrior* in Auckland harbour, causing one death; and external powers with no traditional links with the region – including the (then) Soviet Union and Libya – showed heightened interest.

Meanwhile the predominance formerly exercised in much of the region by Australia and New Zealand was reduced by their other concerns, by increased assertiveness on the part of the island states, and by increased attention to these states by the United States, France, Japan and other powers. In addition a major revolt erupted on Bougainville island in the North Solomons province of Papua New Guinea, and the economic problems of several island states worsened.

Then, by around 1990, changes in the wider world, especially the end of the Cold War and the increasing economic dynamism of Northeast and Southeast Asia, embodied new challenges. Henceforth the island states were obliged to respond to the implications of the end of superpower rivalry, of increasing multipolarity, of the enhanced influence of international and regional organisations and of international law, and of the greater emphasis on economic issues in international affairs.

As a result of these various changes, the Pacific islands region ceased to be a place apart. The region had become less insulated from the wider world. And its similarities to some other parts of the developing world had become both more pronounced and more evident. Nowadays the Pacific islands are very subject to the waves of change. Environmentally, the very existence of some of them may be threatened by global warming. Economically, their chronic problems mostly imply continued dependence. Politically and constitutionally, they are seeking to merge new institutions and ideas with old customs and values. And strategically, they are no longer subject to the 'strategic denial' umbrella of the Cold War era and are increasingly open to ripple effects from trends and developments in Northeast Asia, Southeast Asia and the wider world. Meanwhile, with the end of the Cold War era, the strategic importance of the Pacific islands region in the wider Asia–Pacific context, which had already been modest, rapidly dwindled, helping reduce the interest and involvement of the United States and the United Kingdom. Many of these changes were inevitable. Some were for the better. The overall outcome, however, is that the region has become more politically complex and in some respects more potentially volatile.

This book is a study of security and defence issues and trends in the Pacific islands region, and of the challenges which the Pacific island states face to their security and sovereignty. In recent years, largely in response to the conflicts and tensions evident in the 1980s, numerous articles and several collections have been published dealing with various aspects of the security of the region. This volume is, however, among the first more extended examinations of the subject by a single author. It is also perhaps the first lengthy study which seeks to take account of post-Cold War circumstances.

I give particular attention to political and military issues and trends. I do, however, interpret the concept of security broadly, and thus include some consideration of environmental, economic and other general aspects of the defence of the national interests of the island states. Yet I avoid stretching the elastic concept of security so far as to render it so comprehensive as to be useless. In particular, I do not concern myself with matters of primarily internal concern in the island states, except insofar as they have wider implications for the security of the state concerned, including with respect to its relations with its neighbours, or have become items on the regional security agenda.

My emphasis is on trends and issues over the last decade, and on prospects over the next. In what is a broad-ranging study, intended for both a general and an academic readership, I have generally sought to keep detail to a necessary minimum. But I have chosen to consider in greater depth three topics which have attracted special attention from policy-makers and commentators, both in the island states and elsewhere. These topics are: French nuclear testing and related nuclear issues (Chapter 5), the role of Australia and New Zealand in the region (Chapter 7), and military and paramilitary intervention in the states of the region (Chapter 8).

I focus on the governments of the Pacific island states as central actors in the international affairs of the region. This approach is especially relevant with respect to the Pacific island states, in part because of the general lack in most of them of domestic awareness of, and interest in, external affairs. In addition most of them lack powerful business and other domestic interests and lobbies operating independently of government. But I have sought to ensure that my approach is also informed by an awareness of the importance of non-government actors, interests and influences, both domestic and transnational.

My standpoint is that of an Australian commentator who has had the opportunity, since 1982, to follow developments in the region closely, first as a public servant and then as an academic. I have endeavoured to understand and describe the attitudes and assessments of island governments and islander commentators, but make no claim to speak on their behalf.

We must of course distinguish between the security perspectives and aims of governments, and the security interests of the populations under their (real or putative) authority. In our world there is sadly no shortage of cases in which the security of a government is maintained at the cost of the security interests, broadly defined, of all or part of the population concerned. Fortunately, examples of this phenomenon in the Pacific islands region have been infrequent. But this tension does exist, especially because the structures and systems of the modern state are a recent imposition on the many and varied societies of the region. In Fiji following the military coups in 1987, which protected established interests and asserted indigenous Fijian primacy, the security of the non-Fijian section of the population was in some respects diminished. In Papua New Guinea in the late 1980s and early 1990s, some of the measures employed by government forces to combat the secessionist movement on Bougainville reduced the security, broadly regarded, of local communities on that island.

But consensual traditions are present in several island societies, while more or less democratic forms of government are to be found throughout most of the region. Accordingly, we can assume, for the purposes of this study, the existence of a reasonably broad area of commonality between the security concerns of island governments and those of the populations under their administration.

In this book I use the term 'the Pacific islands region', conceived as a broad strategic and political zone, to refer to the island states and territories and the intervening ocean in a vast area. This predominantly maritime zone is bounded by but also includes Kiribati and the various entities of 'American' Micronesia to the north, the island of New Guinea to the west, and French Polynesia to the east. To the south it is bounded by, but does not include, New Zealand. Its component states and territories have a population which numbers, including the inhabitants of Irian Jaya, some eight million.

My main concern is with the island states, but I also give some attention to the dependent territories in the region. I generally differentiate between the island states and the island territories, but in some instances use the term 'entities' to refer to both the states and/or the territories as a group. I have avoided the term 'South Pacific', because in some usages it is inclusive of New Zealand, and because it is at times used to refer only to those island states and territories south of the equator, excluding those to the north.

Though extensive, the Pacific islands region as defined above is less all-inclusive than the concept of Oceania. I have chosen not to use the term Oceania, because in its broadest usage this term incorporates all the insular areas between the Americas and Asia. Even in its narrower usages, it often refers to Australia and New Zealand as well as to the Pacific islands.

But we should note that there are significant populations of Pacific islanders outside or on the fringes of the Pacific islands region as I have here defined it. They are to be found in New Zealand (or 'Aotearoa,' to give it its Maori name), the Hawaiian islands and Easter Island, all of which were originally settled by Polynesian peoples, and in the mainly Melanesian islands of the Torres Strait. These entities have, however, become or been incorporated into states dominated by non-Pacific Islanders, respectively New Zealand, the United States, Chile and Australia. New Zealand's Polynesian peoples make up around 12 per cent of the total population and comprise both indigenous Maori and immigrants from other parts of Polynesia. The Polynesian communities in New Zealand have attained significant cultural and social recognition. But in its overall population, values, culture, institutions and economy, New Zealand remains distinct from the island states. In the Hawaiian islands – as happened by the way in most of Australia – the indigenous population has been swamped by immigrants. On Easter Island the population, although mostly Polynesian by descent, numbers only a few thousand. The Torres Strait Islands also have only a small population, and many of these islanders have migrated to the Australian mainland. Some Torres Strait islanders have argued for self-determination and independence, but overall, nationalist and secessionist sentiments have been muted by economic dependence, cultural recognition and increased participation in local self-government. With the important exception of New Zealand, these entities neither play a role in nor have substantial direct relevance to Pacific islands affairs. Accordingly, with the exception of a consideration of New Zealand's role in the region, I do not discuss them except in passing. The same goes for the Pitcairn Islands, a remote British possession to the southeast of French Polynesia with a population of mixed European–Polynesian descent of less than one hundred.

I begin this study with a review of the general features of the Pacific islands region and in particular of the island states (Chapter 1). The Pacific island states and territories are more diverse in history, culture, traditions and present circumstances than outsiders often appreciate. But despite their variety, they are also united in some respects by common experiences, common problems and common interests. Accordingly, they have been able to cooperate with considerable effect in various regional bodies.

I suggest that, from an Australian perspective, the states and territories of the region, and their surrounding ocean areas, may usefully be considered as belonging to one of three sub-regions, with respect to their security and defence characteristics. These sub-regions are: 'American' Micronesia, Melanesia and Fiji, and Polynesia and 'Commonwealth' Micronesia. American Micronesia includes the Micronesian entities presently or formerly under American rule. Melanesia and Fiji includes the three Melanesian states, Fiji and the French territory of New Caledonia, which has a Melanesian indigenous population. Polynesia and Commonwealth Micronesia includes the Polynesian entities and the two Micronesian entities, namely Kiribati and Nauru, which were formerly part of the British imperial system.

I next examine the potential for military conflicts between the states of the region and for the emergence of external military threats (Chapter 2). Overall, despite the presence of bitter conflicts in particular states and territories, and despite intermittent tensions between Indonesia and Papua New Guinea over the activities along their common border of the OPM (*Organisasi Papua Merdeka* – Free Papua Movement), the region seems likely to remain relatively peaceful. This is because of the combination of traditions of cooperation with the absence of external and intra-regional military threats, of border and territorial disputes, of disputes over resources, and of armed forces with offensive capabilities.

I then discuss the security perspectives of the island governments (Chapter 3). In the absence of military threats, and in view of their other problems, these governments have generally employed a broad definition of what national security entails. They regard it as involving environmental, economic and other dimensions additional to more traditional defence and military concerns. In this chapter I also review the role of the South Pacific Forum, the main regional organisation, in fostering security and other cooperation, and in seeking to defend the interests of the island states.

In the following chapters I review several of the key issues and trends relevant to the security and sovereignty of the island states. In Chapter 4, I discuss the way in which the island governments have generally upheld indigenous and local rights and have supported decolonisation. In particular they have focused on the French territory of New Caledonia, where the indigenous Melanesian community – the largest ethnic group in the territory, although in a minority overall – has been campaigning for independence. They have given less attention to the other French Pacific territories, namely French Polynesia and Wallis and Futuna, where pressures for independence have been weak or absent. They have generally accepted continued United States sovereignty over American Samoa, Guam and the Commonwealth of the Northern Mariana Islands, largely because of the absence of independence movements in these entities. They have welcomed the constitutional evolution of the Federated States of Micronesia and the Republic of the Marshall Islands, and more recently Palau, towards a qualified form of sovereign independence. They have mainly chosen not to focus attention on the status of the Indonesian province of Irian Jaya, and on the vexed question of Bougainville in the North Solomons province of Papua New Guinea.

Next I consider nuclear, environmental and resource issues (Chapter 5). The island governments have denounced the French nuclear testing programme in French Polynesia, criticised plans to dump nuclear waste in the region and endorsed the Treaty of Rarotonga, which embodies the South Pacific Nuclear Free Zone. Their stance on nuclear issues reflects the strong concern in the island states over threats to their vulnerable environment. Although the dramatic risks associated with global warming have attracted particular attention, the island governments have also focused on the management of forestry and fishing resources and on the general dangers of waste dumping; and are becoming conscious of the environmental dangers associated with economic development and population growth.

Of course the Pacific island states are subject to a broad range of external pressures and influences. Often they must adjust to circumstances and trends not of their making. Accordingly, I also discuss the interests and activities of external actors in the region (Chapter 6). Until the late 1980s the Western powers pursued a policy of strategic denial, but this policy has been outmoded by the end of the Cold War, by the collapse of the Soviet Union and by the increased interest of the island states in diversifying their external connections. In addition to discussing external states, I also note the role of non-government actors, including business firms, lobby groups, international development bodies and criminal groupings. Next I examine the manner in which, among the Western and associated states, Australia and New Zealand have played a special role in the region because of their proximity, relative scale and historical connections (Chapter 7). Both these states are regarded by the island governments as being closely associated with but not *of* the islands region. In 1971 however they accepted an invitation from the island governments to join the island states as founding members of the South Pacific Forum. I also discuss the question of possible military or paramilitary interventions in the island states by Australia and/or New Zealand, focusing on the risk that their capabilities may not be appropriate to some of the prospective scenarios (Chapter 8).

Finally (Chapter 9), I sum up my findings and consider prospects over the next decade. My main conclusions are as follows. Direct military threats to the island states from outside or within the region are unlikely to increase – except conceivably from Indonesia with respect to Papua New Guinea over OPM activities along their common border. Conversely, continued strong emphasis is likely to be placed on environmental, economic and other 'non-military' challenges to security. The end of the Cold War, despite its obvious benefits, has nonetheless been a mixed blessing for the island states and territories. The attention of aid donors and investors has in some measure been diverted elsewhere. The island states are now less able than some of them were hitherto to attract attention and aid because of their strategic location, or more generally to profit from Western concern that they might respond to overtures from non-Western powers. Declining interest by traditional aid donors may not, in the longer term, be compensated for by assistance from those powers, notably Japan, which in recent years have assumed a somewhat larger role in the region. For its part, Australia in the longer term may be less able and willing to assist than is often assumed.

The island states will face some difficult security and associated problems over the next decade or so. Ultimately, responsibility for grappling with the problems ahead will rest with their governments. These governments will need good leadership and good fortune. They will also need an understanding, by external policy makers and commentators, of the complex circumstances and issues involved. My hope is that this book will contribute to that understanding.

Canberra   STEPHEN HENNINGHAM

Acknowledgements

I am grateful to several people for assistance during the preparation of this book. Julie Gordon and Jude Shanahan of the Pacific and Asian History Division in the Research School of Pacific and Asian Studies (RSPAS) at the Australian National University provided word-processing and other practical assistance with several of the draft chapters. Keith Mitchell, head of the Cartography Unit, RSPAS, drew the maps, with his usual skill and care. My thanks also go to Richard Wright, who prepared the index.

Several friends commented on an earlier draft. I did not in all instances agree with their particular views, but they provided several corrections, and some very helpful perspectives and suggestions. I am indeed most grateful to Peter Larmour, Ken Ross, Bill Standish, Karin von Strokirch and Stewart Woodman. Much of Chapter 8 of this book appeared in an earlier version in an article co-authored with Stewart Woodman in *The Pacific Review*; Dr Woodman should be regarded as the co-author of this chapter.

In preparing a book of this kind one draws on the work of many researchers, as I trust the references and the bibliography will attest. I also benefited greatly from working in the stimulating ambience provided by the Research School of Pacific and Asian Studies, and by the rest of the Australian National University. And I have learnt much from numerous conversations, in several locations and over several years, with a broad range of participants in, and commentators on, Pacific islands affairs. Meanwhile, at home, Kate, Elizabeth, Patrick, David and Minou helped me keep my feet on the ground. They, or at least Kate, also helped in many much-appreciated practical ways. I have dedicated this book to them, and to my father, H. Paul Henningham, who has always encouraged and guided my writing. To all those who have helped, I owe sincere thanks. But I retain responsibility for the facts and personal opinions presented herein.

STEPHEN HENNINGHAM

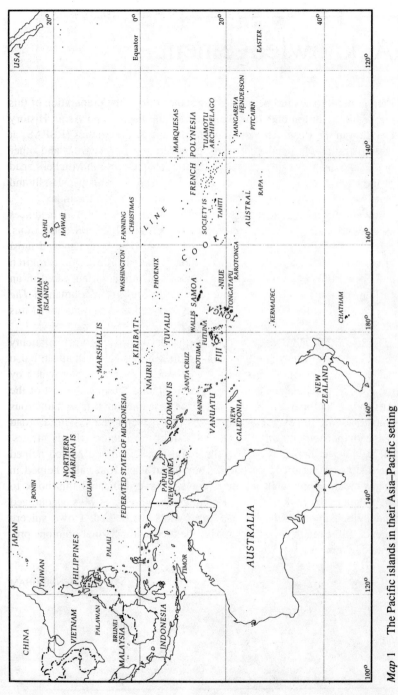

Map 1   The Pacific islands in their Asia–Pacific setting

xvii

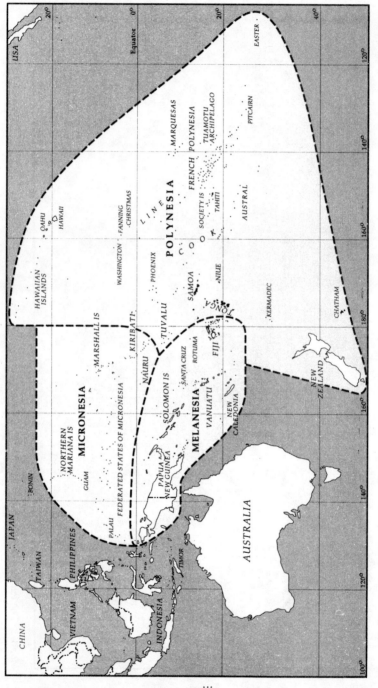

Map 2 The Pacific islands: Micronesia, Polynesia and Melanesia

xviii

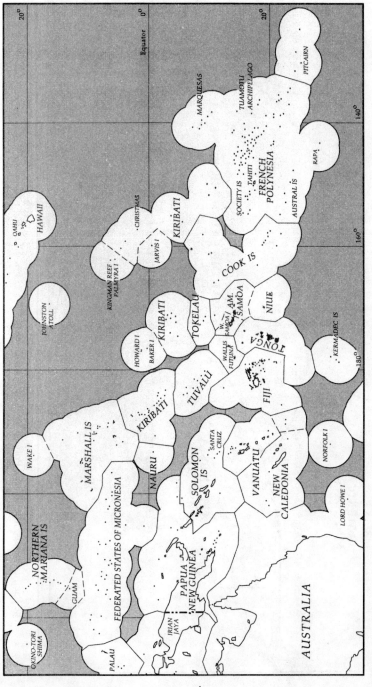

Map 3   The Pacific islands – Exclusive Economic Zones

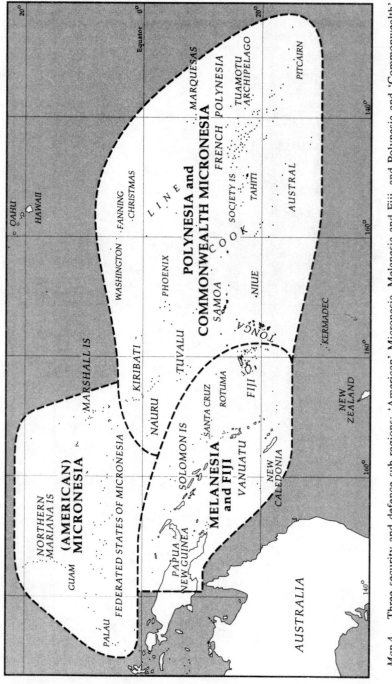

Map 4 Three security and defence sub-regions: 'American' Micronesia, Melanesia and Fiji, and Polynesia and 'Commonwealth' Micronesia

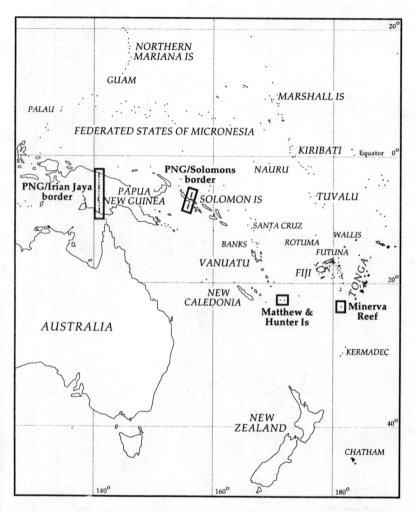

Map 5 The Pacific island states – troubled border zones and disputed maritime areas

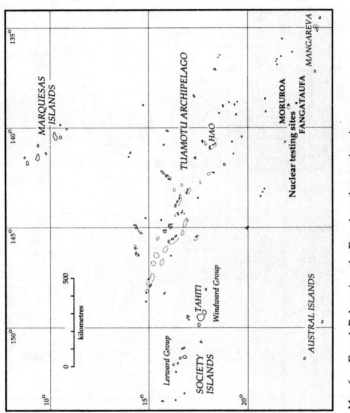

Map 6   French Polynesia – the French nuclear testing sites

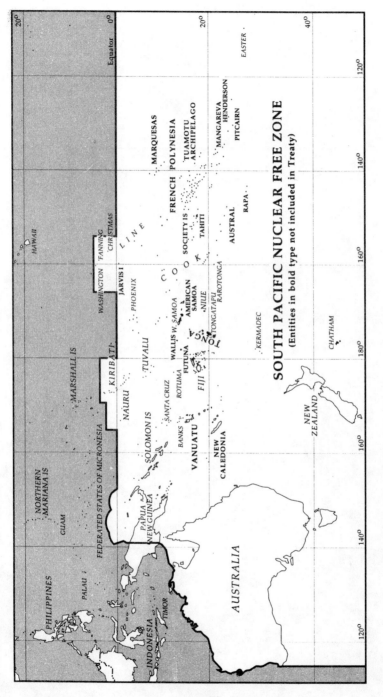

Map 7 The treaty area of the South Pacific Nuclear Free Zone

1 Introduction: Diversity but Common Interests

For many outsiders the phrase 'the Pacific islands' prompts confused images of swaying palms, sparkling lagoons, suns setting into tropical seas, and happy smiling 'natives'. Beyond the picture postcard and tourist brochure images, however, the Pacific islands region is diverse and complex. Its main characteristics, with respect to the concerns of this volume, are as follows.

A MARITIME REGION

Less than 3 per cent of the Pacific islands region is land. This land is fragmented into thousands of islands, distributed across a vast area (Map 1).

SMALL SCALE

The island states are relatively small in population and land area (Table 1.1). In 1990, apart from Papua New Guinea with its then population of 3.5 million, Fiji (population: 725 000) and the Solomon Islands (population: 324 000), all the island states had populations of less than 160 000, ranging from Western Samoa (157 700) to Niue (2500). The average (arithmetic mean) population of the island states was just over 400 000. If Papua New Guinea is excluded, the arithmetic mean was some 130 000. In the range from Papau New Guinea down to Niue, the median state was Tonga, with a population of just under 100 000.[1] The average land area of the island states is some 4000 square kilometres.

A COLONIAL HERITAGE

Western navigators and those who followed them ended the previous isolation from the wider world of the peoples of the Pacific islands. At first contacts with the newcomers were sporadic, except in Guam and nearby islands where Spain established a presence from the 1680s. From around 1800, however, Western missionary, commercial, beachcomber and

Table 1.1   Member states of the South Pacific Forum – basic data

States	Population (mid-1990)	Land area (sq km)	Sea area ('000 sq km)	GDP per capita[a] (A$, c. 1990)
Pacific Island States				
Cook Islands	16 900	237	1 830	3 943
Federated States of Micronesia	101 200	701	2 978	1 600
Fiji	725 000	18 272	1 290	2 181
Kiribati	71 800	690	3 550	654
Republic of the Marshall Islands	46 200	181	2 131	1 514
Nauru	9 300	21	320	8 000 (GNP)
Niue	2 500	259	390	1 600
Palau[b]	15 200	488	629	3 400
Papua New Guinea	3 528 500	462 243	3 120	1 376
Solomon Islands	324 000	27 556	1 340	725
Tonga	96 300	747	700	1 256
Tuvalu	10 200	26	900	767
Vanuatu	146 400	12 190	680	1 283
Western Samoa	157 700	2 935	120	939
Other states				
Australia	17 000 000	7 686 848	8 600	18 500
New Zealand	3 400 000	268 700	2 222	14 500

Notes: [a] The GDP figures used for this and the following tables have several
              imperfections but are broadly indicative.
          [b] Palau became independent in free association with the United States in
              1994, and is expected to become a member of the Forum from 1995.
Sources: South Pacific Commission, South Pacific Economies, Statistical Summary
          Number 12 (Noumea: 1991); Australian and New Zealand government
          figures.

official involvement in the region increased. Islander leaders and communities at times played one power off against another, but the longer-term
advantage lay with the outsiders.

By the first decade of the twentieth century, all of the islands of the
region had become colonies or protectorates of the Western powers. The
relations of island communities with the exterior were henceforth shaped
by their connection with one or another colonial power. British involvement was substantial, either directly or through its dominions of Australia
and New Zealand, but other powers were also present. These patterns of
domination were amended from time to time by shifts in the fortunes and
policies of the colonial powers.

Spain's presence in the Pacific islands ended with its defeat in the Spanish-American war of 1898. Spain ceded Guam to the United States and, short of funds, sold its other possessions and claims in Micronesia to Germany. The German presence in Micronesia, New Guinea and Samoa was in turn eclipsed by the First World War. Japan acquired Germany's possesions in Micronesia, but lost them to the United States when defeated in the Second World War. The French presence in the region was unsettled by that war, but de Gaulle's Free French movement managed to maintain French sovereignty in New Caledonia and in Tahiti and its islands. The Dutch mounted a rear-guard action in West New Guinea in the 1950s, but were eventually obliged to accept the incorporation of that region by Indonesia.

Around the same time as the Netherlands, in response to Indonesian and international pressure, was reluctantly relinquishing West New Guinea, other Western powers began to diminish their control over other parts of the region. Pressures for change came mostly from outside the islands region; nationalist and autonomist movements were present in only a few places. The tide of decolonisation that had previously swept through Asia and Africa began to ripple through the Pacific islands (Table 1.2).

Table 1.2   Decolonisation in the Pacific islands region

State	Year of independence	Colonial power
Western Samoa	1962	New Zealand
Cook Islands	1965 (Free Association)	New Zealand
Nauru	1968	Australia (with New Zealand and the UK)
Tonga	1970 (formerly a protectorate)	United Kingdom
Fiji	1970	United Kingdom
Niue	1974 (Free Association)	New Zealand
Papua New Guinea	1975	Australia
Solomon Islands	1978	United Kingdom
Tuvalu	1978	United Kingdom
Kiribati	1979 (formerly linked with Tuvalu)	United Kingdom
Vanuatu (formerly the New Hebrides)	1980	France/UK (Condominium)
Marshall Islands Association)	1986 (Compact of Free America	United States of
Federated States of Micronesia	1986 (Compact of Free Association)	United States of America
Palau (Belau)	1994 (Compact of Free Association)	United States of America

The first new state to emerge was Western Samoa: in 1962 it became independent from New Zealand, which had ruled it since the First World War. Over the next two decades, New Zealand, Australia and the United Kingdom established self-government in their possessions in the region, and then transferred sovereignty to almost all of them.

These three colonial powers had responded to changing domestic and international climates of opinion about colonial rule. They had also reached the conclusion that the costs and inconveniences of maintaining their rule generally outweighed the advantages. By 1980, when the former Anglo-French Condominium of the New Hebrides became independent as the Republic of Vanuatu, eleven states had emerged. They included two, namely the Cook Islands and Niue, which were independent in 'free association' with New Zealand.

In contrast, France continued to believe in the benefits of maintaining its control, especially because of the importance to it of its nuclear testing facilities in French Polynesia. It resisted the momentum towards independence in the New Hebrides. It retained its three territories, despite the challenge to its position in New Caledonia in the late 1970s and the 1980s from the Melanesian Kanak nationalist movement.

For its part the United States wished to secure its strategic interests in Micronesia, but initiated processes of self-determination in the components of its Trust Territory of the Pacific Islands. The Northern Mariana Islands opted to become a self-governing 'Commonwealth' of the United States. The Marshall Islands and the Federated States of Micronesia entered into Compacts of Free Association, which made them (more or less) independent in 'free association' with the United States. The United Nations Security Council endorsed the new status of these three entities in December 1990. But efforts to reach a settlement with Palau (Belau) were delayed until 1994 because that entity's 'nuclear free' constitution was in conflict with United States defence requirements.

VARYING LEVELS OF SOVEREIGNTY

The Pacific island states consisted, in early October 1994, of nine states which had full political independence, along with five states whose independence was qualified in some respects under special arrangements with the former colonial power. The fully independent states were Western Samoa (independent in 1962), Nauru (1968), Fiji (1970), Tonga (1970), Papua New Guinea (1975), Solomon Islands (1978), Tuvalu (1978), Kiribati (1979) and Vanuatu (1980).

The five states whose independence was in some respects qualified were the Republic of the Marshall Islands and the Federated States of Micronesia, which had entered their Compacts of Free Association with the United States in 1986; Palau, which had entered a Compact of Free Association with the United States in late 1994; and the Cook Islands and Niue, which had become states in 'free association' with New Zealand in 1965 and 1974 respectively. The links of these states with external powers have sometimes constrained their international acceptance. For example, the relationship which the Cook Islands has with New Zealand has resulted in the rejection of the Cooks' request to be covered by the Lomé Convention as part of the African-Caribbean-Pacific group of former colonies which receive special market access to and development assistance from the European Union. Meanwhile some commentators have argued that the Marshall Islands, the Federated States of Micronesia, and Palau lack genuine independence.

These states are nonetheless recognised as independent actors in regional affairs and are members, along with the other island states, of the South Pacific Forum, the annual meeting of regional heads of government. Over the next decade or so, broadly similar forms of 'free association' may also provide solutions to the constitutional future of the French Pacific territories of New Caledonia and French Polynesia, and possibly also of Bougainville and the adjacent islands which comprise the North Solomons province of Papua New Guinea.

LINKS WITH FORMER ADMINISTERING POWERS MOSTLY REMAIN STRONG

Established patterns of aid, trade, investment and, in some instances, migration have tended to endure, as have institutional frameworks. The 'Compact of Free Association' states are closely linked to the United States. Western Samoa, the Cook Islands and Niue have maintained close connections with New Zealand, including by substantial migration. Australian aid to Papua New Guinea comprised half of the new state's government revenue for the first few years after independence in 1975. As of the early 1990s it still comprised around a seventh.

THE PRESENCE OF SEVERAL DEPENDENT ENTITIES

These entities include the Indonesian province of Irian Jaya; the three French territories of New Caledonia, French Polynesia and Wallis and

Futuna; the United States territories of Guam, the Commonwealth of the Northern Mariana Islands and American Samoa; and the New Zealand territory of Tokelau. With the exception of Irian Jaya, which the Indonesian government does not regard as forming part of the Pacific islands region, all of these entities are members, along with the island states, of the South Pacific Commission, a regional economic development organisation (discussed below). Most of these entities exercise some measure of self-government.

LOCAL TRADITIONS MODIFY REPRESENTATIVE DEMOCRACY AND THE RULE OF LAW

Island leaders mostly set great store on traditional ways of leadership and conflict management, although at times appeals to tradition and custom provide a convenient rationale for the protection of vested interests. Constitutional rule and liberal institutions are generally well established, but traditional values and customs are often given formal recognition in constitutions and legislation. These values and customs have a strong influence on how government and society operate. In Papua New Guinea most parliamentarians regard themselves as representing themselves and their own kin and clan group supporters, rather than their electorate and the wider public. The other island states include the 'elected oligarchy' of Western Samoa, wherein all adults can vote but only those of chiefly rank can stand for office, and the neo-traditional monarchy of Tonga, in which the king and his government are accountable in only a modest fashion to the electorate. They also include the Republic of Fiji, in which the political system established following the 1987 coups, in order to help ensure overall Fijian dominance, privileges Fijian chiefs and rural Fijians to the disadvantage of the Indian community and urban residents.

ETHNIC AND CULTURAL DIVERSITY

Following ripples of settlement over many centuries, the indigenous population of the Pacific islands region is diverse. It is conventionally, though somewhat simplistically, divided into three broad ethno-cultural categories: the Micronesians of the northern islands; the Polynesians of the eastern islands; and the Melanesians of the western islands (Map 2). Between these broad categories there are significant connections and similarities; within them there is extensive internal social and cultural differentiation, on linguistic, community, regional and other lines, especially in Micronesia and Melanesia. Fiji comprises a transition zone between Melanesia and Polynesia, and the indigenous Fijians have both Melanesian and Polynesian affinities.

Significant non-indigenous groups are also present in the region, notably the Fiji Indians or 'Indo-Fijians', who comprise just under half of the population of Fiji; the people of European descent who form a third of the population in New Caledonia; the Filipinos and Japanese in parts of American Micronesia; the immigrants to Irian Jaya from other Indonesian provinces; and the small but commercially significant Chinese communities in several states and territories.

LOCAL IDENTITIES ARE STRONG, NATIONAL COHESION OFTEN WEAK

Before the colonial era, political units were small, fluid and often at odds. The hill forts on the Polynesian island of Rapa, which is now part of French Polynesia, attest to chronic feuding between rival chiefdoms. In Melanesia, linguistic diversity prevails. In the archipelago of the New Hebrides (now Vanuatu), for example, some 100 languages were present in the nineteenth century, of which about 80 are still in use, providing a focus for distinct identity. Throughout the island states and territories, people identify strongly with their kin group and native place. Their commitment to the overarching political unit within which they find themselves is often weak, in part because most of these units were only recently invented.

ECONOMIC DIVERSITY AND VULNERABILITY

Despite some similarities, the economies of the island states also vary, because of differences in scale, resource-base and historical background. These 'developing' economies contrast with the modern market economies of the neighbouring states of Australia and New Zealand. The subsistence sectors of the island state economies can generally provide adequate standards of nourishment and shelter. Absolute poverty has been rare, but is increasing because of urban drift and the decay of communal traditions. Overall, the island states are gravely handicapped by their distance from markets, by poor transport and communications, by the impact of cyclones and other natural disasters, by their limited range of exports, by their lack of economies of scale, and by stiff competition in world markets from other suppliers of the commodities which they can produce. They are price-takers not price-makers. They have suffered from long-term downward tendencies in commodity prices, combined with upturns in the prices of fuel and other essential imports. With the exception of phosphate-rich Nauru (discussed below), all of the island states rely on aid, in most instances to a large extent, for the provision of modern infrastructure and services, and for measures intended to modernise their economies.[2]

Yet there are significant differences between the island state economies. The more populous and resource-rich states of Melanesia and Fiji have the potential to become economically self-reliant, provided internal political problems can be contained, whereas the other states – except, for the time being, Nauru, seem destined to remain aid-dependent indefinitely.

The two states with the best prospects for economic self-reliance in the short to medium term are Fiji and Papua New Guinea. Both these states, however, face significant problems. The Fijian economy recovered quite well from the downturn which followed the coups in 1987, and in the late 1980s the Fiji government instituted some important structural reforms. But continued economic progress will require careful management and an enduring political settlement between the Fijians and the Indo-Fijians. Fiji remains significantly dependent on preferential market access under the Lomé Accords and other trade agreements.[3] Similarly, most of the other island states benefit from Lomé and/or other concessional trade agreements. The island governments would prefer the consolidation of such arrangements so as to provide assured markets and returns. Several of them are finding it difficult to adjust to trends towards more liberal international trading arrangements.

Papua New Guinea has great mineral and other resource wealth. But its government faces pressing social and political problems, with which it has a limited capacity to deal, because of weaknesses in this state's institutions and infrastructure, and because of the fractiousness and cupidity of many of its leaders. The government has the hard task of managing resource use and economic development so as to maintain economic and social stability and bring lasting benefits.

The island states have put special emphasis on the actual and potential resources of their exclusive economic zones (EEZs – see Map 3). But for most island states, high costs, the lack of infrastructure and skilled personnel and variations in the migratory movements of the main fish stocks have blighted early hopes of high returns. Efforts to establish domestic fishing industries have generally had disappointing results, and the main return for island states from the resource have comprised licence fees paid by foreign fishing fleets. In the longer term, the island states may benefit from the exploitation of seabed and marine mineral resources within their EEZs. But undersea mining faces technical, cost and environmental constraints. It is unlikely to begin before the early decades of the next century, if then, and will require massive capital investment. Rather than exploiting them directly, the most the island states can hope for are rental returns on these resources.[4]

SOME OF THE ISLAND STATES ARE JURIDICAL RATHER THAN EMPIRICAL ENTITIES

The emergence of the island states as sovereign entities despite their lack of cohesion and/or economic weakness needs to be put in historical perspective. As Robert H. Jackson points out, the transition of these former colonies, and of many colonies elsewhere, to independence resulted much more from changes in international morality and international law than from internal pressures.[5]

Up until the Second World War it was widely accepted among the great (mostly European) powers that these powers and in some instances their former settler colonies had the right to rule peoples and territories acquired by conquest and cession. From the end of the war onwards, however, the way was opened for the decolonisation of almost all of the former colonies and protectorates. Egalitarian, democratic, anti-colonial and anti-racist convictions strengthened; support grew for the self-determination of subject populations; the European powers displayed reduced strength and/or will; and nationalist movements gathered strength and eventually triumphed in several imperial possessions, notably in the Dutch East Indies, India and French Indochina. The trend gathered momentum as numerous new states joined the United Nations.

In the 1950s administrators in most of the island territories generally thought that independence was a distant or else unattainable goal. From the 1960s, however, views and policies changed. As noted earlier, the United Kingdom and its former dominions of Australia and New Zealand arranged for the transition to independence or else 'free association' of their island possessions. Meanwhile the United States arranged for a transition to self-government and either integration or 'free association' for the components of its trust territory in Micronesia. France alone resisted the trend.

Several of these new states, in the Pacific islands region and elsewhere, consisted: 'not of self-standing structures with domestic foundations – like separate buildings – but of territorial jurisdictions supported from above by international law and material aid – a kind of international safety net. In short, they often appear to be juridical more than empirical entities.'[6] The Pacific island states possess 'negative sovereignty', in the sense of enjoying formal rights of non-intervention and other international immunities. Some of them trade on their sovereignty, earning revenue by selling stamps and operating tax havens and flags of convenience. Several of them however do not possess the 'positive sovereignty' held by older, more developed and more fully empirical states, in the sense of the wherewithal on the basis of their own resources and cohesion to deter intervention, to play a relatively individual and independent part in international affairs and to provide socioeconomic welfare.[7]

VARIED SECURITY AND DEFENCE IMPORTANCE

During the Second World War, the island groups in the region became of strategic significance to Japan and its adversaries. Many of the islands in the north and west of the region were directly affected by the hostilities. Other islands more remote from the centres of conflict became supply and staging bases. Since the war, the importance of the islands as 'stepping stones' has declined because improvements in transport and communications now permit military operations to be more easily mounted over longer distances. But, as discussed below, the various entities presently or formerly under American administration in Micronesia have retained substantial wider strategic importance, while some of the other island groups have some strategic significance.

Indeed, in the case of the atolls of Moruroa and Fangataufa in French Polynesia, their very remoteness and isolation encouraged their selection in the late 1950s as sites for the French nuclear testing programme. For their part the United States and the United Kingdom, in the period from the late 1940s to the early 1960s, had chosen remote locations in Micronesia and Polynesia as nuclear test sites. As Stewart Firth comments with respect to a testing site in the Marshall Islands, 'Remoteness, which had once served to insulate Bikini atoll from the rest of the world, now made it the centrepiece of American military action. To the people of Bikini, who numbered 160 in 1946 [and who were relocated before testing began], their atoll was not remote. It was home, the centre of all they knew.'[8]

THREE SECURITY AND DEFENCE SUB-REGIONS

Given their diversity, it is often difficult to generalise about the island states and territories. For the purposes of my examination, from an Australian perspective, of security and defence concerns in and associated with the region, and on the basis of the location and general features of the island states and territories, they may be grouped, along with their surrounding ocean areas, into three sub-regions: 'American' Micronesia; Melanesia and Fiji; and Polynesia and 'Commonwealth' Micronesia (Map 4).[9]

This categorisation, it should be stressed, is intended merely to serve as a descriptive and explanatory device: in other contexts other lines of division and other connections would be given greater salience. For example, although Fiji is mostly grouped in this study with the Melanesian states, it maintains strong social and cultural links with the Polynesian states to its east. Similarly, although the 'American' and the 'Commonwealth' Micronesian entities are here treated separately, these entities have historical and cultural connections.

'American' Micronesia is located in the northwest of the region. Its components are those island groups in the Micronesian cultural zone which are presently or were formerly under United States rule (Table 1.3). It thus includes three (more or less) independent states, namely the Federated States of Micronesia, the Republic of the Marshall Islands, and Palau (Belau). It also includes the dependent territories of Guam and the Northern Marianas.

These various entities have strategic significance for the United States and its allies and associates because they are located adjacent to key lines

Table 1.3   Entities of 'American' Micronesia – basic data

Entity	Population (mid-1990)	Land area (sq km)	Sea area ('000 sq km)	GDP per capita (A$, c. 1900)
Federated States of Micronesia	101 200	701	2 978	1 600
Guam	133 400	541	218	12 334
Republic of the Marshall Islands	46 200	181	2 131	1 514
Commonwealth of the Northern Mariana Islands	44 200	471	777	11 558
Palau	15 200	488	629	3 400

Sources: As for Table 1.1.

of communication between the United States and Asia. The United States maintains defence facilities in both Guam – which has an excellent harbour – and in the Northern Marianas. In addition, it conducts its intercontinental ballistic missile-testing programme in the Marshall Islands, firing the missiles from Vandenberg Air Force Base in California to Kwajalein atoll.

The reforms within and then the disintegration of the Soviet Union ended the importance of the American Micronesian states and territories in relation to superpower conflict. But they remain important with respect to the involvement of the United States in the Asia-Pacific region and to its missile testing programme. These entities have few natural resources, and receive substantial funding from the United States.

In addition to Fiji, the components of the 'Melanesia and Fiji' subregion consist of the states of Papua New Guinea, the Solomon Islands and Vanuatu, and the French territory of New Caledonia (Table 1.4). These entities are located to the west of the region. Overall they are by far the largest of the various island entities in land area, resource base and population. They have considerable strategic importance, especially for Australia and New Zealand, because of their location close to the Australian continent and adjacent to lines of communication between Australasia and Northeast Asia and the United States. Although they are all aid recipients, they also have a broad range of resources, which should permit them in the longer term to attain a substantial measure of economic self-reliance, provided political problems can be contained.

The states and territories of Polynesia and 'Commonwealth' Micronesia (Table 1.5), are located in the north and the east of the region. These entities generally have greater political coherence but fewer eco-

Table 1.4   Entities of Melanesia and Fiji – basic data

Entity	Population (mid-1990)	Land area (sq km)	Sea area ('000 sq km)	GDP per capita (A$, c. 1900)
Fiji	725 000	18 272	1 290	2 181
Irian Jaya	1 400 000	420 000	NA	700 (est.)
New Caledonia	167 600	19 100	1 740	16 354
Papua New Guinea	3 528 500	462 243	3 120	1 376
Solomon Islands	324 000	27 556	1 340	725
Vanuatu	146 000	12 190	680	1 283

Sources: As for Table 1.1.

Table 1.5   Entities of Polynesia and 'Commonwealth' Micronesia – basic data

Entity	Population (Mid-1990)	Land area (sq km)	Sea area ('000 sq km)	GDP per capita (A$, c. 1990)
American Samoa	46 800	200	390	6 663
Cook Islands	16 900	237	1 830	3 943
French Polynesia	196 300	3 521	5 030	19 000
Kiribati	71 800	690	3 550	654
Nauru	9 300	21	320	8 000 (GNP)
Niue	2 500	259	390	1 600
Tokelau	1 800	10	290	NA
Tonga	96 300	747	700	1 256
Tuvalu	10 200	26	900	767
Wallis and Futuna	13 700	255	300	NA
Western Samoa	157 700	2 935	120	939

Sources: As for Table 1.1.

nomic resources and higher levels of aid-dependence than their neigh-bours in the Melanesia and Fiji sub-region. The entities in this sub-region include the Polynesian states of the Cook Islands, Tonga, Western Samoa and Niue, as well as several dependent territories in the Polynesian cultural zone, namely the American territory of American Samoa, the New Zealand territory of Tokelau, and the French territories of Wallis and Futuna and of French Polynesia. In addition the sub-region includes the 'Commonwealth' Micronesian states of Kiribati and Nauru. These latter two states are ethnically Micronesian. I have employed the adjective 'Commonwealth' with respect to them to indicate that they formerly were part of the British imperial system, and are now associated with the Commonwealth. Kiribati is now a member of the Commonwealth; it was formerly under British rule. Nauru was administered by Australia as an Australian, British and New Zealand Trust Territory, and is now an associate member of the Commonwealth.

The scanty resources of the entities of Polynesia and Commonwealth Micronesia include their labour power. Some of them maintain economic equilibrium and reasonable living standards in large part because of remittances from communities living and working abroad. Their remoteness, small size and limited resources mostly mean that they have little wider strategic significance, except insofar as the remoteness of some of the islands in the sub-region has made them attractive to external powers as nuclear test sites. Nauru is at present a special case among these entities, because of its phosphate deposits. But the phosphate will run out over the next decade or so, leaving severe ecological damage. A decline in living standards seems inevitable, the severity of which will depend on the wisdom and good fortune with which the phosphate profits have been invested. Although returns on invested wealth will help sustain the economy, in the absence of other resources Nauru is likely to become a significant recipient of aid. In the post-phosphate era, Nauru can be expected to become more like the other smaller island states.

CONNECTIONS DESPITE DIVERSITY – THE 'PACIFIC WAY'

Despite the diversity of the island states and territories, there are also close connections between them. Their governments are aware of common characteristics and interests. In culture and ways of life there are important similarities between the island peoples of the region. Christian missionaries had a major influence in the islands, converting most of their populations, at least nominally, and establishing the first educational and health services. The churches continue to play an important part. The élites of the region are narrow. Links between them have been strengthened through similar backgrounds of education, often in church schools, followed by higher education at the University of the South Pacific, the University of Papua New Guinea, or in the United States, Australia or New Zealand.

All the island states are former colonies or protectorates of Australia, New Zealand, the United Kingdom or the United States, except for Vanuatu, which formerly was the Anglo-French Condominium of the New Hebrides. This background has left broad similarities in institutions and élite attitudes. Ideological and religious differences between and within states are generally either not present or else are of limited wider political importance, and thus are not a factor in regional relations. With the exception of Vanuatu, the transitions to independence were mostly amicable, encouraging the maintenance of strong connections with the former administering powers.

The governments of the island states and territories have expressed their sense of common interests and have sought to increase their economic well-being through regional cooperation. This interaction has reinforced a sense of common identity and interests. There are limits to what can be achieved within the region, because the island state economies lack complementarity. But the island governments have recognised benefits in scientific and technical exchange and cooperation, and advantages in presenting a common front on political and security issues.

Indigenous traditions, especially in Polynesia, favouring the consensus resolution of disputes have encouraged this emphasis on cooperation. Island leaders have referred to a 'Pacific Way', whereby issues are talked through in an unhurried fashion in informal meetings, in pursuit of a consensus acceptable to all involved. This commitment to cooperation has been strengthened because the individual island states lack the resources to set up a network of diplomatic posts and to engage in extensive bilateral diplomacy.

The two key regional organisations are the South Pacific Commission and the South Pacific Forum. The South Pacific Commission (SPC) was founded in 1947 by the colonial and administering powers, namely Australia, France, Great Britain, the Netherlands, New Zealand and the United States. (The Netherlands withdrew in 1962, after Irian Jaya's incorporation into Indonesia.)

Nowadays the SPC comprises the independent island states as well as the dependent entities in the region, apart from Irian Jaya, as well as the present and former administering powers of the post-war era, except for the Netherlands. In late 1993, however, the United Kingdom advised that it intended to leave the Commission. At the time of its formation, France and the Netherlands had insisted that the SPC should not concern itself with political questions. When the former colonies in the region attained independence from 1962 onwards, their leaders expressed frustration with this constraint.

In 1971, in part in a response to this frustration, the independent and self-governing island states formed the South Pacific Forum. Realizing, however, that their influence on their own would be limited, they at that time also invited their large neighbours Australia and New Zealand to join. The Forum has operated through annual meetings of the heads of government of the member states, at which issues of concern are considered. Between meetings, the Forum Secretariat (formerly SPEC – the South Pacific Economic Cooperation Bureau) provides continuity and acts on Forum decisions.

Both the Forum and the SPC have focused on economic cooperation and development. But security issues, broadly defined, have also surfaced on the Forum's agenda and have been discussed in the corridors at SPC meetings. As we shall see in the next two chapters, these issues have rarely involved concern over external or intra-regional military threats. Instead they have generally focused on non-military threats and challenges to security and sovereignty.

2 Pacific in Nature as well as Name?

The Pacific Ocean was so named, it seems, because of its tranquillity when Magellan first sailed on it.[1] But just as this ocean has its storms and cyclones, so too do the Pacific islands have a history of conflict and violence.

In pre-colonial times conflict was endemic within and between the numerous communities of Melanesia. In Micronesia and Polynesia social units were in many instances larger and social cohesion stronger, but violence within and between groups was common. Western expansion into the region was supported with military force. The warm welcome given by some Polynesian societies to the new arrivals was in part informed by an awareness of Western technological strength, especially the destructiveness of naval gunfire.[2] Christian missions did much to 'pacify' the peoples of the region, but so too did punitive patrols, especially in Melanesia. Colonial rule was usually established and consolidated against local resistance.

Western expansion into the Pacific islands incorporated them into the international system, making them subject to rivalries and conflicts between external powers. In 1899 for example the Samoan islands were divided between Germany (Western Samoa) and the United States (American Samoa). Britain withdrew its claims in return for concessions elsewhere, notably with respect to the Solomon Islands, Tonga and Niue. In the late nineteenth century France hoped to acquire the New Hebrides. But its ambitions were checked by Great Britain. When France and Britain became allies against Germany under the *Entente Cordiale* of 1902, an uneasy compromise was reached whereby the New Hebrides and the nearby Banks and Torres groups became from 1907 the Anglo-French Condominium of the New Hebrides – a sort of joint protectorate. The United States acquired Guam as a spoil of war from its victory over Spain in 1898.

Early in the First World War, the German possessions in the region were taken over by Australia (Papua New Guinea and Nauru), New Zealand (Western Samoa) and Japan (the Micronesian islands other than Guam, Nauru and the Gilbert Islands [now Kiribati]). During the Second World War, parts of the region became battle grounds in the conflict between Japan and the United States and its allies. Following allied victory, the United States was given the former Japanese possessions in Micronesia as a United Nations trust territory. Soon after the war the Netherlands reluctantly accepted the emergence of the new state of Indonesia, which embodied most of the former Dutch East Indies. But it retained control until 1961 of the western half of New Guinea, until obliged to relinquish it to Indonesia under military and diplomatic pressure.

Of course, conflicts between external powers involving the region were sporadic, and were interspersed with long periods of peace. The strategic and economic assets and potential of the islands were often only of minor importance; instead the islands were affected by larger rivalries and conflicts. Consistently, the presence or absence of military threats to the Pacific islands region depended on circumstances and trends elsewhere, both in the wider Asia–Pacific region and globally.

EXTERNAL MILITARY THREATS IN THE CONTEMPORARY PACIFIC ISLANDS

Despite this troubled background, in the post-1945 era potential external military threats to the islands region, except for the risks and disruption associated with nuclear testing and other defence activities, have largely been absent. In order of importance, there are four main reasons for this.

First: following allied victory in the Second World War, the Pacific islands – and especially those islands of Micronesia which were granted to the United States as a strategic trust territory – became or were reconfirmed as an integral part of the United States and Western sphere of influence. They have retained this status. During the Cold War era, the United States, Australia and New Zealand pursued what Richard Herr and others have described as a policy of strategic denial. This contributed to the absence of great power intervention to exploit local disputes and conflicts, except to some extent in propaganda and rhetoric. Accordingly, in contrast to what happened in several other parts of the world during this era, these disputes and conflicts were mostly not 'internationalised.'

Second: the new international norms which have come into operation since the Second World War have opposed external military intervention and upheld the sovereignty of the successor states to the colonial empires. In this context, and despite some misgivings, including among Pacific island leaders, Indonesia's incorporation of West New Guinea was generally accepted internationally as legitimate, because Indonesia was the successor state to the Netherlands East Indies, rather than as an act of external aggression.

Third: most external states which conceivably could have acted aggressively against the island states have been preoccupied with other concerns.

In any case, they also have lacked the requisite force projection capabilities, given the remoteness of most of the islands.

And fourth: in recent times most of the states of the region have lacked the strategic relevance or economic resources liable to attract hostile outside interest. Circumstances might have been somewhat different if they had become major producers of oil or of other relatively scarce and valuable resources.

The only external military threats which could possibly have directly affected parts of the region over the last twenty or so years have related to tensions between Indonesia and Papua New Guinea and to the role played in western defence and security arrangements by facilities located in American Micronesia.

The intermittent tensions between Indonesia and Papua New Guinea have related to their common border (Map 5). The boundary itself is not in dispute. It was agreed on between the Netherlands and Britain in 1895, and reconfirmed and clarified by Australia and Indonesia in 1974 and by Indonesia and Papua New Guinea in agreements concluded in 1979 and 1984. Similarly, the maritime boundaries between the two states have been settled amicably. But because of the harsh terrain, which comprises vast swamps, dense jungle and rugged mountains, demarcating the actual boundary has not been easy. In the 1950s the Dutch mistakenly administered villages later found to be in Papua New Guinea. In 1983 Papua New Guinea surveyors discovered that the trans-Irian Jaya highway being built by Japanese contractors for the Indonesian authorities had strayed across the unmarked border at two places: after negotiations the two sections of road were closed.[3]

The prompt resolution of the highway issue demonstrated the acceptance by both governments of the established border and their unwillingness to dispute over it. Nonetheless the boundary line is 'artificial', in that it fails to 'correspond with any of the major divisions of the physical or cultural landscape.'[4] The border is highly porous and the linguistic and cultural identities of the Melanesian groups in the border region often traverse the boundary line. Both governments accept the right of 'traditional border crossers' to cross the frontier temporarily for customary and social reasons and to engage in farming, hunting and fishing in accordance with their traditional rights. The Indonesian government has been vexed, however, by the activities in the border region of the *Organisasi Papua Merdeka* (OPM – Free Papua Movement).

The OPM is a loose, factionalised nationalist movement. It comprises a variety of dissident individuals, groups and local communities opposed to the implications of the incorporation of Irian Jaya into Indonesia. The active membership of the OPM and similar movements seems to amount to only a few hundred, at most. Sympathy for their activities is, however, much more widespread in Irian Jaya. This expresses, the late Peter Hastings has pointed out, 'the continuing problems of Melanesians throughout the whole island [of New Guinea] in reaching accommodation with the demands of... powerful and alien civilization[s].'[5]

OPM militants and their supporters have sought sanctuary across the border. Papua New Guinea, in an assertion of its sovereignty, has refused to grant Indonesian forces the right of 'hot pursuit' across the border in operations against OPM forces. But on occasion Indonesian units have either strayed across the poorly-marked border or else have mounted cross-border raids and patrols. This has led to exchanges of fire between Indonesian and Papua New Guinea patrols, although without any casualties so far. In early 1984, for example, Indonesian army patrols and combat aircraft engaged in operations against the OPM 'strayed into PNG territory and tensions rose to high levels.'[6]

In addition to OPM activists, hundreds of other Melanesians from Irian Jaya have crossed over into Papua New Guinea on various occasions, and for various reasons. These reasons include experience of or else fear of military repression, dissatisfaction with social and economic change in Irian Jaya, including the acquisition of their land for immigrants from other provinces in Indonesia, and encouragement to move by the OPM. Their numbers peaked at some 11 000 in 1984, following an abortive OPM uprising earlier that year.[7] Many of these people have eventually been resettled in Papua New Guinea, while others have been repatriated to Irian Jaya.

Considerable sympathy exists in Papua New Guinea for the OPM and for its opposition to Indonesian rule in Irian Jaya. This sympathy has also been expressed elsewhere in the Pacific islands region, notably by Father Walter Lini's government in Vanuatu in the early and middle 1980s and by non-government organisations. The question of Irian Jaya has not however become accepted as a regional 'decolonisation' issue (see Chapter 4).

Successive Papua New Guinea governments have wished to maintain good relations and reach an accommodation with their country's large and powerful neighbour. Senior leaders have argued that colonialism was responsible for the division of the island of New Guinea into two, and that 'Papua New Guinea now has no choice but to comply with the historical facts of life.'[8] They have declined to support the OPM, and have sought to resolve difficulties with Indonesia through negotiation.

The first government under the prime ministership of Paias Wingti, which held office from November 1985 to July 1988, put special emphasis on conciliation. It deported the key OPM leaders who had taken refuge in Papua New Guinea, arranging for their resettlement as refugees in Africa and Europe. Meanwhile, the Indonesian government set out to ensure good relations, including by fostering personal links with Papua New Guinea leaders. In one incident, Indonesian Army Commander General Benny Murdani 'donated' US$ 140 000 to Ted Diro – at that time Papua New Guinea Foreign Minister and formerly the commander of the Papua New Guinea army – for the campaign funds of his People's Action Party.[9] In 1986, the two governments concluded a 'Treaty of Mutual Respect, Friendship and Cooperation' designed to put the relationship on a new and cordial footing.

This increased cordiality in part reflected increased confidence in Papua New Guinea that Indonesia was not 'inherently expansionist', despite the apparent evidence of the incorporation of Irian Jaya, the *Konfrontasi* (confrontation) with Malaysia in the early 1960s, and the invasion of East Timor in 1975. As Mackie and Crouch have pointed out, these episodes need to be understood in their particular contexts and in relation to the ending of colonial rule in the region. The process of European decolonisation is now, however, 'complete in this part of the world. Indonesia has no basis for claims to Papua New Guinea – and no desire for it or sense of need for it – as she had in two [namely Irian Jaya and East Timor] of these three cases.'[10]

Indeed, Indonesia recognised the forthcoming independence of Papua New Guinea nearly two years before it took place.[11] Moreover Indonesia has engaged in normal diplomatic relations with its neighbour and has never questioned Papua New Guinea's right to exist or its sovereignty over its territory. The present Indonesian regime has given no indication whatsoever that it harbours designs on Papua New Guinea, and Indonesia has no clear motive for mounting a major attack.

Even if Indonesia did wish to conquer Papua New Guinea, the practical difficulties involved in mounting an invasion and consolidating control would be awesome. This is because of the difficult terrain and the certainty of strong resistance, as Indonesia's experience in the much smaller entity of East Timor has made clear.[12]

Should intermittent tensions escalate into major hostilities, Australia would very probably regard itself as implicated because of its close links with Papua New Guinea and its interest in promoting peace and stability in its northern approaches. Indeed, any potential opponent 'would need to face the stark reality that a major attack on Papua New Guinea could only succeed with Australia's primary air and naval capacities neutralized first. This would be extremely difficult, especially given the probability of substantial United States logistic and other assistance to Australia.'[13] Any

Indonesian aggression against Papua New Guinea would also attract strong censure from the other island states, the South Pacific Forum, and the international community generally. In particular, the links that Papua New Guinea has established with the ASEAN countries could serve as a restraining influence on Indonesia.

On present indications, border tensions between Indonesia and Papua New Guinea are likely to remain low-level, and thus are unlikely to pose a wider threat to regional security and stability. For the situation to alter significantly, one or more of the following changes would be necessary: the emergence of a new leadership in Indonesia with expansionist and interventionist ambitions; the adoption by the Papua New Guinea leadership of a combative stance contrasting with the tradition of seeking accommodation with Indonesia; and a sharp upturn in the strength and effectiveness of resistance in Irian Jaya, especially if this depended in part on the use of cross-border sanctuaries. Even if circumstances changed in these directions, however, neighbouring states and the international community would encourage conciliation. So an increase of incidents and violence in the border region would be considerably more likely than the outbreak of major hostilities between Papua New Guinea and Indonesia.

The American Micronesian entities have also been open to possible external threat, because of their location and because of the part that the facilities on their territory play in the United States and Western defence and security system. The American territory of Guam has naval and air bases; missile testing is conducted in the Marshall Islands; and other parts of this sub-region host defence and defence-support facilities.

During the Cold War era, in the scenario of a superpower confrontation, armed conflict could conceivably have destroyed lives and property in these islands, as it did so devastatingly in the Second World War. Such a confrontation was, however, always of limited likelihood, even though the superpower balance was less stable in the North Pacific than in Europe. And even had such a conflict taken place, its centre would very probably have been far to the north and west, with American Micronesia less subject to the direct impact of hostilities. This risk has receded with the end of the Cold War and the break up of the Soviet Union. But it will continue to be present in some measure while these islands remain part of the American defence and security network, especially with respect to developments in North Korea.

Yet although they would be unlikely to be much affected immediately and directly in the unlikely scenario of a nuclear war, the Pacific islands, along with much of the rest of the world, would suffer severe medium and longer-term economic, environmental and other effects. So the peoples and governments of the islands region, like their counterparts elsewhere, have an interest in continued progress with arms control and disarmament.

Not by accident, the conceivable external threats relating to Papua New Guinea and American Micronesia affect the north-western part of the Pacific islands region, where it abuts with or fringes on the populous, dynamic and potentially volatile regions of Southeast and Northeast Asia. Overall, no forseeable military threat comes from the other adjoining regions: Australia and New Zealand to the south and west; and – across a vast ocean gap – North America and Central America to the northeast and Latin America to the southeast. The only exception concerns the possibility of armed Australian or New Zealand intervention to protect and evacuate nationals, or to counter terrorist activity, or else, in certain circumstances, to assist a broadly-supported constitutional government under violent internal threat. Rather than a military attack, however, such intervention would probably be small-scale, limited in duration, implemented so as to minimise civilian casualties, and only likely to go ahead with both domestic support in the intervening power and broad regional acceptance (see Chapter 8).

INTRA-REGIONAL THREATS

The overall absence of plausible external threats to the region is complemented by a lack of violent conflicts between the Pacific island states. In contrast with most other regions of the world since 1945, in the islands region the intra-regional use or threatened use of armed force to help shape relations between states has been absent.

This absence of intra-regional threats has resulted in part from the lack of border and territorial disputes. Except for the land border between Papua New Guinea and Irian Jaya (discussed above), all the international boundaries in the islands region are maritime. Because the islands and island groups of the region are scattered over a wide area, there are considerable distances between almost all of the various island states, compared with circumstances in some other insular regions, notably insular Southeast Asia and the Caribbean. The one exception is the distance of only a few kilometres between the northern islands of the Solomon Islands and Bougainville island in the North Solomons province of Papua New Guinea.

Until the late 1970s the island states could only claim their territorial seas out to a twelve nautical mile limit, so questions of maritime demarcation did not arise, except between the Solomon Islands and Papua New

Guinea. But the negotiation of the United Nations Convention on the Law of the Sea, which was completed in 1982, and its ratification over the following decade, stimulated the island states to claim exclusive economic zones (EEZs) up to a limit of 200 nautical miles (Map 3). Agreed boundaries between abutting EEZs have been arrived at amicably in almost all cases. Yet although disputes over maritime boundaries have been rare, there are three instances of the disputed ownership of particular reefs and islands (Map 5).

First, both Tonga and Fiji have claims to the Minerva Reefs, which are located to the south of Fiji and the southwest of Tonga. Fiji regards the reefs as lying within its EEZ, whereas Tonga claims an historical association with them, including by means of traditional fishing.[14] If its claims were recognised Tonga would be entitled to an expanded EEZ. The question has not been actively disputed, and is likely to be resolved amicably in due course.

Second, France and Vanuatu have differed over the tiny, barren and uninhabited islands of Matthew and Hunter, which lie southeast of Vanuatu and east of New Caledonia. The Vanuatu case is that these islands formed part of the jurisdiction of the New Hebrides, and that people from the southern islands of the archipelago sometimes visited them to fish. France's claim is based on arrangements made before the New Hebrides became independent. Thus a 1965 exchange of letters 'recorded that Britain was content with the view that the islands formed part of New Caledonia.'[15]

The islands are of no value in themselves, but their possession entails ownership of an expanded EEZ covering some 60 000 square nautical miles. A Vanuatu expedition visited Hunter in March 1983, conducted a custom ceremony, raised the flag and removed a plaque left earlier by France. But French forces arrived a week later and removed the Vanuatu flag, and since then a French outpost has remained in these islands to enforce the French claim. Vanuatu's claim was supported by the Kanak nationalist movement in New Caledonia, but opposed by the anti-independence, pro-France majority in that territory.

For some months this issue increased the tension in relations between France and Vanuatu. These relations had already been difficult following France's obstruction of the transition of the New Hebrides to independence in 1980. Since then, however, the dispute has become at most only a minor irritant in French/Vanuatu relations. It did not become a major or an enduring issue in the domestic politics of either state, and since 1983 has scarcely been mentioned by either side in official statements. It seems unlikely to lead to a clash of arms, because of its lack of immediate practical importance and because Vanuatu completely lacks the capability to challenge the military strength of France. Relations improved following the December 1991 elections, at which the Francophone-based Union of Moderate Parties (UMP), led by Maxime Carlot, became the dominant partner in a new governing coalition, bringing an end to the rule of the Anglophone-based Vanua'aku Pati, which had held office since 1979. The new government has established warm relations with France, and has not given any public indication of a wish to pursue the claim.

Third, the Republic of the Marshall Islands has argued that it rather than the United States should have jurisdiction over Wake Island. This island is located about 500 miles north of the closest island in the Marshall's Ratak chain and about 2300 miles west of Honolulu. The Marshallese 'have long maintained that Wake, which they call *Enen-Kio*, is traditionally part of their territory. It was historically used for turtle hunting, fishing, and as a refuge.'[16] The question came to a head in 1990 in response to a suggestion that jurisdiction over Wake be transferred from the United States government to that of its territory of Guam. Although many Marshallese feel strongly about the matter they have so far chosen to pursue it cautiously, and it seems unlikely to became a dominant issue in relations with the United States.[17]

Apart from these three minor cases, there are no disputed land or maritime territories in the region. Nor are there any other significant irredentist sentiments and claims. Irredentist sentiment has existed in the past in the Solomons in relation to Bougainville, but it has been muted in recent years. Geographically, Bougainville and its offlying islands are part of the Solomons archipelago, and there have been significant cultural, trade and historical links between Bougainville and the Solomon Islands. In the early 1970s, when Papua New Guinea and the Solomon Islands were moving towards independence, there was substantial support in the Solomons for the suggestion that Bougainville be separated from Papua New Guinea and become part of the jurisdiction of the Solomon Islands. Solomon Islands leaders were aware that the income from the giant copper mine on Bougainville would have greatly improved the economic viability of the Solomons. But at no stage has the Solomon Islands government endorsed the view that Bougainville should be incorporated into the Solomons.

Tensions have arisen however in relation to the Papua New Guinea/Solomon Islands border zone. Since the late 1980s many Solomon Islanders, including several members of parliament, have been sympathetic to the Bougainville insurgents, and to their demand for independence. Some inhabitants of the Western Provinces of the Solomon Islands have assisted the insurgents, including by providing supplies in defiance of the Papua New Guinea blockade. They have been motivated both by sympathy for the insurgents and by the opportunity for lucrative returns. In addition, representatives of the Bougainville Revolutionary Army (BRA – also known as the Bougainville Republican Army) have been allowed to operate freely in the Solomon Islands, including by opening an office in the capital, Honiara. One result has been repeated criticisms of the approach of the Solomon Islands government by Papua New Guinea spokesmen.

There has been strong discontent in the Solomon Islands about Papua New Guinea's handling of the Bougainville question and over the way in which the dispute has impinged on the sovereignty of the Solomon Islands. In 1991 and 1992 tension mounted when Papua New Guinea units, apparently exceeding their instructions, raided into Solomon Islands territory to disrupt supply routes to the rebels and to punish villagers who had been aiding them. In May 1992 the then Papua New Guinea Foreign Minister, Sir Michael Somare, expressed his dissatisfaction with the attitude and approach of the Solomon Islands government to the insurrection, especially with respect to the BRA office in Honiara.[18] For some months Solomon Mamaloni, the (then) Solomon Islands Prime Minister, refused to engage in talks with the Papua New Guinea government.

But although tensions arising from the revolt continued into the early months of 1993, there was no indication that Solomon Islands intended to change its policy to one of active support for the insurgents. From mid-1993 Solomons/Papua New Guinea relations improved. Following the Solomon Islands elections in June, the cautious Francis Billy Hilly replaced the combative Solomon Mamaloni as Prime Minister. By the end of 1993 most of Bougainville was under the control of the Papua New Guinea defence force and/or of local 'resistance' militias opposed to the BRA. By this time the BRA had squandered much of its earlier support by fractiousness, human rights abuses and an inability to provide services. Papua New Guinea's confidence that a resolution was in sight increased, so its concerns about infractions of its embargo on the island diminished. Meanwhile the supply of the insurgents had become less of an issue, because the authorities and their allies now had greater control over the coastal areas. Though indiscipline and human rights abuses by Papua New Guinea forces continued, the national government had established more reliable control over them, ending cross-border incursions.

In late 1993, building on earlier agreements, the two governments signed an accord aimed at restoring good relations. Under the new arrangements the former Bougainville Revolutionary Army office in Honiara was converted into a Bougainville Humanitarian Issues Centre, and Papua New Guinea agreed to pay A\$ 300 000 in compensation for casualties and damage inflicted during incursions into the Solomon Islands. Relations remained generally good over subsequent months. When negotiations between the Papua New Guinea government, the Bougainville Revolutionary Army and other parties recommenced in August/September 1994, the meetings took place in Honiara, the capital of Solomon Islands, with Solomon Islands Prime Minister Francis Billy Hilly chairing the key meeting. At least so far, the Papua New Guinea and Solomon Islands governments had put earlier troubles over the border area behind them.

Despite its irritation with Port Moresby, and notwithstanding the presence of strong sympathies for the rebels in the Solomon Islands, the Solomon Islands government has chosen to seek to limit damage to its bilateral relations with Papua New Guinea over this issue. Other island governments have taken the view that the Bougainville question is a domestic issue for Papua New Guinea. One constraint which has inhibited support for the Bougainville revolt by the Solomon Islands government is the fear of encouraging secessionist tendencies in the Solomon Islands themselves.

ISLAND STATE MILITARY CAPABILITIES

Because of the absence of external or intra-regional military threats and of border and territorial disputes, because of their economic weakness, and because they assume that an informal American, Australian and New Zealand 'security umbrella' operates in some measure with respect to the region, the island governments have spent little on defence. Only Papua New Guinea, Fiji and Tonga have armed forces, numbering respectively, in mid-1993, 3800, 3900 and 350 personnel. Their neighbours, Australia and New Zealand, have defence forces numbering, respectively, 63 200 and 10 800.[19]

In addition to army forces, Papua New Guinea and Fiji also have small naval and air units. All three island state armed forces lack the capability to mount operations beyond their home territories, and are substantially oriented to internal security, although Fijian units have served with distinction in international peacekeeping operations. In a major internal crisis, the effectiveness of these three armed forces would be constrained, among other things, by equipment, logistical and communications weaknesses, as has been shown with respect to Papua New Guinea during the Bougainville conflict. Among the other island states, Vanuatu and the

Solomon Islands have small paramilitary police units, while the other states rely exclusively on small police forces.

Following Papua New Guinea's intervention in 1980 to help quell the revolt on Espiritu Santo in Vanuatu, Sir Julius Chan, who was then serving his first term as Prime Minister of Papua New Guinea, proposed the establishment of a regional peacekeeping force under the aegis of the South Pacific Forum. This possibility has since then been raised from time to time. But the establishment of such a force would require the resolution of several difficult practical and political problems.[20] Who would fund and provide personnel for such a force? Where would it be stationed? Under what circumstances and conditions and with what safeguards would it be employed? Would it be used sufficiently often to make its formation and cost worthwhile? Could it cloak neo-colonial intervention by Australia and New Zealand, the two powers which presumably would provide most of the funding and some of the personnel? Would individual Forum governments be able to veto its use? Would its use clash with the sovereignty of particular states, especially in relation to essentially internal disputes?

In view of the practical problems and the potential divisiveness of the proposal, the island governments have so far been disinclined to pursue it. They have preferred instead to consider whatever *ad hoc* measures may become appropriate from time to time in particular circumstances.

In early 1994 elements in the Papua New Guinea government expressed interest in the possible establishment of a special Pacific islands multilateral force to assist with peacekeeping in Bougainville. The plan was pursued actively from early September 1994, after negotiations had recommenced between the Papua New Guinea government, its local allies on Bougainville, and the secessionist forces. A special multilateral force was set up in late September 1994, comprising personnel from Fiji, Tonga and Vanuatu. Australia provided training, logistical and the main financial support, at a cost of over A\$5 million. An Australian officer assumed overall command, but with a Tongan officer serving as ground commander. New Zealand provided some training assistance. The task of the force was to help maintain peace and order on Bougainville for two weeks in October 1994, during which peace talks would be pursued.

CONCLUSION

In the Pacific islands region in recent times the virtual absence of external and intra-regional military threats has been complemented by traditions of regional cooperation. In addition, the security and defence of the region has been underwritten to a considerable extent by the Western powers. This arrangement, which was established during the Cold War era, is likely to continue indefinitely.

Of course internal tensions and bitter conflicts are present in several island states. Under certain circumstances, conflict in the Papua New Guinea–Indonesia border region could increase. Conflicts in the neighbouring, and potentially volatile, regions of Southeast Asia and Northeast Asia, which could develop in a complex and fast-moving fashion, could also have implications for and ripple effects on parts of the Pacific islands region, especially on American Micronesia and Papua New Guinea.

Yet overall in recent years, at least with respect to both external and intra-regional military threats, the region has been pacific in nature as well as in name. This is certainly so in comparison with most other regions of the world. So the states of the region have been at liberty to focus much of their attention on non-military aspects of regional security.

3 Beyond 'Whose Sail...on the Horizon': Island State Security Perspectives

In pre-colonial times, most Pacific islander communities were economically self-reliant and introspective. This was so despite trade, migration and warfare. According to one prominent Tuvaluan, 'Ours was largely a struggle with the limitations of the environment – although once or twice we did need to keep an eye on exactly whose sail was on the horizon.'[1] During the Second World War, however, some of the Pacific islands 'provided the battleground', and their populations found themselves 'caught by the inescapable tides of global politics.'[2] Nowadays, the island states are directly subject to global economic and political circumstances and trends. They are obliged to define and pursue their national interests in this broader context. In this chapter I review the external policy stances of the island states. I begin by reviewing general policy orientations, and then discuss sub-groupings of states, and individual states.

GENERAL ORIENTATIONS

Island governments are conscious that their states' small scale and lack of economic and military strength leaves them potentially vulnerable. Almost all of the island states 'do not even have the military and weapon capacity to defend against an invasion by a well-armed, well-trained...mercenary group.'[3] The island governments' awareness of their potential vulnerability and their view that the international community should protect the sovereignty of small states informed their strong support for the United States and its allies in the Gulf War.[4] The island states do not form part of any overarching security pact. Several of them however have close connections, including in some instances by means of treaty links, with the United States, Australia or New Zealand. Most of the island states would expect one or more of these powers to come to their aid in a crisis.

Yet island government attitudes to these larger powers have often been ambivalent. In early 1987 Prime Minister Lini of Vanuatu claimed that Australia and New Zealand posed a potential threat to the small states of the region, because of their neo-colonial attitudes and their development

29

of ready reaction forces. Following the Fiji coups, and the subsequent deterioration of relations between Fiji and both New Zealand and Australia, a senior Fijian official commented to a mid-1989 conference that the development of New Zealand capabilities in the region:

> raises fears that we can have here in the South Pacific what is now happening in the Indian Ocean where India, by invitation, helped militarily with the situation in the Maldives and is now involved in Sri Lanka. That, I imagine, would always be a reminder to the people of Fiji, that it could also happen in our own region. I was interested to hear the statement that there is no perceived military threat in the region. From the perspective of one or two island countries the threat of military intervention cannot be discounted in the light of what has occurred or is happening in other areas.[5]

The island governments responded in varied ways to the partial unravelling of ANZUS in the mid-1980s because of the unacceptability to the United States of New Zealand's ban on port visits by nuclear-armed or nuclear-powered ships (see Chapter 7). Several senior islander politicians and officials, notably in Vanuatu but also in Papua New Guinea and elsewhere, were impressed by what they saw as New Zealand's show of independence. At a conference in 1990, Margaret Taylor, Papua New Guinea's (then) Ambassador to Washington, praised New Zealand's 'tough stance' on the nuclear issue. She commented that the 'New Zealand position is admired and respected...', and compared New Zealand's approach to regional issues favourably with that of Australia.[6]

But several island governments were concerned about frictions within an arrangement which they had assumed also provided them with some informal security guarantees. In mid-1989 Taufa Vakatale, the Secretary of the Fiji Foreign Affairs Ministry, after commenting that the security of Australia and New Zealand encompassed as well the security of the smaller states of the region, argued that among the Pacific island states, 'there should be great concern...over the future of ANZUS, [as] a regional security arrangement involving Australia, New Zealand, and the United States of America.'[7]

The island states look to the United States and its Western partners for aid and other assistance, but are also resentful of the size, wealth and leverage of these powers. During the Cold War era most of the island states implicitly aligned themselves with the Western association of nations. Strong Christian traditions have encouraged anti-Communism but have also at times discouraged pragmatism, fostering instead an idealistic – sometimes moralistic – approach. The experience of the island states has been mostly with the Western association of states. Western companies, organisations and individuals have had a major impact on the region, for better and worse, so memories and perceptions of exploitation and injustice colour the attitudes of island governments. Island leaders are conscious that, when there is a clash in interests and priorities, the Western powers are generally inclined to put their own economic and strategic interests ahead of those of the island states and their peoples. In 1989 Tony (now Sir Anthony) Siaguru, a senior Papua New Guinea lawyer and political commentator, and formerly a government minister and a departmental head, charged that:

> It is the very nations which would have us submissively follow their parental guidance as elder nations that are most involved in ripping us off economically and ripping us up environmentally. Clockwork-orange admirals from America visit us in Papua New Guinea and warn us against Russians bearing gifts. But our experience is that it is our assumed friends and allies we should be wary of: they are the ones destroying our forests and marine environments, they are the ones exploding nuclear devices around us and trying to dump their nuclear waste in our backyards. Those are the concerns we have to face.[8]

Statements such as this are at times exaggerated for rhetorical effect and for bargaining and political purposes. But they do reflect views which are widespread in the region, even if often qualified and balanced by other considerations.

The ambivalence felt in several of the island states towards the United States was reinforced in the early 1980s by conflict over tuna fishing by American vessels in island state exclusive economic zones (EEZs). At this time the refusal by the United States to accept the Law of the Sea Convention, along with the cavalier approach of the American tuna industry, sparked opposition to what the island governments regarded as 'tuna piracy'. From 1986, however, the signing of a multilateral fisheries agreement, and its subsequent renewal, repaired the strains in relations between the island governments and the United States. The island governments have continued to take a strong stance on fisheries issues. Later in the 1980s the island governments, along with Australia and New Zealand, condemned drift-net fishing by Japanese, Taiwanese and other trawlers, and took part in the successful campaign for the banning of this fishing technique.

As new generations have come to power in the island states, with weakening connections with the colonial past, and as island governments have sought to expand and consolidate their sovereignty, a new assertiveness has become evident. This development has been associated with the questioning and revision of the institutions and arrangements set in place at the time of independence, because these are now seen as less appropriate to local traditions and customs and to changing circumstances.[9] On the other hand the newer generations of island political and community leaders are better-educated than their predecessors. They include many able people with a technocratic and pragmatic orientation, who provide a counter-balance to some of the more maverick leaders.

Because military threats to national security have largely been absent, and because of their economic preoccupations, most of the Pacific island governments have interpreted the concept of security broadly. They have often given emphasis to the economic and other non-military challenges to sovereignty and well-being. This emphasis has been strengthened by the distance of most of the island states from the flashpoints of great- and middle-power rivalry and tension and has been further encouraged by the end of the Cold War and the disintegration of the Soviet Union.

Yet while mostly secure from direct military threats, the island states have in recent years become increasingly connected with, and to a considerable extent dependent on, the wider world. Island leaders believe that donor states have an obligation to provide aid to redress historical wrongs and to correct present imbalances. But they resent the dependence of the island states on aid. And they are also resentful that their states, because of their small scale and lack of economic and political power, are subject to but have little influence over international political and economic trends.

Accordingly, island governments generally want to diversify their aid and trade partners. In part the aim is to increase the level of assistance. But island governments also want to increase their freedom of manoeuvre – and hence the degree, in practical terms, of their political and economic independence – by reducing reliance on any one aid/trade partner.

So far we have discussed the general external policy orientations of the island states. These generalisations, however, need to be qualified, modified, and fleshed out by a consideration of the variations in views and approaches in particular parts of the region and in particular states.

THE MELANESIAN STATES AND FIJI

The policies of the governments of Papua New Guinea, Solomon Islands and Vanuatu in part reflect the sense of common Melanesian identity which has emerged in these three states. This consciousness is based on ethno-cultural similarities and similar historical experiences. It has been facilitated by the presence of the various forms of 'Neo-Melanesian', a pidgin English which combines an essentially English word-stock with an Austronesian syntax. These languages are known as *Tok Pisin* in Papua New Guinea, *Pijin* in the Solomon Islands and *Bislama* in Vanuatu.

The sense of common Melanesian identity has been strengthened by a range of personal contacts, including church connections and the links formed by young people while studying abroad, notably at the University of Papua New Guinea in Port Moresby and at the the University of the South Pacific in Suva. It was given expression in 1985 by the formation by these three states of the 'Melanesian Spearhead Group'. Initially the Spearhead was intended as a bloc to lobby on the New Caledonian question at meetings of the South Pacific Forum. It later assumed a more general role as a grouping pursuing what are seen as shared Melanesian interests. It lost much of its initial momentum in the late 1980s and early 1990s because of the reduced salience of the New Caledonian issue following the interim peace settlement in that territory embodied in the Matignon Accords of 1988, and because of changes of leadership in the three states.

The diverse communities of the Melanesian states are more volatile, and often less conservative, than those in most of the other Pacific island societies. The Melanesian entities mostly became subject to external contact and colonial rule and exploitation relatively later than the Micronesian and Polynesian entities. Initial contacts and conflicts often remain strong in local tradition. The interiors of some of the larger Melanesian islands were not 'opened up' to the modern world until the 1940s and 1950s. Several Melanesian societies experienced brutal treatment during the colonial era. This heritage helps shape present thinking. In 1988 the Solomon Islands Minister for Finance, after recalling early conflicts between his ancestors and outsiders, noted that one of his great-uncles had been kidnapped, 'protesting violently, direct from his canoe' to go as an indentured labourer to Queensland.[10]

In addition, Melanesian cultures seem to be somewhat more inward-looking and suspicious of outsiders and external influences than those of Polynesia and Micronesia. In Polynesia and Micronesia, those of mixed local and other ancestry are generally accepted more or less readily as part of, or at least as connected with, the community, despite some tensions, whereas this is not always so for those of mixed ancestry in parts of Melanesia.

Moreover the Melanesian states attained political independence relatively later than their Polynesian counterparts and Fiji. The intellectual formation of their leaderships was influenced by the more radical sentiments present on university campuses and more generally in intellectual discussion in the late 1960s and the early 1970s. And as new players in the regional game, aware of a Fijian and Polynesian inclination to patronise them, they may have felt the need to act more independently and assertively.

Contrasts in approach between the Melanesian states and the other island states can be overemphasised, but it is clear that the Melanesian states have generally taken a more militant line than their Polynesian and Micronesian neighbours. They expressed some reservations about the decolonisation process in American Micronesia, although ultimately they went along with the regional consensus.[11] They were also critical of the Treaty of Rarotonga, which instituted the South Pacific Nuclear Free Zone, believing that the treaty was insufficiently radical in scope and aims (see Chapter 5). They have taken a strong line on issues relating to the French presence, giving these issues prominence in their foreign policies. As well as condemning nuclear testing and the handling of New Caledonia, they have also been inclined on occasion to condemn the French presence in itself, arguing that its continuation is an anomaly.

The Melanesian governments were more robustly critical of the French nuclear testing programme, until its suspension in April 1992, than the Polynesian governments. They took this stance even though the Melanesian states are located further from the test sites, and hence further from any immediate risks, than the Polynesian states. The Melanesian governments have on occasion criticised testing not merely because of possible health and environmental risks, but more importantly because they saw testing as expressive of, and integral to, what they regarded as continued French colonialism in the region.

Their stance on New Caledonia has reflected the strong sympathies felt by many in the independent Melanesian states for the campaign of their Kanak 'brothers' for independence. In their views on New Caledonia, the Melanesian governments have generally given little attention to the rights and interests of the non-indigenous communities, regarding them as interlopers. The position of the Melanesian governments on the French presence has been important to them as a matter of principle. It may also have fulfilled political/diplomatic and psychological purposes, by providing a set of issues on which these governments could agree heartily, at least until Vanuatu shifted its position in the early 1990s, following the coming to power of a coalition government in which the majority party had strong French connections. In doing so they could overlook their dissimilarities and different interests, while expressing that sense of distinctive Melanesian identity which forms part of the image they hold of themselves. These differences have included the contrasting stance of Papua New Guinea and Vanuatu on the OPM, a movement which received diplomatic support from Vanuatu until the late 1980s, as well as the tensions over Bougainville which developed in the late 1980s between Papua New Guinea and the Solomons (see Chapter 2).

But despite the similarities between the foreign policies of the three states, there are also some important differences and nuances. Papua New Guinea's approach has been influenced by the view of its leaders that Papua New Guinea should play a leading part in regional affairs. They have assumed that this role naturally falls to Papua New Guinea because in size, population, resource base and potential wealth it dwarfs the other island states.

Papua New Guinea's wish to exercise leadership also in part reflects its intention to demonstrate the genuine nature of its independence from Australia, its former colonial power. Australia is by far Papua New Guinea's leading aid donor. Over the fifteen years from 1976 to 1990, Australian budget and balance of payments support averaged 25.6 per cent per year of the Papua New Guinea budget.[12] Although the overall trend was downward, as of 1991 Australian aid still provided some 15 per cent of the budget. Australia is the major supplier of Papua New Guinea's imports and investments, and there are some 15 000 Australians resident in Papua New Guinea.

Successive Papua New Guinea governments have sought to assert their independence against the risk of overwhelming Australian influence. At independence, the government of Papua New Guinea adopted a policy of 'universalism,' whereby Papua New Guinea should have relations on an equal footing with all states with which such links could be mutually beneficial. This policy was amended in 1981 into one of 'active and selective engagement', under which external relations were to be oriented towards states and organisations selected because of 'their utility to Papua New Guinea's economic and political development.'[13] Successive governments have sought to diversify their aid and trade contacts, so as to reduce dependence on Australia. The wish to reduce dependence on Australia was reinforced when Australia, because of its own economic difficulties, reduced its aid by A$ 10 million in 1986, arbitrarily and without consultation. In the mid-1980s the government of Prime Minister Paias Wingti put Papua New Guinea's relationship with Australia on a more formal footing, as a partnership between equals in terms of sovereignty, by negotiating a 'Joint Declaration of Principles', which was ratified in 1987.

As part of its efforts to break with the past and to lead the island states towards a more assertive stance, Papua New Guinea governments expressed disapproval during the early and mid-1980s of the South Pacific Commission, denouncing it as an outmoded colonial institution. The location of the Commission's headquarters in Noumea, the capital of the French territory of New Caledonia, was a particular irritation, and encouraged fears of undue French influence.

To replace the Commission, Papua New Guinea proposed that a 'Single Regional Organisation' should combine the functions of the Commission, the Forum and other regional organisations. The members of this proposed body would come exclusively from the island states and territories, although it was envisaged that funding would come from the present and former administering powers and from other donor countries. But proposals for a Single Regional Organisation did not win wide support, in part because the donor states were reluctant to endorse an organisation in which their participation would be limited to providing funds.

From around 1987, however, the heat went out of the issue, because the Forum responded to Papua New Guinea's concerns as well as to more general dissatisfaction with a lack of coordination and overlapping activities between the various regional organisations. It did this by expanding the role of the Forum Secretariat and by restructuring an earlier coordinating committee so as to improve liaison with and coordination of the various regional bodies. This new body, which is entitled the South Pacific Organisations Coordination Committee (SPOCC) held its first meeting in Suva in February 1989.

The shift in Papua New Guinea's position on the South Pacific Commission was evident in 1990–92, when the question of changing the location of the headquarters of the Commission arose. This shift also reflected improved relations with France, following the restoration of peaceful conditions in New Caledonia, as a result of the signature of the Matignon Accords in June 1988 (see Chapter 5). Papua New Guinea supported the continued presence of the Commission in Noumea, relocated to a new site provided by the French government. It did so against a Fijian proposal that the Commission be shifted to Fiji, because of lower operating costs there and because France and New Caledonia, in their high-handed push to relocate the Commission and use the site for tourist development, had treated the island states disrespectfully. At a special conference held in Noumea in March 1992 to resolve the question, the Papua New Guinea delegate commented that:

> his government's position had been arrived at independently and had never changed. The South Pacific Commission had been a useful venue for consultations for members on issues affecting New Caledonia. In

other fora, many Pacific Islands countries had expressed support for the Kanaks. We should therefore be consistent in the South Pacific Commission and not deny their right to be associated with other Pacific Islanders through the presence of SPC headquarters in Noumea.[14]

Attitudes to the South Pacific Forum have varied, but Papua New Guinea's interest was strongest during the early post-independence years, when its (then) Prime Minister, Michael Somare, struck up a good working relationship with the (then) Prime Minister of Fiji, Ratu Sir Kamisese Mara. From 1985 to 1988, when Prime Minister Paias Wingti held office in Port Moresby, the Papua New Guinea government's interest in the Forum declined. It put emphasis instead on the Melanesian Spearhead Group. In March 1988 it set out to formalise relations within the Spearhead Group by arranging the signature of 'Agreed Principles of Cooperation Among Independent States in Melanesia.' As well as confirming continuing interest in the New Caledonian question, these principles sought to encourage economic links between the member states.

Later on, however, Papua New Guinea reaffirmed its interest in the Forum, while reducing its emphasis on the Spearhead Group. The reasons for this shift included the coming to power from July 1988, after a successful no-confidence motion against Wingti, of a government under the prime ministership of Rabbie Namaliu, with Michael Somare as Foreign Minister; the negotiation of an interim settlement in New Caledonia, which took the heat out of this issue; the tensions which arose between Papua New Guinea and the Solomons over the Bougainville revolt; and the change of government in Vanuatu in late 1991 which brought a more conservative, pro-French government to power under Prime Minister Maxime Carlot (now Maxime Carlot Korman).

The stance of Papua New Guinea has also been shaped by the awareness that it fringes on Southeast Asia. Papua New Guinea has been described as the 'bridge' between Southeast Asia and the South Pacific. But Papua New Guinea's former Foreign Affairs Department head Bill Dihm has riposted that: 'I don't see Papua New Guinea as a "bridge nation" between Asia and the South Pacific. People walk over bridges.'[15]

Papua New Guinea has set out to contain intermittent tensions with Indonesia over the *Organisasi Papua Merdeka* (OPM) and the border (see Chapter 2). Negotiations with Indonesia resulted in a Treaty of Mutual Respect, Friendship and Cooperation, ratified in 1987. This treaty is intended to provide the basis for the defusing of tensions and the peaceful negotiation of contentious questions. Papua New Guinea's approach has been conditioned by its awareness of its economic and military weakness relative to that of Indonesia and has embodied a willingness to accept a post-colonial settlement not of its own making.

In contrast, Papua New Guinea's support for Kanak independence in New Caledonia has carried few risks for Papua New Guinea. In addition, France is an easy target because it can be readily represented, albeit in some respects misleadingly, as upholding old style European colonialism in its Pacific territories. Although circumstances in Bougainville differ greatly from those in New Caledonia, the Papua New Guinea government does not regard the ethnic nationalism of some of the inhabitants of Bougainville as legitimate, whereas it supports Melanesian ethnic nationalism in New Caledonia (see Chapter 4).

Papua New Guinea has also made special efforts to develop good relations with the ASEAN states, in part to help insulate itself against Indonesian pressure. As well having attended ASEAN meetings since 1976 as a special observer, in July 1989 Papua New Guinea became the first non-member state to accede to the ASEAN Treaty of Amity and Cooperation. It has welcomed investment from the ASEAN states. After Indonesia, Malaysia is the ASEAN state which has developed the closest links with Papua New Guinea. Several Malaysian timber companies have engaged in operations in Papua New Guinea, at times in an irresponsible and exploitative fashion, and other commercial links have developed. In 1991 Papua New Guinea and Malaysia signed a defence Memorandum of Understanding. This provided a basis for Malaysian defence aid to Papua New Guinea, especially in relation to measures to check insurgency and civil unrest, although as of late 1994 no implementation of this arrangement had taken place.

For its part, Vanuatu aspired during the 1980s to a role of moral leadership in the region. During this period the policies of the Vanuatu government were shaped in part by memories of France's obstruction of the coming of independence, and of the support by local French officials and businessmen for the secession attempt on Espiritu Santo in 1980. As in many other former colonies, but in contrast to the peaceful transition to independence in most of the other Pacific island states, in Vanuatu a difficult process of decolonisation has left legacies of bitterness and suspicion. Under the nationalist *Vanua'aku Pati* (VP – 'Our Land Party'), which held power from 1979 until it lost government in the December 1991 elections, Vanuatu was often at odds with France, but it also generalised its stance by strong criticism of colonialism and neo-colonialism and by suspicion of the Western association of states.

During the 1980s Vanuatu, although its radicalism should not be exaggerated, generally took a more radical position on foreign policy issues than the other states of the region. For several years it was the only island state to have become a member of the Non-Aligned Movement, although Papua New Guinea later also joined this organisation, in 1992. In the 1980s Vanuatu also established diplomatic relations, albeit rather insubstantial ones, with Vietnam and Cuba, based on the moral support which these states gave to the VP during its campaign for independence. In the mid-1980s, elements in the Vanuatu leadership showed considerable interest in the prospect of developing relations with Libya, and in 1987 Vanuatu conducted a fishing agreement with the Soviet Union. These contacts were not however consolidated in subsequent years. While under VP rule Vanuatu sought to be even-handed in relation to the superpowers, although relations with the United States improved in the late 1980s. Under VP rule Vanuatu also took an absolutist line on nuclear issues, expressing strong reservations about and declining to sign the Treaty of Rarotonga, which established the South Pacific Nuclear Free Zone.

Vanuatu's stance has also been affected by the domestic political implications of its relations with France. This domestic dimension interacts with broader questions of principle and national interest in the shaping of Vanuatu's foreign policy. Before independence, France supported the Francophone and *Kastom* ('Custom') parties which coalesced into the UMP (Union of Moderate Parties). Since the Santo Rebellion and the attainment of independence the UMP has suffered politically because of VP charges that it is subversive and pro-French. Playing the 'French Card' helped keep the VP in power from 1979 to 1991. But the VP lost momentum from the late 1980s, and experienced bitter personal rivalries which led to splits and defections. The weakening of the VP permitted the UMP to emerge as the single largest party following the December 1991 elections, and to form a governing coalition soon afterwards.

During the period of VP rule the importance of French aid to Vanuatu had constrained the VP government, despite the domestic political advantages that criticism of France could bring, and despite the scars of decolonisation. In 1979 and early 1980 the VP favoured the idea of letting the New Caledonian Kanak independence movement set up a 'Provisional Government' in Vila. But it changed its mind after the French government warned that if this step was taken, then French aid would cease.[16] In 1980–81 a schism emerged within the VP leadership. Some leaders urged a complete break with France, if necessary at the cost of no more aid, whereas others, because of the importance of the aid contribution, especially with respect to Francophone education, favoured reaching a compromise. Those favouring compromise eventually won, and French aid continued.[17]

Vanuatu's relations with France were difficult throughout the 1980s, especially because of strong support by Vanuatu for Kanak nationalism in New Caledonia. They deteriorated sharply in October 1987, when the VP government, seeking to discredit the UMP in advance of the November elections, claimed that it had proof that France was funding the UMP.[18] Vanuatu expelled the French Ambassador, France cut its aid spending, Vanuatu expelled further French diplomats, and France reduced its aid even further. The size of the French mission declined from over thirty expatriate staff to only two, with the Vanuatu government declining to accord diplomatic status to the head of mission.

A 'normalisation' of the relationship with France was delayed by a bitter political conflict between the governing VP, led by Father Walter Lini, and an alliance between the UMP and a small, dissident group of former VP legislators led by Barak Sope. In late 1988, having consolidated its position, the Lini government set out to reduce tensions with France. Although Vanuatu remained critical of French nuclear testing, tensions over New Caledonia had by then been reduced by the Matignon peace process. At the United Nations General Assembly in October 1988, Vanuatu commended France on reaching a settlement in New Caledonia. The following year the Vanuatu Foreign Minister travelled to France for talks.

In a press interview in March 1990, Lini said that he wanted the re-installation of a French Ambassador in Port Vila and a return to normal relations. He emphasised the prospective importance of renewed French educational, technical and financial aid to Vanuatu, and noted that while Australia and New Zealand were supplying aid according to what was feasible for them, France had a larger economy than these states.[19] His remarks indicated Vanuatu's need for aid because of its economic problems. But they probably also resulted from a wish to counter the suggestions of his political rival, Barak Sope, that a renewal of French aid would depend upon a victory by Sope's Melanesian Progressive Party and his (then) UMP allies in the elections due in 1991.

By the end of the 1980s, in concert with the improvement of relations with France, Vanuatu had opted for a more cautious and pragmatic foreign policy. Some of the more adventurous initiatives of the VP government in the 1980s seemed to have brought more costs than benefits. Thus the interest some prominent ni-Vanuatu showed in early 1987 in relations with Libya waned when hoped-for aid did not eventuate, and when the connection caused internal dissent, attracted Australian criticism, and reduced investor confidence and tourist arrivals. Barak Sope, the politician most associated with the Libyan connection, had become a bitter rival of Lini, and was eventually forced out of the VP in mid-1988. At one stage during the political disturbances of May 1988 (see Chapter 8), which mainly arose out of the rivalry between Lini and Sope, Lini had been obliged to request support from Australia and New Zealand, the two states which he had earlier condemned for alleged neo-colonialism.

Despite the progress under the VP government towards 'normalisation', relations between Vanuatu under a VP or other Anglophone-dominated government and France are always likely to have undercurrents of tension. Bilateral relations with France improved sharply, however, after the UMP was the most successful party in the late 1991 elections, and formed a governing coalition in which it was the dominant partner. The closer and more cordial relations which the new government established with France was a major diplomatic breakthrough for France in the Melanesian part of the region.

But in the elections the UMP had won only 19 of the 46 seats. In order to form a government it had negotiated a coalition with the National United Party (NUP), a group comprising Lini and his supporters which had split from the VP a few weeks earlier, and which had won 10 seats. Over the following years, although the precise composition of the coalition altered several times, the basic pattern whereby the Francophone UMP held office in coalition with several Anglophone parliamentarians continued. The necessity for the UMP to govern in coalition with the one of the (continually squabbling) Anglophone parties provided a restraint on too close an indentification by the UMP with French interests and aims.

For its part France handled its relations with the coalition government fairly cautiously. It discouraged unrealistic expectations of substantial increases in French aid, and encouraged Vanuatu to look for support from New Caledonia and Australia. In mid-1994, Maxime Carlot Korman, although he had earlier been sceptical of the more strident claims of some anti-nuclear campaigners, announced his opposition to a renewal of French nuclear testing in the Pacific islands region. This stance indicated an awareness that his government needed to be conscious of domestic and wider regional imperatives.

Unlike Papua New Guinea and Vanuatu, the Solomon Islands has not aspired to a leadership role, although in 1984 the (then) prime minister, Solomon Mamaloni, in one of the initiatives that contributed to the eventual formation of the Melanesian Spearhead Group, did call for the formation of a separate Melanesian grouping. The Solomon Islands comprises the third most populous of the island states (after Papua New Guinea and

Fiji) and has, after Papua New Guinea, the second-largest land area. It also has a wide range of natural resources, and considerable potential for economic development. But infrastructure and services are poor, living standards are low, ethnocultural and regional differences are strong, and its governments have faced serious development problems.

The approach of Solomon Islands, although it has been broadly similar to that of its Melanesian neighbours, has tended be more cautious and introspective, despite occasional dramatic rhetoric from some leaders. A mid-1985 statement on foreign policy commented that, as a small state dependent on, and vulnerable to, changes in the world economy, and lacking military power, the Solomon Islands had adopted 'a broadly-based multi-dimensional approach to foreign policy which seeks to develop equal partnerships bilaterally, regionally and multilaterally.' Accordingly, the Solomon Islands had supported the United Nations and the Commonwealth, and had endeavoured to be 'both selective and cautious' in opening and developing diplomatic relations with other states.

The Solomon Islands has also taken a firm stance against nuclear testing and the dumping of nuclear and other toxic wastes. It has opposed 'all forms of colonialism'. Yet in a formulation which shows caution and an awareness of the political obstacles involved, the foreign policy document states that Solomon Islands has set out to do 'whatever *is possible and sensible* to assist the colonised peoples in the South Pacific region to gain their independence' [emphasis added].'[20]

Since attaining independence in 1978, the Solomon Island has enjoyed generally cordial relations with Papua New Guinea, until tensions arose over the Bougainville revolt in the late 1980s and early 1990s (see Chapter 2). These tensions were in due course contained however, and meanwhile the positions taken by the Solomon Islands on regional security issues remained broadly consistent with those of Papua New Guinea.

Unlike the Solomon Islands, Fiji has both expected to play and has often been accorded a leadership role among the Pacific island states. Fiji attained independence relatively early, in 1970, in advance of Papua New Guinea, the Solomons and Vanuatu. It played the leading part in establishing the South Pacific Forum and has been prominent in other regional organisations and initiatives. This role reflected Fiji's standing as the second most populous island state after Papua New Guinea, its relative economic strength, its central location in the region, and its character as a transition zone between the Melanesian and Polynesian cultural worlds. Fiji has come under strong Polynesian influences, particularly in the development of its chiefly system. Indigenous Fijian culture combines Melanesian and Polynesian elements, with Polynesian influence strong in the eastern parts of the island group. The indigenous Fijians have cultural and chiefly links with the Polynesian states and territories, especially Tonga. Though the Fijians also have some affinities with Melanesia, they have been inclined to regard themselves as distinct from the Melanesian world, although this stance changed somewhat in the late 1980s.

Fiji has generally taken a strongly conservative, pro-Western stance on security and defence issues. The exception to this came in April/May 1987, when a more radical government briefly held power after a narrow election victory. The new government, which was led by the late Dr Timothy (Timoci) Bavadra, was a coalition between the militant, trade union-based Fiji Labour Party, and the more conservative National Federation Party, which represented the Indian cane farmers and Indian business and professional interests. But this government was deposed a month after its election by Lieutenant-Colonel (later Major-General) Rabuka's first coup on 14 May 1987. Following several weeks of uncertainty, Colonel Rabuka mounted a second coup in September 1987. Henceforth a military-backed administration headed by Rabuka held power, proclaiming itself the champion of indigenous Fijian interests. Fiji returned to constitutional rule following elections in May 1992, under an electoral and political system designed to ensure Fijian dominance. Rabuka's party performed well in the elections, and he formed a new government.

Because it was ousted from office, the Bavadra government had only limited opportunity to implement its policies. These policies included a ban on port visits by nuclear-armed and nuclear-powered ships, along with other measures designed to make Fiji's stance more distinct from that of the Western powers. In practice, however, the Bavadra government's conduct in office, if it had been permitted to continue, probably would have been milder than some of its election rhetoric had suggested, both because the responsibilities of office have a restraining influence, and because it was based on a coalition of diverse interests, some of them conservative.

Successive Fijian governments have expressed a strong commitment to the Forum and other regional activities, but have also tended to have wider horizons than some of the other island state leaderships. In part this has been because of long-serving Prime Minister Ratu Sir Kamisesi Mara's experience as a delegate at the negotiations of the Lomé Conventions, and in a range of other international meetings. It also in part results from the deployment of Fijian troops and police in peacekeeping duties in the Middle East and elsewhere.

Fiji's formerly close relations with Australia and New Zealand cooled as a result of the condemnation of the 1987 coups by these powers, though they improved from around 1990. Fiji responded to the tensions with Australia and New Zealand by developing closer links with France and the United States and by seeking to diversify its links further, including with the ASEAN states. Because of its close links with Polynesia, and its strong commitment to the South Pacific Forum as the premier regional organisation, the government of Fiji has responded cautiously to invitations to become a member of the Melanesian Spearhead Group. Fijian leaders, notably Prime Minister Rabuka, have expressed interest in the idea, but at least for the time being, the Fiji government has not taken the matter further.

THE POLYNESIAN AND COMMONWEALTH MICRONESIAN STATES

The policies of the Polynesian and the Commonwealth Micronesian states have generally contrasted with those of the three Melanesian states. Their populations are smaller and are generally more cohesive than those of Melanesia. Compared with their Melanesian counterparts, they have been subject for a longer period to modern and western influences, especially from the churches. They mostly attained independence or self-government somewhat earlier, in an intellectual environment less influenced by criticisms of colonialism and charges of neo-colonialism. In several of these states, chiefly systems and respect for elders help maintain social discipline and encourage conservative policies. Outsiders tend to be viewed with somewhat less suspicion than in Melanesia.

As smaller states with narrow resource bases, these states are inclined to caution. They support the South Pacific Commission, in part because it unites not only sovereign and self-governing but also dependent territories in a single organisation. This permits a strengthening of the cultural and other connections – notably those between Western Samoa and American Samoa, between the Cook Islands and French Polynesia, and between the Commonwealth and the 'American' Micronesian states and territories – which transcend differences in colonial history, constitutional status and political organisation.

These small states have been wary of Melanesian aspirations to regional leadership, whether based on size (Papua New Guinea) or on moral authority (Vanuatu in the 1980s). Some of them were irritated by the formation of the Melanesian Spearhead Group. They believe that the formation of blocs within the Forum is not conducive to consensus, and tended to resent the assertion of Melanesian independence via the Spearhead group. With

French encouragement, some Polynesian leaders have considered the idea that the Polynesian states and territories form a Polynesian 'community' or confederation, to express their strong sense of shared identity and also in part as a counterweight to the Spearhead. Some leading figures in the Cook Islands, Tonga, French Polynesia, American Samoa and Niue showed some interest in this idea. Tuvalu and Tokelau would also be eligible for membership. Its proponents have also suggested that the proposed organisation should encompass the New Zealand Maoris and the indigenous Hawaiians.[21] But support for the proposal waned from around 1989 when the Spearhead Group lost much of its earlier momentum.

Compared with the Melanesian states, and despite strong concerns over nuclear testing and New Caledonia, the Polynesian and the Commonwealth Micronesian states, along with Fiji, responded more positively to France's aid and diplomatic drive from 1987, which was intended to contain and reduce opposition to the French presence. The more cautious Polynesian stance on the French presence was illustrated in the comments made by Tupuola Efi, Western Samoa's then Deputy-Prime Minister, during a stopover in Auckland while returning from Paris in late October 1987. After calling for a calm dialogue rather than the maintenance of rhetorical positions on New Caledonia, he also commented that: 'The French, who have a Polynesian Minister [that is the Tahitian, Gaston Flosse], which in itself is a considerable step ... are talking with states of the South Pacific outside their traditional sphere of influence, in a way they did not before. In the Cook Islands and in other countries, they are offering their aid constructively.' He added that differences over nuclear testing and other issues remained, but that France, if it intended to play a more positive role in the region, should be permitted to do so.[22]

The most conservative Polynesian state is Tonga, which was a British protectorate until 1970. Tonga is a monarchy in which the chiefly class dominate the parliament. The Tongan government has adopted a conservative foreign policy. It has refused to sign the Treaty of Rarotonga, which established the South Pacific Nuclear Free Zone, because in its view the treaty compromises Western strategic interests (see Chapter 5). It has given cautious support to Forum positions on nuclear testing and New Caledonia, but with reservations and in part for the sake of preserving regional consensus. But despite this conservatism, the at times idiosyncratic influence of King Taufa'ahau Tupou IV, and of his son, Crown Prince Tupouto'a, and the lack of formal mechanisms of government accountability, can give Tongan policies a maverick character.

The former New Zealand colony of Western Samoa is also conservative, but is more pragmatic and moderate in style and orientation than

Tonga. From independence in 1962 until 1990, only those of chiefly rank could vote and hold office. After a referendum in 1990, the suffrage was extended to commoners, but parliamentary candidates must still be of chiefly rank. But the proportion of those holding *matai* or chiefly titles has been expanded in recent years, to encompass over an eighth of the population. Chiefly dominance in the parliament and government encourages caution, and Western Samoa has been 'content to move within the broad consensus established by annual South Pacific Forum discussions and the deliberations of the United Nations General Assembly and the Commonwealth Heads of Governments Meetings.'[23] Western Samoa has close links with the neighbouring United States dependency of American Samoa. Although Western Samoa is glad to be independent, there is some envy among Western Samoans of the material benefits enjoyed by the American Samoans because of their American connection, whether directly through development aid and welfare benefits or indirectly through remittances from American Samoans resident in the United States.

As noted earlier, the Cook Islands (since 1965) and Niue (since 1974) are self-governing and independent in free association with New Zealand. They are both heavily dependent on New Zealand aid and on remittances from their communities resident in New Zealand. Both Cook Islands and Niue generally take a moderate line and support the Forum consensus. Because of the close kin and cultural links between the Cook Islands and French Polynesia, the Cook Islands government has been keen to develop connections with that territory, and has also been positive in its attitude to the French presence in the islands region, including by signing a treaty of friendship with France in 1993. Cook Island governments have encouraged the Forum to take moderate positions on New Caledonia, and have taken a cautious, nuanced stance on French nuclear testing. They also have had reservations about New Zealand's policy on nuclear ship visits, and about the resulting rift in United States/New Zealand relations in the mid-1980s (see Chapter 7).[24]

The final Polynesian state is Tuvalu, which, like the Cook Islands and Niue, is one of the world's smallest states. It has a population of about 10 000. Yet even the smallest island states display pride and a wish to increase their self-reliance. In an effort to escape perpetual mendicancy and to increase its freedom of manoeuvre, Tuvalu has successfully negotiated with its main donors the establishment of the 'Tuvalu Trust Fund'. This investment fund, which came into operation in 1987 with a capital of about A$ 30 million, is intended to produce sufficient interest to permit Tuvalu to cover its basic costs. The returns on the fund during its first few years were disappointing, but have since stabilised, though some problems have continued. Successive Tuvaluan governments have taken a cautious stance on security and foreign policy issues, and have supported the consensus positions reached by the South Pacific Forum.

Like the Polynesian governments, the governments of the two Commonwealth Micronesian states of Kiribati and Nauru have usually pursued moderate and cautious security and defence policies. In the South Pacific Forum, they have generally supported consensus positions. As noted earlier, these two entities were both formerly part of the British imperial system, Kiribati as part of a British colony and Nauru as a British–New Zealand–Australian territory under Australian administration.

Kiribati, a collection of widely-dispersed atolls, is a very poor state. Its key resource in colonial times, phosphate, had been exhausted before independence was granted. It has sought to be as self-reliant as possible, including by means of a fishing deal with the Soviet Union in 1985, which however was not renewed. But for the foreseeable future it will continue to depend on aid even for basic services and infrastructure. In contrast Nauru still had rich phosphate reserves when it became independent. This wealth, its social implications, and the grave ecological damage to the island from mining, all make Nauru a special case, even though its cultural and political links with the other states and entities of the region have been maintained. But the phosphate will run out in about a decade or so, depending on the rate at which extraction continues, and Nauru will become more like the other smaller island states. Meanwhile substantial assistance will be needed to repair the ravaged environment.

The two Commonwealth Micronesian states have generally been pro-Western in orientation, although Nauru's relations with Australia, the United Kingdom and New Zealand have at times been clouded by the legacies of phosphate mining in the colonial period (see Chapter 7). When the government of Kiribati reached a fishing agreement with the Soviet Union in 1985, it did so despite the concern of Australia, New Zealand and other powers that the agreement could open the path for further Soviet expansion in the region. But the Kiribati government was neither attracted by the Soviet 'model' nor interested in developing a more substantial relationship. Instead, its motive was to increase its self-reliance by taking advantage of the generous fees offered. In addition, it was keen to assert its independence of judgement and exercise its sovereignty. So external criticism strengthened rather than reduced its commitment to the deal. Irritation with 'tuna piracy' by US trawlers was also a factor. Kiribati did all it could to ensure that the Soviet Union honoured the agreement to the letter, and declined to renew the agreement when the Soviets did not agree to continue to pay a high premium.

AMERICAN MICRONESIA

The other states in the Micronesian cultural zone are the 'free association' states of the Federated States of Micronesia, the Republic of the Marshall Islands, and Palau. These states are tied closely to the United States through substantial aid and subsidies. In addition, their citizens have the right to reside and work in the United States, and thus in due course to qualify relatively easily for citizenship. The Federated States of Micronesia and the Marshall Islands entered into their compacts in 1986, while Palau acceded to its compact in 1994. The compacts are for fifteen years, but they incorporate military agreements which run for fifty years, thus imposing longer-term constraints on the independence of these entities. So their sovereignty is likely to remain under question, in some measure, because the United States remains responsible for their defence and security and because they are obliged to conduct their external relations in ways which are broadly compatible with United States interests.[25]

In 1987 the Federated States of Micronesia and the Republic of the Marshall Islands became members of the South Pacific Forum, on the basis that they were fully internally self-governing and able to implement Forum decisions within the region. Palau is expected to join the Forum from 1995. The outlook and policies of these three states are shaped by their close links with the United States, their complex colonial history, their geographical location, and their economic links with the Asian countries, especially Japan.

Despite some tensions, notably in the Marshall Islands over compensation for the victims of nuclear testing, relations with the United States have generally gone smoothly in the first two of these entities since the adoption of the compacts. Palau had only just entered its compact at the time this book went to press, but it too can be expected to have reasonably good relations with the United States, now that the vexed question of its constitutional status has finally been settled.

In July 1988, during a visit by Vice-President Bush to the Marshall Islands, acting-President Henchi Balos expressed gratitude that United States protection had 'enabled the Marshall Islands to develop in its own way without threats from the outside.'[26] Some three years later, the (then) Marshall Islands Foreign Minister Tom Kijiner commented that US/Marshalls relations were 'going smoothly.'[27] Similarly, when he addressed the General Assembly of the United Nations in 1991, the Federated States of Micronesia President Bailey Olter said that the United States deserved 'unqualified praise for its singular commitment and generosity' in bringing his country to self-determination.[28]

Both the Federated States of Micronesia and the Marshall Islands wish to be accepted as full participants in Pacific islands affairs. Their conduct as members of the South Pacific Forum has been cautious and generally conservative. In their first few years after acceding to the compacts, they concentrated on obtaining international diplomatic recognition, a goal made easier to achieve because of their acceptance by the other island states.

Outside the region, several governments, including that of the United Kingdom, had reservations about granting diplomatic recognition to the Marshall Islands and the Federated States of Micronesia because of their close defence and other links with the United States. At first it was doubtful whether their transition from components of a trust territory to new states would be endorsed by the Security Council of the United Nations. The Soviet Union was inclined to use its veto both to pursue its rivalry with the United States and because it believed that under the compacts these two entities remained *de facto* United States colonies. But East/West détente and the end of the Cold War opened the way for the Soviet Union to accept the new arrangement. The Security Council endorsed the Compacts in late 1990, and in 1991 both states joined the United Nations, with near-universal support.[29] Palau will be similarly welcomed into the international community, now that it has completed its transition to free association status.

The acceptance of these new states by the South Pacific Forum has facilitated the strengthening of links between them and the other island states, including with the other Micronesian members of the Forum, Nauru and Kiribati. The various Micronesian states were thus able to reaffirm some historical and cultural connections. But no sense of overall unity between them exists. There has been no indication of any propensity by the various 'American' and non-American Micronesian states to form a bloc within the Forum, or to seek to develop a distinctive identity by other means. Compared with 'Polynesia' or even 'Melanesia,' 'Micronesia' has been, at least so far, more a convenient label than a term accurately denoting shared characteristics. In 1987 the (then) Federated States of Micronesia President John Haglelgam commented that 'so far I have not seen any issue where we would come together and act as a bloc.'[30]

Both the Federated States of Micronesia and the Marshall Islands have put strong emphasis on increasing their economic self-reliance and reducing their dependence on the United States. Palau is likely to take a similar stance. All three states lack resources, except for fisheries and tourism potential. But the Federated States of Micronesia has some agricultural potential, while the Marshall Islands has benefited financially from compensation for nuclear damage and from the presence of the Kwajalein missile-testing base. These three states are unlikely to attain economic independence before their compacts come up for renewal or abolition, or indeed for many years thereafter. In each of these states, the American connection and the benefits it brings have considerable popular support, despite bitterness about the colonial past, despite the tragic legacy of nuclear testing in the Marshalls, and despite the presence of regional rivalries linked to strong reservations about the American connection in some parts of the Federated States of Micronesia. Because of the material advantages of the American connection, and because of the constraints imposed by the compacts, these states can be expected to remain closely aligned with the United States in their external policy orientations.

THE SOUTH PACIFIC FORUM AND WIDER SECURITY/ ECONOMIC COOPERATION

The Pacific island states have endeavoured to express their sense of shared identity and to pursue their common interests through involvement in the South Pacific Forum. For the smaller states, which have limited resources to devote to diplomacy and little leverage on their own account in regional and world affairs, the Forum has provided a means of pursuing their aims and policies in a more effective manner at a reduced cost. In relation to environmental, decolonisation, nuclear and other issues relevant to regional security, the Forum has sought to encourage the development of a broad consensus. It has been wary however of intruding into what it regards as the internal affairs of its members, so that it has given some major political issues, including those relating to Fiji and Bougainville, little or only informal attention.

The Forum has also sought to represent its members' views in international meetings and negotiations. Thus it has tabled the New Caledonian case before the United Nations, campaigned strongly against driftnet fishing, and expressed concern over the possible risks of chemical weapon disposal at Johnston Atoll. In addition, starting with the Forum meeting held in Tarawa in July 1989, it has engaged in formal multilateral and bilateral discussions with several 'Dialogue Partners', namely external states and agencies. These discussions take place immediately after the meetings between the Forum heads of government.

As efforts continue, in the post-Cold War era, to develop greater security and economic cooperation in the wider Asia–Pacific region, the South Pacific Forum and individual island states have responded with a mixture of interest and apprehension. Because of their modest size, wealth and power, the island states would not expect to take a leading part in the development of these initiatives, but would wish to be consulted. Several of the island states would regard membership of, or association with, broader regional initiatives and organisations as another useful means for reducing dependence on a narrow range of established aid donors and economic and security partners.

The Forum will seek to ensure that account is taken of the needs and interests of the island states. Island governments are aware that the focus of these initiatives is located outside the Pacific islands region, and that the needs and interests of the island states are easily overlooked. One senior island official has observed that: 'The apparent indifference to island countries' aspirations and needs, displayed by some proponents of new forms of Asian–Pacific cooperation will need to be overcome if the South Pacific is to be orderly, stable and secure.'[31] Indeed, several island leaders have been annoyed that the Asia–Pacific Economic Community (APEC) concept has been developed by Australia and other countries without reference to island state concerns and opinions. Meanwhile, if progress with the establishment of an Asia–Pacific Security Forum is consolidated, and presuming it was extended to embrace the Pacific islands, island leaders would probably see it as a useful additional means in which to pursue their concerns. They would probably, for example, seek to use such a body to put additional diplomatic pressure on France over nuclear testing, should testing be resumed.

4 Decolonisation, Indigenous Rights and Internal Conflicts

The positive external security circumstances of the island states have permitted their governments to define security broadly. Yet though free in recent decades of the threat or actuality of intra-regional armed conflict, as well as of serious direct external threats, the region has had no shortage of internal tensions and conflicts.

In Irian Jaya, various groups of local Melanesians have resisted Indonesian rule. Around the time of Papua New Guinea's accession to independence, several 'micro-nationalist' movements flourished, representing attempts by small communities to go their own way.[1] Larger secessionist movements, in Papua, East New Britain, and especially Bougainville, inspired Papua New Guinea's decision, soon after independence in 1975, to devolve power to provincial governments. In 1989 a major secessionist revolt developed on Bougainville island. Secessionist tendencies have been expressed elsewhere in the region, including, to give only a few examples, in the island provinces of Papua New Guinea, the Western Provinces of the Solomon Islands, in Espiritu Santo and Tanna in Vanuatu, on Rotuma island in Fiji, and in Pohnpei, one of the components of the Federated States of Micronesia. In the French overseas territory of New Caledonia, the indigenous Melanesian Kanaks have campaigned militantly for independence, sparking two bouts of conflict during the 1980s which left over 40 dead.

In the absence of external or intra-regional threats, state force has mainly been used *within* the island states and territories rather than to deter aggression or defend against attack. It has been employed against nationalist and secessionist movements and to contain other internal tensions. In addition, in Fiji in 1987, military force was used to overthrow a reformist, mainly Indian-supported government in order to defend established interests and reassert indigenous Fijian authority.

Since religious or ideological cleavages are mostly absent, minority movements in the region have generally not been able to look for support to co-religionists or fellow believers in neighbouring states and territories. This has reduced the extent to which local conflicts have created a regional and wider resonance.

A sense of ethnic identity has however contributed to the success of efforts by the Kanak nationalist movement in New Caledonia to gain regional support. The Kanaks have attracted support from the Melanesian states because of a sense of common Melanesian identity, while gaining sympathy more generally in the region because of anti-colonial sentiment. In contrast the Bougainville conflict, although its scale is much greater than that of the tensions in New Caledonia, has not become a burning issue in regional affairs, although it has led to bilateral tensions between Papua New Guinea and both the Solomon Islands and Australia (see Chapters 2 and 7).

In this chapter, I examine decolonisation issues, indigenous rights issues, and secessionist and other internal conflicts in the region, and explore the reasons why some conflicts have assumed importance in regional affairs, whereas others have had only local impact.

DECOLONISATION

The contrast in attitudes towards New Caledonia and Bougainville illustrates the extent to which the outlook of island governments is shaped by their acceptance of the post-colonial order established in the region, within the broader context of the attitudes and norms concerning decolonisation established in recent decades by the international community (see Chapter 1). From the time of the Second World War, support evaporated for the notion that the 'advanced' European and European-descended peoples had an inherent right to rule others. And it became widely accepted that a newly-independent state has the right to assume control over the territory administered by the former colonial power.

In the Pacific islands region, as elsewhere among recently-independent states, a marked reluctance exists to challenging the post-colonial order. Any tinkering with that order threatens the legitimacy of existing states, conflicts with the norm in international politics of non-interference in the internal affairs of other sovereign states, and could encourage a variety of dissident and secessionist tendencies within particular states.

As recognised successor states, both Papua New Guinea in relation to Bougainville, and Indonesia in relation to Irian Jaya, are generally regarded by the island governments as having a legitimate right to contain dissent and rebellion, albeit if concerns are expressed over human rights abuses. In contrast, the island governments have often seen France's continued rule over its Pacific territories as a vestige of old-style European colonialism. Some of the island governments have also viewed the process and outcome of the decolonisation of American Micronesia with some scepticism.

During the decolonisation process, some of the former colonial jurisdictions were revised, at least in instances where such revisions did not conflict with the interests of the decolonising power. The British colony of the Gilbert and Ellice Islands was split into the successor states of Kiribati and Tuvalu, because of rivalries and ethnic differences between the Micronesian i-Kiribati and the Polynesian Tuvaluans. The vast United States Trust Territory of the Pacific Islands was broken into four entities, namely the Commonwealth of the Northern Mariana Islands, the Federated States of Micronesia, the Republic of the Marshall Islands, and Palau (Belau). This fragmentation resulted in part from cultural differences and differing political and economic aims among the various American Micronesian entities. But it was readily accepted and to some extent encouraged by the United States because it made it easier overall to negotiate settlements securing American defence and strategic interests.

In the Anglo-French condominium of the New Hebrides, in contrast, the 1980 attempt by Jimmy Stephens to split Espiritu Santo from the emerging state of Vanuatu was defeated. Stephens had support from local French and mixed-race settlers, from land speculators and some American business interests, and from local French officials. But he and his 'government' lacked credibility, and had active support from only a portion of the island's population. Meanwhile the nationalist *Vanua'aku Pati* (VP) had earlier performed strongly in the 1979 elections, demonstrating that it had substantial support in most parts of the New Hebrides archipelago, including on Espiritu Santo. The right of the VP government to assume control of the successor state and to confirm its jurisdiction over Espiritu Santo was supported by the United Kingdom, the South Pacific Forum states and the international community, and was grudgingly accepted by France.

Once the process of decolonisation was completed in relation to particular states, jurisdictions were regarded as set in concrete, both in individual states and across the region as a whole. These attitudes were reinforced by the considerable sea gaps dividing almost all of the island states, and by the absence of irredentist claims. As well as supporting the specific outcomes of the decolonisation process in the region, the island governments have wanted this process to be continued, in those instances where island entities remain under Western rule.

Their commitment to decolonisation relates to their determination to assert their own political independence. Of course, coping with the challenges of independence has proved more difficult than expected, leading to frustration and disillusionment.[2] Island leaders are conscious that the

French and American territories receive substantial funding, and thus have a higher average standard of living than their independent neighbours. But they are also conscious of the sharp inequalities in the distribution of wealth in some of these territories, especially as in several instances the indigenous communities in a particular territory are disadvantaged relative to many of the non-indigenous residents. And they are concerned by the adverse social and cultural effects of continued dependence. Accordingly, the island states have generally favoured the decolonisation of the remaining territories, provided that decolonisation is sought by the majority of the indigenous population of the territory. So long as the arrangements for the ending of external rule have broad support within a former entity, the island governments have been relaxed about the nature of the new relationship established. Thus they have accepted 'free association' arrangements as well as full independence. Where the local indigenous community has not generally favoured a transition to independence or free association, as has been the case for example in the Northern Marianas, in French Polynesia and in American Samoa, the island states have mostly accepted the continuation of external rule.

Regional support for decolonisation initially focused on the New Hebrides, where Britain accepted and encouraged, but France resisted, an early transition to unitary independence. The Forum island states gave diplomatic support to the *Vanua'aku Pati* government which won office in 1979, and welcomed Vanuatu to membership of the Forum in 1980. Despite the reservations of some of the island states about intervention in the internal affairs of a particular state, Papua New Guinea troops, with Australian diplomatic, logistical and communications support, helped quell the French-encouraged secessionist movement on Espiritu Santo.

In New Caledonia, conflict has developed between the indigenous Melanesians, known as Kanaks, who comprise some 45 per cent of the population, and who mostly want independence, and the non-indigenous inhabitants, most of whom oppose independence.[3] Regional interest in New Caledonia began to develop in the late 1970s, and was sharpened when a *Front Indépendantist* (Independence Front) delegation from New Caledonia was present at the time of the Forum meeting at Honiara in 1979.[4] Since then representatives of the Kanak nationalist movement, which in 1984 was reorganised into the FLNKS (*Front de Libération Nationale, Kanak et Socialiste* – National Kanak Socialist Liberation Front), have been on hand at every Forum. New Caledonia, being neither independent nor fully self-governing and in clear transition to independence, does not qualify for Forum membership. Moreover the Kanak nationalist movement represents only a portion of New Caledonia's population. Nonetheless, while not attending the Forum's formal sessions, the Kanak delegations have met separately with the Forum leaders. In addition the FLNKS, representing the Kanak people, has been a member of the Melanesian Spearhead Group since 1989.

The Forum cautiously welcomed the reforms implemented in the territory by the French Socialists after they won government in 1981, and delayed the tabling or 'reinscription' of New Caledonia by the United Nations Committee of Twenty-Four on Decolonisation. But when the conservative government which held power in France from 1986 to 1988 reversed its predecessor's policies for New Caledonia, the Forum decided to support reinscription. This led to the censure of France by a majority of United Nations members. The Forum responded positively to the Matignon Accords of mid-1988, whereby a new Socialist government led by Michel Rocard established an interim peace settlement.

Under this settlement, which will culminate in a referendum in 1998 on the territory's future, some powers have been devolved to three provincial governments, two of which are under the control of the nationalist movement; massive spending has been directed to improving infrastructure and services in the interior and outer islands, where the majority of the Melanesian population lives; and programmes have been established to improve the educational attainments of the Melanesians and their level of participation in the public service and the private sector.[5] This interim settlement has been reasonably successful, at least so far, so New Caledonia has receded in importance on the Forum agenda. But the Forum is monitoring developments: if conflict breaks out again New Caledonia is bound to return as a prominent issue at Forum meetings.

Australia, New Zealand, Fiji, and the Polynesian and Micronesian states were at first cautious about the United Nations reinscription of New Caledonia. This was despite pressure from the Melanesian Spearhead states to move quickly. When the reinscription process was set in train, however, Australia and New Zealand provided indispensable administrative and diplomatic support to implement the Forum's policy. Australia, New Zealand and the island states also backed Rocard's policy for New Caledonia, which from mid-1988 established an interim peace, although the Spearhead states had reservations.

In contrast to continued interest in New Caledonia, the attention of the island governments has turned only intermittently to circumstances in French Polynesia, the other large French territory in the region. A strong nationalist movement emerged in French Polynesia in the late 1940s and early 1950s, but was obstructed by the French administration, by fair means and foul. Since the 1960s, although sentiment in favour of increased self-government has been strong, only a minority of French Polynesians have supported complete independence. Despite reservations about the nuclear testing programme, most French Polynesians have welcomed the massive influx of funds associated with the programme and with a more general effort by France to consolidate its presence. In each of the 1986 and 1991 elections to the local Territorial Assembly, parties calling for independence won only some 15 per cent of the vote.

In Wallis and Futuna, France's other territory in the region, no public expressions of pro-independence sentiment have been made. The territory has a population of only some 14 000, and limited resources. It is heavily dependent on French funding. Under the constitution adopted in 1961, local custom and tradition and the Catholicism adhered to by almost all of the population are protected. In recent decades many Wallisians have migrated to New Caledonia, and the majority of the Wallisian community there has voted against the Kanak nationalist movement, because its interests are tied up with the French presence. Despite tensions between the local people and the French administration, and support for expanded local autonomy, a large majority of the population of Wallis and Futuna favours continued close connections with France.

Wallis and Futuna attracts little international attention, even from critics of the French presence in the region. French Polynesia has assumed more salience. From time to time criticism of French nuclear testing in the region and of French control of New Caledonia has been generalised into calls for independence for French Polynesia. But in the absence of a strong nationalist movement in French Polynesia, the question of that territory's constitutional evolution has not become an major issue in regional affairs.

Attitudes to French Polynesia have also been moderated because the closer neighbouring states, namely the Cook Islands, Western Samoa and Tonga, have been moderate to conservative in their attitudes. In contrast New Caledonia is part of the more volatile Melanesian region, and throughout the 1980s the government of its closest neighbour, Vanuatu, regarded the campaign for the independence of New Caledonia from external rule as a continuation of that which had taken place in the New Hebrides.

Decolonisation has also been at issue in relation to the United States Trust Territory of the Pacific Islands, the collection of Micronesian islands formerly held by Japan which the United Nations granted to the United States to administer after the Second World War. As noted earlier, its successor components are the Northern Mariana Islands, which opted in 1975, with 79 per cent of voters in favour,[6] for political union with the United States as a self-governing 'Commonwealth'; the two entities which in

1986 entered into free association compacts for fifteen years with the United States, namely the Federated States of Micronesia and the Republic of the Marshall Islands; and Palau, which in late 1994 also acceded to free association status. When this resolution of Palau's status is approved by the United Nations, the Trust Territory will cease to exist.

The close links of the Micronesian free association states with their former administering power have at times attracted criticism.[7] Unlike New Zealand's associated states, the Cook Islands and Niue, the Micronesian entities are unable to proceed without delay to full independence, should they wish to do so, simply by passing the appropriate legislation in their legislatures. Instead they are required to wait until their compacts with the United States come up for renegotiation or cancellation. And even if they choose full independence at that time, they would still require United States assent to cancel the defence provisions of the compacts, which run for fifty years.

In December 1990 the United Nations Security Council endorsed the status of the Federated States of Micronesia and the Republic of the Marshall Islands, together with that of the Commonwealth of the Northern Mariana Islands, as an appropriate fulfilment of the United States' obligations to these entities as parts of the Trust Territory of the Pacific Islands. This decision was only possible because, in the post-Cold War spirit of détente, the Soviet Union decided not to employ its veto, as it had earlier intended to do.[8] Australian diplomats in Moscow, consistent with Australia's alliance with the United States and with its particular interest in the Pacific islands region, had played an active part in getting the Soviet government to focus on the question. In 1991 the Marshall Islands and the Federated States of Micronesia were accepted into the United Nations.

The United States had also encouraged Palau to proceed to free association status. But this outcome was blocked for some twelve years from 1979 because the defence and security provisions of the proposed compact were in conflict with the anti-nuclear provisions of Palau's constitution. The Palauans' anti-nuclear sentiments had been shaped by bitter memories of suffering during the Second World War.[9] They were also concerned about the prospective diversion of scarce land to military purposes. They had legitimate concerns, and the United States has been justifiably criticised for exerting heavy-handed and coercive pressures. But some accounts are one-sided. The inclusion of the anti-nuclear provisions in the Palauan constitution may in part have also reflected a wish to improve Palau's bargaining position relative to the United States. In addition the question of Palau's constitutional future was complicated by the complex and bitter rivalries within Palauan society. In several referenda a substantial majority, ranging from 61 to 72 per cent, voted for the free association compact. But none of these referenda attained the 75 per cent of votes then required to override the nuclear-free provisions of the constitution.

In 1992, however, Palau responded to changing circumstances by taking the action required to enter into a Compact of Free Association with the United States. In November 1992 its voters approved, by 62 to 38 per cent, a constitutional amendment which reduced the requirement for a vote amending the anti-nuclear provisions of the constitution to 50 per cent. Next, in a referendum held on 9 November 1993, Palauans voted 68 per cent in favour of the Compact to 32 per cent against. The voter turnout was high.

The referendum result thus permitted the resolution of the status of the last remaining portion of the former United States Trust Territory of the Pacific Islands. Palau should become a member of the South Pacific Forum from 1995, assuming that legal challenges initiated by opponents of the compact do not succeed. The resolution of the Palau question was facilitated because, since the end of the Cold War, Palauan concern over the defence implications of the Compact has diminished.

During the Cold War era, the United States had envisaged that, under a free association compact, Palau would provide a possible locale for the redeployment of some military assets and facilities, albeit on a modest scale, in the scenario of a United States withdrawal from the Philippines. But this scenario has lost much of its relevance, for several reasons. These include the end of the Cold War period, supplemented by budget difficulties in the United States; the resulting intention of the United States to wind down its West Pacific military presence, in part by deployments outside the region; and technological and communications improvements which facilitate long-distance operations and reduce the need for substantial forward deployments and for the employment of island bases as strategic 'stepping stones'.[10]

In addition, in recent years the United States government, partly because of the difficulties which have arisen in relation to the Philippines, Palau and elsewhere, has decided that henceforth, unless special circumstances apply, substantial bases and facilities will only be established either on undisputed United States territory or else in places where their presence will not result in local opposition. The question was posed sharply in the early 1990s by the closure of the Clark Air Base as a result of the eruption of Mount Pinatubo, and by the American departure from the Subic Naval Base. In response, the United States redeployed some assets and facilities, on a modest scale, to its territory of Guam, but has otherwise largely withdrawn back to Hawaii and the mainland United States. It also arranged to use ship repair and servicing facilities, on a commercial basis, in Singapore, and may develop similar arrangements, on a small scale, elsewhere in Southeast Asia.

As a result the relevance of Palau in United States contingency planning has declined. This decline was confirmed when the United States indicated in late 1990 and early 1991 that it did not intend to build new bases in Palau. Accordingly, Palau was somewhat less subject to pressure from the United States, but also had less bargaining power in its efforts to negotiate an attractive settlement. In the early 1990s some Palauan leaders were told that should they continue to reject the Compact, the attractive financial deal offered therein might no longer be available, given Palau's reduced strategic importance and the budgetary difficulties of the United States. In June 1992 the United States government informed the United Nations Trusteeship Council that it would give Palau another opportunity to accept a free association compact, failing which it would turn its attention to the independence option.[11] Subsequent negotiations between the governments of the United States and Palau paved the way for the successful vote in November 1992 to facilitate the amendment of the constitution.

As well as facing obstacles and criticism in Palau, United States policy concerning American Micronesia has also attracted some criticism in both the Commonwealth of the Northern Mariana Islands and in Guam. The Northern Marianas, impressed by the economic and other benefits flowing from the United States connection, chose commonwealth status in 1974. As a Commonwealth of the United States, the Northern Marianas has full internal self-government and full access to federal funding programs. The United States assumes responsibility for the defence and foreign affairs of the Northern Marianas, but nonetheless this entity has been able to exercise considerable autonomy in the development of its external economic relations, especially with nearby states in Asia.

Although wishing to remain an integral part of the United States, the Northern Marianas has called for a revision of the commonwealth arrangements, to give it greater freedom in its external relations as well as control over the exclusive economic zone around its territory. In addition, many of the residents of the Northern Marianas, like those of the other United States insular entities in the Pacific islands region and in the Carribean, complain that in some respects they are second-class citizens. Thus they are not eligible to vote in the process to elect the president of the United States, and their elected representatives in Congress do not have full voting rights in that body. Indeed the 'Resident Representative' of the Commonwealth of the Northern Marianas in the Congress 'has no rights or privileges in Congress, except the same right to present testimony that any person has'. For their part, the 'delegates' elected by American Samoa and Guam can introduce bills and vote in committee, but do not have the vote in plenary sessions.[12]

When, in December 1990, the Security Council agreed that the Strategic Trusteeship should be dissolved in relation to the Northern Marianas, the Federated States of Micronesia and the Republic of the Marshall Islands, the President of the Northern Marianas complained that the decision had been taken too quickly. He had wanted more time for the Northern Marianas to champion its view before the international community that its constitutional relations with the United States needed some revisions.

In Guam, as in the Northern Marianas, connections with the United States remain strong and extensive. But demands for the revision of relations with the United States have been given impetus by the cultural and political revival in recent decades among the Chamorros people, who comprise approximately 42 per cent of the population. The Chamorros are of mixed indigenous-Spanish descent. There are some parallels between their situation and that of the Kanaks in New Caledonia: both groups comprise an indigenous grouping which has become a 'minority in its own country'. The United States took over Guam in 1898 after winning the Spanish-American war. The Chamorros complain that despite Guam's colonial history, first under Spanish and then American rule, punctuated by the Japanese occupation during the Second World War, its inhabitants have never been permitted to take part in a proper act of self-determination. In contrast the other entities in American Micronesia, as successor components of the Trust Territory of the Pacific Islands, have been through a process of decolonisation observed and endorsed by the United Nations.

At present the Chamorros and other Guamanians are negotiating with the United States for a change in Guam's status from that of a dependent territory to that of a United States 'Commonwealth'. They hope that such an arrangement will provide for complete internal self-government and the return of federally-held property, and will give Guam substantial control over the application of federal legislation.[13] The would also like Guam to have control of the surrounding exclusive economic zone. So far the United States government has resisted the efforts of the Guamanians to expand on the content of the proposed Commonwealth arrangements. The negotiations are likely to take several years, and tensions will increase if the United States government fails to offer a settlement which is acceptable to the Guamanians.

In response to the decolonisation process in American Micronesia, one commentator has raised the possibility of the Polynesian territory of American Samoa proceeding to independence as 'Eastern Samoa' under a free association compact with the United States.[14] American Samoa has remained predominantly Polynesian in population. Its people govern their own local affairs and are conscious of the present benefits of the American connection. Neither the United States government nor the American Samoan government has shown interest in the possibility of the territory proceeding to free association status. But the notion could possibly be pursued at a later stage by American Samoans keen to protect their cultural identity and increase their self-governing and external relations powers while preserving advantageous connections with the United States. Should at some stage a freely-associated state of 'Eastern Samoa' emerge, it would no doubt be welcomed as a member of the Forum.

The island states have broadly endorsed the handling by the United States of its obligations with regard to both the components of the former Trust Territory of the Pacific Islands and the territories of Guam and American Samoa. At least in the short term, it does not seem likely that differences and tensions between the United States and these various entities will surface as issues on the regional political and security agenda, in particular in discussions at South Pacific Forum meetings.

Around the turn of the century, however, the relations of the Marshall Islands and the Federated States of Micronesia with the United States could attract some attention, as the fifteen-year duration of their compact arrangements nears completion in 2001. And efforts by the Northern Marianas, Guam and American Samoa to increase their self-governing powers and constitutional freedoms in relation to the United States could also attract sympathetic attention.

So far, despite tensions and difficulties, the United States has maintained reasonably cordial relations with its Pacific island territories and with its associated states, in part because these communities rely heavily on the financial and other benefits of their American connection. The governments of the Pacific island states accept the United States as a legitimate and valued participant in Asia–Pacific affairs. They have not generally regarded the United States, despite bitterness over some issues, with the kind of suspicion and hostility which often has been directed against France and its presence in the Pacific islands region.

INDIGENOUS NATIONALISM, THE FIJI COUPS, AND SECESSIONIST MOVEMENTS

The emphasis of island leaders on self-government and political independence for former colonies and their opposition to colonialism and its legacies reflects their sympathy with indigenous aspirations. They generally

define the boundaries and content of the 'national' community in terms of
the jurisdictions of the established states of the region, but within this
context they strongly support the rights and interests of indigenous
peoples. In several of the Pacific island states, as elsewhere, an unresolved
tension exists between the ethno-nationalist conception of the nation as
essentially comprising a single ethnocultural community, and the territorial conception of the nation as comprising the populations resident and
under a single administration in a particular territory.[15]

The island governments had reservations about the coups in Fiji in
1987. Yet once the coups had taken place, they mostly took the view that
the interim administrations established in Fiji should not be subject to
external pressure. Most of them interpreted the coups in an uncomplicated
fashion, as a reassertion of indigenous rights and interests against
encroachments by the immigrant Indian community. They believed that
this reassertion should take precedence over democratic principles and the
rights of non-indigenous nationals. They showed little sympathy for inter-
pretations of the coups that presented them as more complex phenomena,
fueled in part by personal ambitions and anxieties and by a wish to defend
class and regional interests. In several island states and territories the
leader of the coups, Sitiveni (or 'Steve') Rabuka, was regarded as a hero.
In Papua New Guinea, for example, the (then) Secretary of the Foreign
Affairs Department named his newborn son after him. In New Caledonia,
the leaders of the Kanak nationalist movement indicated sympathy and
support for Rabuka's assertion of Fijian primacy.

In the Papua New Guinea parliament, soon after the first coup, some
parliamentarians made strong attacks on the small but commercially
significant Chinese community in Papua New Guinea, depicting it negatively and describing it as similar in some respects to the Indian community in Fiji. In late September 1987 the (then) Prime Minister Paias Wingti
told parliament that Papua New Guinea had deep sympathy for the problems of Fiji, believed that these problems were an internal matter which
only the Fijians could resolve, and thought that there should be no attempt
by external parties to interfere in Fiji. Overall, there was a sharp difference
in perceptions of and responses to the coups between the island states and
Australia and New Zealand. Indeed, the outrage at the coups expressed by
the Australian and New Zealand governments was not shared by the island
governments.

In Fiji the focus on indigenous rights has been at the expense of Fiji
Indians (also know as Indo-Fijians). Militant Fijians have argued that the
Indians were imposed on the indigenous Fijians during the colonial era in
pursuit of commercial interests. But 'locals' versus 'immigrants' tensions

also exist throughout the region between groups of islanders, at local, regional and 'national' levels. Conflict often focuses on rights to land. Examples over the last decade include tensions between the indigenous Melanesians and the Polynesian immigrants, mostly from Wallis and Futuna, in New Caledonia; differences between the peoples of the different states of the Federated States of Micronesia; tensions between the long-established residents of Efate island in Vanuatu and migrants to Efate from elsewhere in the archipelago; and, bitterness and conflicts between the local people on Bougainville and the 'redskins', a term describing Papua New Guinea immigrant workers, who characteristically are of lighter skin colour than native Bougainvilleans. The tensions on Bougainville contributed to the mass departure, following violence, of the redskins in the late 1980s. Similarly, tensions have arisen between the native Polynesians of New Zealand, the Maori, and Polynesian immigrants to New Zealand.

Antipathy to outsiders and a strong sense of local nationalism have been central to the conflict in Bougainville (see also Chapter 2). From 1964, when the CRA mining company began operations at Panguna, there were intermittent tensions and secessionist demands related to mining activities, environmental destruction and the arrival of workers from elsewhere in Papua New Guinea. Disputes over compensation and royalties also developed. The local land owners disputed over the division amongst them of their share of the royalties and other returns. They also complained that their share was derisory, compared with the shares going to the provincial and national governments, and given the environmental devastation and social disruption involved in the mining operations. Other local people, who were not eligible to receive a share of the proceeds, but whose lives had been disrupted by the mine, complained that they had received no or only trifling compensation.

In 1975, on the eve of Papua New Guinea's independence, Bougainville leaders declared the independence of 'The Republic of the North Solomons'. They backed down however when the central government reinstated a recently-suspended interim provincial government, and established a system of provincial government throughout Papua New Guinea.[16] Simmering discontents resurfaced from 1988. Attacks on mining operations which forced the closure of the mine were combined with violence against both local people and outsiders. The politics of the dispute were complex, as May points out:

> in a pattern not unfamiliar to students of Melanesian politics, what
> appears at first to be a straightforward case of a landowner group

seeking increased compensation from a mining company turns out to be a multi-layered mass of shifting elements whose motivations range from a broad Bougainville nationalism to internal family fighting.[17]

In early 1989 Francis Ona, the leader of the militants among the traditional landowners, announced that the 'Republic of Bougainville' had been established. Efforts by the Papua New Guinea government to contain the revolt failed, and the situation rapidly deteroriated. Extensive human rights abuses were committed by both government and rebel forces, and various criminal groupings took advantage of the breakdown in public order. But in due course the Bougainville Revolutionary Army squandered much of its earlier support by fractiousness, human rights abuses and an inability to provide services.

By late 1994 the direct casualties from the conflict numbered in the hundreds, thousands more people had died or suffered serious illness because of the absence of health and welfare services, and there had been extensive damage and destruction to infrastructure and property. The province, formerly one of the most prosperous and advanced parts of Papua New Guinea, had become a disaster zone. In August 1994 the (then) Papua New Guinea Minister for Finance, Masket Iangalio, estimated that the costs of the conflict included 'more than A\$ 100 million annually in direct expenditure alone'.[18] The indirect costs, including revenue foregone and damage to plant, equipment and infrastructure, ran into billions of dollars. By this time the Papua Guinea defence force, in loose association with various local 'resistance' militias opposed to the Bougainville Revolutionary Army, had regained control over much of the island, paving the way for a renewal of negotiations, which Sir Julius Chan pursued actively after he replaced Paias Wingti as Prime Minister in late August 1994.

While essentially local in their roots, conflicts reflecting indigenous and localist aspirations can impinge on international relations within the region. The Fiji coups, political tensions in Vanuatu, and the conflict in Bougainville have all become issues in regional or bilateral diplomacy. These and other domestic conflicts have on occasion created circumstances conducive to the use or potential use of force, or to the provision of military assistance from another island state or from a neighbouring state, in particular Australia (see Chapters 7 and 8). Since the late 1980s Australia has provided assistance to Papua New Guinea in its efforts to cope with the Bougainville conflict, despite concerns about human rights abuses, but has sought to limit its involvement.

There has been strong discontent in the Solomon Islands about Papua New Guinea's handling of the Bougainville question and over the way in which the dispute has at times impinged on the sovereignty of the Solomon Islands (see Chapter 2). Yet despite its irritation with Port Moresby, and notwithstanding the presence of strong sympathies for the rebels in the Solomon Islands, the Solomon Islands government has chosen to seek to contain damage to its bilateral relations with Papua New Guinea over this issue. Other island governments have taken the view that the Bougainville question is a domestic issue for Papua New Guinea.

Neither have powers and organisations external to the region involved themselves significantly in the conflict, although the Commonwealth Secretariat has sought to play a mediating role, and Amnesty International and other bodies have condemned human rights abuses. If the conflict had erupted some years earlier the (then) Soviet Union and its clients and associates may have been tempted to seek to turn it to propaganda advantage. On the other hand the Soviets would have been wary about damaging relations with Papua New Guinea, the largest island state, and with Australia. At an earlier stage Libya, too – which in the mid-1980s had provided some 'security training' assistance to Kanak nationalists from New Caledonia, and to OPM supporters and members of the *Vanua'aku Pati* in Vanuatu – may have offered some support as part of its interest in 'liberation' movements.

The Bougainville conflict has been on an unusually large scale, involving heavy casualties and extensive material damage. But similar conflicts can be expected to develop or resurface elsewhere in the Pacific islands region, amidst diverse, plural societies which do not mesh neatly with the structures and values of recently-invented states. This is especially true of Melanesia, but it also applies to other parts of the region. In American Micronesia, for example, there are ethnic and other rifts between and within the four 'states' which have been grouped together in the Federated States of Micronesia, and between them and their 'national' government. Glenn Petersen has commented that:

In time, I believe, unhappiness with the central government, which has been growing steadily since its inception, will result in a concerted effort, quite possibly accompanied by some violence, to wrest power from it. When this happens, however, relations among the states themselves will have so deteriorated that no new accommodation among them will be found. When the current Compact of Free Association with the United States expires in 2001, the Federated States of Micronesia may well disintegrate into a series of microstates, even smaller than their present aggregate population of just over one hundred thousand.

Most likely the early twenty-first century will see a series of political entities forming in [the former Federated States of] Micronesia on the scale of Tuvalu, Tokelau, or...Niue....The historical trajectory of colonialism, which once strung these islands together like so many gems on an empress's necklace, has passed its apogee; the golden chain has snapped and the stones scatter.[19]

Dr Petersen may have overstated his case, but secessionist tendencies could indeed gather strength in the Federated States of Micronesia as the compact arrangements move towards their expiry.

Meanwhile, the determined response of the Papua New Guinea government to the Bougainville conflict has in part been informed by concern lest the secessionist movement there provide a precedent and encouragement for similar movements elsewhere in Papua New Guinea. A transition by Bougainville to independence or independence in association would certainly be regarded as a precedent by dissident groups elsewhere in Papua New Guinea. In late 1994 political leaders from the various island provinces of Papua New Guinea threatened to push for independence from the 'mainland' of Papua New Guinea, unless the Papua New Guinea government acceded to their demands for greater autonomy. They confirmed that they had been closely following developments in Bougainville. Secessionist pressures have also been present in Solomon Islands, notably in the Western Province.

These conflicts will strain domestic resources, and at times will have wider implications, but generally more for particular bilateral rather than for regional relations. The potential for unrest in island states has from time to time prompted calls for the establishment of a permanent regional peacekeeping force. But, as discussed in Chapter 2, the island governments have shown little interest in the creation and development of such a force, though they have been willing to support the *ad hoc* establishment of forces for particular purposes. Thus in September 1994 they supported the setting up a multilateral force to assist with the peace process in Bougainville.

OTHER INTERNAL TENSIONS

As well as the tensions associated with decolonisation, indigenous rights, and secessionism, many other parts of the region are also subject to other forms of violent internal conflict. These conflicts reflect economic, social, cultural and regional cleavages and rivalries. In many instances, they focus on the right to occupy and use land. They often are associated with the erosion of traditional values and institutions by rapid social and economic change, including extensive urbanisation. Population increase has sped ahead of the growth of employment in the cash economy, helping expand unemployment and sharpen competition for resources, thus contributing to social tensions. The processes of economic development, while promising to raise standards of living in the longer term, often bring social, economic, cultural and environmental disruption in the short term. This disruption sharpens conflicts within communities, and between local and regional communities and the central government.

In the Pacific islands region, as elsewhere, people have multiple affiliations and senses of identity which come into play according to the particular contexts in which they find themselves. In much of the region however identity and loyalty is primarily associated with small communities and/or kin groups. Horizons often do not extend far beyond the hamlet or village and the island or valley in which it is located. In several island societies a sense of civic or public duty and obligation, as distinct from, and on occasion in contradiction with, kinship and community obligations, is generally absent.

State and administrative institutions and mechanisms which can contain tensions and disputes and offer possible means for their resolution before they become violent are often weak and ineffective. Indeed, on occasion these institutions and mechanisms create and exacerbate problems more than they help to contain or resolve them. Peter King has pointed out that the police and the military in Papua New Guinea, which are described collectively as the 'disciplined forces', have often in recent years been characterised by their indiscipline.[20] Rather than assuring the security of the population, they have at times been, along with corrupt and exploitative members of the political élite, a source of insecurity.

In the years ahead, moreover, military and police forces may be inclined to intervene in politics. There are precedents, in addition to those provided by the two coups in Fiji in 1987, and their aftermath. On several occasions in Papua New Guinea in the late 1980s and early 1990s, especially though not exclusively in relation to the Bougainville conflict, the military and/or police forces refused to follow government orders and interfered improperly in the political process. The bad case scenarios for the next decade or so include a botched coup in Papua New Guinea, which cripples the national government, paving the way for a collapse of public order and widespread violence and destruction.

Internal unrest and violence have from time to time posed a serious challenge to internal security in some island states. In May 1988 the government of Vanuatu was unsettled by demonstrations and rioting in Port

Vila, the capital, arising out of land issues and political rivalries. In Palau, during the years of wrangling over the compact issue, and in a context shaped by heavy American pressure, one president was assasinated and another committed suicide, and several other violent incidents took place. In Papua New Guinea, the management of internal unrest and violence has become a significant aspect of bilateral relations with Australia. Since 1988 Papua New Guinea has received police training and other assistance from Australia, intended to improve its ability to contain crime and maintain public order. So far, however, these various conflicts, in Papua New Guinea and elsewhere, have not usually had direct wider implications for regional security affairs.

CONCLUSION

The island governments are likely to maintain their interest in decolonisation issues with respect to the American and French territories. In particular, they will follow developments in New Caledonia closely, as the referendum planned for 1998 draws nearer. Their approach will primarily be pragmatic, and will be informed by the attitudes of the indigenous communities in the respective territories. The island governments are also likely to continue to favour the protection of indigenous rights, at the 'national' though not always at the 'subnational' level.

Secessionist movements are likely to surface from time to time. But the island and donor governments can be expected to continue to support the boundaries and jurisdictions established under the post-colonial order, and to regard secessionist disputes as essentially a matter for the state concerned. The various secessionist movements will often have difficulty in establishing their credibility – a task which some existing island governments, despite external recognition and support, themselves find difficult. The secessionist movements are able to mobilize against an externally-imposed state structure, but are often unable to cohere effectively in support of a positive programme of their own. The local loyalties and grievances and the narrow horizons which provide their impetus are also major obstacles to effective organisation and realistic planning. So they will find it hard to attain wider international acceptance and support.

Over the next decade or so, several island governments will need to increase substantially the capacities of their policing and legal systems so as to cope with the stresses and strains of economic development and social change. Some governments will also require increased police and military strength in order to manage secessionist challenges.

Some island governments, especially in Melanesia, will need outside help to assist their military and police forces to operate professionally and effectively, including by respecting human rights and democratic government. Should donors fail to assist sufficiently, they will risk expending their other aid contributions to no lasting purpose.

5 Environmental, Resource and Nuclear Issues

In their thinking about security, island leaders and commentators have often put strong emphasis on environmental, resource and nuclear issues. In doing so, they often take the high moral ground. They point out how unspoiled Pacific island environments have been damaged, and in some instances devastated, by outsiders. They also express resentment that decisions taken and actions implemented in far distant places, in which Pacific islanders play no part, can have catastrophic implications. Thus massive resource use in rich industrial countries has accentuated global warming; defence priorities in the United States, the United Kingdom and France have resulted in the use and abuse of parts of the region for nuclear and missile testing; and the nuclear and chemical industries in the industrialised countries have been attracted by the possible use of parts of the region for waste dumping.

These arguments have much strength. Yet island societies have themselves not always given environmental protection a high priority. In pre-colonial times Polynesian communities drastically altered the ecology of the islands on which they settled. On Easter Island, for example, population pressures led to massive deforestation.[1] In what is now Papua New Guinea, archaeological traces have been found of communities which apparently disappeared after destroying their own resource base by over-cultivation.[2] In recent years some island political and community leaders have been complicit in the environmental destruction wrought by irresponsible mining, forestry and resort development companies. From the mid-1980s, however, the governments of the island states began to give significant attention to domestic environmental problems. The task they face is to match their natural concern over externally-caused environmental dangers with effective local measures to protect the environment and promote sustainable development.

GLOBAL WARMING

Since the mid-1980s the implications of global climatic change, especially the warming of the planet and expected increases in sea levels and in stormy weather, have attracted considerable attention. Long-term natural changes in the temperature of the planet have apparently been accentuated

71

by human economic activity, especially by the heavy use of fossil fuels in the developed countries. The island governments gave these problems a high priority at the 1989 meeting of the South Pacific Forum, and have considered them further at subsequent Forum and other regional meetings.

In addition, the island governments have lobbied to raise international awareness of these problems and to encourage ameliorative action, notably in the international negotiations for a framework convention on climate change. As part of this effort several of the island governments and the South Pacific Forum have sought to use the forums provided by the United Nations and its agencies, and by the Alliance of Small Island States, a body which represents island states from around the world. So far, however, the results of these efforts have been disappointing, because the developed states, in view of the costs involved, are reluctant to move swiftly to reduce their levels of industrial emissions.

Should the predictions of a significant rise in sea levels prove well-founded, the very survival of some island entities will be imperilled. In the short term, their populations may suffer from storm damage and from the contamination of their fresh water tables by sea water. In addition many of the coral reefs in the region, which in a number of areas are already threatened by pollution, could die as a result of relatively small variations in water level and temperature. This would remove the first line of defence against wave damage in coastal areas, and cause a drastic depletion in the fish and other seafood stocks which depend on reef environments.

In the longer term, many islands may be inundated. The highest point on Kiribati, for example, is only a few metres above sea level. Other low-lying states and territories include Tuvalu, the Marshall Islands and Tokelau. Most of the other island entities comprise both high- and low-lying islands. But even on the high islands, a significant portion of the good agricultural land and much of the infrastructure is concentrated in low-lying coastal areas.[3]

Substantial additional aid could be requested by island states to assist in the transfer of populations and the reconstruction of infrastructure. These requests would come at a time when many other parts of the developing world would be seeking similar assistance. The tragic impact of the cyclones on Bangladesh in early 1991 may be a portent. In addition the wealthy countries would have their own costly problems to deal with because of rising sea levels and changing weather patterns. So it may be difficult for donors to respond fully to requests.

In addition, climatic changes may create large numbers of 'environmental refugees' who may seek resettlement in neighbouring island states, or in Australia and New Zealand. In August 1994, after apparently unprecedented tidal waves battered the atoll state of Tuvalu, its prime minister queried whether the tidal waves resulted from rising sea levels. He also criticised Australia for not doing enough to reduce greenhouse gas emissions and hence global warming, and asked whether, if rising sea levels threatened Tuvalu's viability, Australia would be able to host the resettlement of the Tuvaluans.[4] The question of resettlement could strain relations between Australia and New Zealand and the island states, inasmuch as Australia and New Zealand may be reluctant or slow to fulfill island government expectations.

Even if the bad case scenarios about global warming are not borne out, environmental degradation will remain of particular concern to several island states, in view of their limited land areas and resource bases, and of the vulnerability of their land and waters to pollution which could reduce agricultural and fishing yields. As Jeremy Carew-Reid comments:

> Nowhere are the limits to the resource base more acutely felt than on an island. Island systems in their natural state tend to be finely tuned, with a delicate balance maintained between their various parts. This ecological refinement makes them more vulnerable to rapid and irreversible change resulting from natural disasters, such as cyclones, and from human activities.[5]

Many of these problems must be grappled with at the local and state level. Problems in one particular island state will not necessarily have direct repercussions on neighbouring states. But the island states have seen advantages in exchanging information and in seeking to develop common codes of environmental practice in the region. To this end they established the South Pacific Regional Environment Program (SPREP) in 1982; this intergovernmental body now has its headquarters in Apia, Western Samoa. The SPREP has negotiated two international treaties which came into force in 1990: the Convention for the Protection of the Natural Resources and Environment of the South Pacific Region (the SPREP Convention), and the Convention on the Conservation of Nature in the South Pacific (the Apia Convention). These treaties are designed to increase the awareness of, and the constraints against, environmental damage and degradation.[6]

RESOURCES ISSUES

Irresponsible exploitation of resources can bring environmental damage on a scale which threatens the long-term viability of substantial parts of the resource base of the island states.

The South Pacific Forum established the Forum Fisheries Agency (FFA) in 1978 to help monitor and protect the region's fisheries resources. The island governments have also cooperated in an externally-funded intergovernmental organisation, the South Pacific Applied Geoscience Commission, known as SOPAC, which has examined prospects and requirements for the exploitation of marine mineral resources.[7] At present market conditions do not justify the development of this form of exploitation. But if and when it does commence it is envisaged that regional cooperation will help ensure that responsible methods of exploitation are employed, and that the island states get a fair share of the proceeds.

In the 1980s the Forum Fisheries Agency and the island governments campaigned successfully against tuna poaching by American vessels, with the result that in 1986 the United States entered into a multilateral fisheries agreement. The island governments and the Forum and the FFA also campaigned successfully, including through the United Nations, against the use of driftnets in the region, because of the devastating 'strip mining' impact this technique had on fish stocks and other marine life. By around 1990, the states which send fishing fleets to the region had agreed to stop using driftnets.

At the 1994 meeting of the South Pacific Forum, held in late July/early August in Brisbane, Australia, the Forum heads of government agreed to put increased emphasis on exchanging information on fisheries resources, on curbing poaching, and on ensuring that island states got a fair return from the exploitation of these resources. According to one estimate, as of the early 1990s the returns received by the island states amounted to 'only A\$ 74 million of the A\$ 2 billion worth of fish plucked from their waters each year.'[8] The island states have lost out because of illegal fishing and under-reporting. In addition, only the United States has signed a multilateral fishing treaty, under which the island states get back between 8 to 10 per cent of the value of landed catch. In contrast, the income derived by the island states from the other external fishing nations, notably Japan, Taiwan and South Korea, has amounted to only 2 to 4 per cent of the landed catch.[9]

The island governments have also made some efforts to protect land-based resources. Severe environmental damage has occurred over recent decades in several island states as a result of irresponsible forestry and mining exploitation. In some instances controls established during the latter part of the colonial era, when administering governments were more concerned than had often earlier been the case with protecting the interests of the native peoples, have been ignored or diluted by newly-independent governments.

Some politicians and officials have been corrupted, and have turned a blind eye to abuses and malpractice. Some island governments, in their enthusiasm to get much-needed revenue, have been naive in their dealings with mining and timber companies. In 1993, according to one estimate, the three Melanesian states 'lost up to A\$ 350 million in logging revenue...because of overlogging and underpayment by foreign-owned companies.'[10] Some forestry companies, and the village leaders with whom they have dealt, have adopted a 'get rich quick' view which has imperilled attempts to establish harvesting practices which ensure that the forests will be a renewable resource.[11]

The meeting of the South Pacific Forum in Nauru in 1993 discussed the rapacious behaviour of some forestry companies, and this question was again highlighted at the 1994 Forum in Brisbane. Solomon Islands Prime Minister Billy Hilly told the Brisbane Forum that the Solomons was financially dependent on foreign logging. Indeed, timber represented more than half of receipts from exports. He said that 'Project upon project that interact dangerously on the environment are approved in the name of improving the national economy.' But the timber companies failed to fulfill their license conditions with respect to environmental protection. The result, he complained, was 'a ravaged forest, polluted water supplies and coral reefs covered in silt.' At present extraction rates, he warned, the Solomon Islands would be completely logged out within fifteen years.[12]

Mining resources are not of course renewable, but their exploitation has often proceeded at a rapid pace without sufficient effort to minimise and counter environmental damage and social dislocation. Ciaran O'Faircheallaigh comments that:

> Modern resource projects, and particularly mining projects, have the potential to create enormous environmental damage...[M]any...projects are on a huge scale, and consequently dispose of very large quantities of waste, particularly waste rock and tailings, but also sulphuric acid (from smelting) and other by-products which cannot be profitably recovered...Bougainville Copper Limited removed 83.5 million tonnes of rock and ore from the Panguna open pit in 1988 alone; of this amount, 35.3 million tonnes was disposed of on waste rock dumps, and approximately 48 million tonnes (the ore residue after removal of some 200,000 tonnes of copper) was disposed of into the Jaba River system in the form of tailings. Much of the waste generated by resource exploitation is highly toxic, containing heavy metals and other substances which can be very destructive if released into the environment.[13]

O'Faircheallaigh accepts that mining inevitably produces massive amounts of waste material, some of which is highly dangerous. But he points out that:

the technology is available which can reduce environmental pollution; many mines in developed countries have very little detectable impact on the environment (for example uranium mines in North Australia, zinc/lead mines in the Republic of Ireland). It is also possible to minimize the impact on subsistence activity of those environmental effects which are unavoidable; for example by timing exploration activity and locating mine facilities and infrastructure in ways that minimize their effects on wildlife. Yet some resource development activities in the South Pacific continue to have devastating effects that seriously threaten the livelihood of indigenous peoples.[14]

Several companies have indeed relaxed their standards of conduct in the region, whereas their operations elsewhere, where institutional, legal and political safeguards are stronger, have been more responsible.

The Commonwealth Micronesian state of Nauru, which comprises only a single island, has been heavily affected by the environmental and social impacts of extensive mining. Indeed, much of the interior of this small island is gravely damaged, and requires substantial rehabilitation. Shortly before the meeting of the South Pacific Forum in Nauru in August 1993, Australia and Nauru reached an out-of-court compensation settlement of a Nauru claim for damages for the devastating environmental impact of phosphate mining on Nauru during the colonial period (see Chapter 7). Unfortunately, since Nauru attained independence in 1968, only a limited amount of money and effort has gone into environmental rehabilitation.

Ultimately the environmental and social problems raised by the conduct of many mining and forestry companies must be dealt with within particular states. At the 1994 Forum, however, island heads of government agreed that sharing information and establishing guidelines would be helpful. With respect to forestry, they undertook to support greater information exchange within the region on irresponsible companies and on responsible techniques of exploitation, and to support the development of 'a common code of conduct governing logging of indigenous forests'[15]

NUCLEAR TESTING

Island governments have also expressed strong concerns about nuclear testing, especially its potential health and environmental implications. Until 1961, when their tests were shifted to underground sites in Nevada in the United States, the United States and the United Kingdom conducted atmospheric nuclear tests in the Pacific islands region.[16] Because their testing in the region was concluded before the Pacific island colonies began to attain political independence, the United States and the United Kingdom have escaped substantial criticism of their testing programmes from independent island governments. The tragic legacies of nuclear testing have however had great influence in parts of the former Trust Territory of the Pacific Islands, in those islands directly affected by the the tests, which are located in what is now the Republic of the Marshall Islands. The United States government has paid out massive sums in an effort to provide compensation and redress for the destruction, dislocation, suffering and death caused in parts of the Marshall Islands by atmospheric nuclear testing.

French testing in the region has taken place above and below the isolated atolls of Moruroa and Fangataufa in French Polynesia (see Map 6). France conducted atmospheric tests from 1966 to 1975, and then shifted its testing programme underground. President Mitterrand announced a suspension of the programme in April 1992, reducing tensions over the issue. This decision was, however, essentially a gesture to environmentalist sentiment in metropolitan France, rather than a response to criticisms of the tests from island and other governments and from regional and international lobby groups. As of late 1994 it was not yet clear whether the tests would be renewed.

Meanwhile the French government continued to maintain that it had the right to resume the tests on its own sovereign territory in the region when and if it so wished. Since around 1990 the French authorities have been involved in a process of strategic and defence reassessment, in the light of the new circumstances prevailing in the wake of the Cold War. This process has potential implications for the future of the testing programme. French spokespersons have indicated that, should the programme be renewed, it would probably only continue for a limited number of years, in order to generate further data and permit the completion of the development of particular weapons systems, rather than proceeding indefinitely.[17]

Although the French testing programme was suspended in early 1992, it merits careful consideration, for three reasons. The programme may be resumed, it may already have had substantial health and environmental implications, and the opinions on it expressed by the island governments provide further insights into their security perspectives.

France has in part reduced regional concerns over nuclear testing by offering reassurances that the testing programme entails no health or environmental risks, by inviting regional leaders to French Polynesia for briefings on the tests, and by providing information to research missions. The first of these missions, known as the Atkinson mission after its leader, undertook enquiries in October 1983 on behalf of Australia, New Zealand and Papua New Guinea. After a brief visit to the testing sites it produced a report which, while it expressed concern over the possible longer-term leaching of radioactive materials, did not endorse the more dramatic claims made by some anti-nuclear campaigners about the health and environmental risks of French testing.[18]

But concerns persisted, focused on the possible leaching of radioactive materials, which conceivably could already be taking place, albeit at a minimal level. In any case island leaders have argued: 'If the tests are safe, why not conduct them in metropolitan France?' To the island governments the tests are a colonial issue. They take this view because France has continued the tests despite regional opposition, and because the tests take place in a territory which was acquired in the nineteenth century, and which remains firmly under French control, despite its exercise of a measure of self-government. Only a plebiscite confined to the locally-born population of French Polynesia would show whether the people of the territory accept the continuation of the tests. So far no French government has been willing to take such an initiative, mainly because of the view that a small part of the 'indivisible French Republic' should not decide questions of national defence, but also because of the possibility that the voters would opt against testing.

The governments of most of the island states have shown little sympathy for French arguments that the nuclear deterrent is essential to the defence of France; and that during the Cold War period it made an important contribution, in particular by complicating the planning of the Soviet Union, to the central strategic balance and hence to the avoidance of nuclear and world war. The end of the Cold War, progress with arms control, and the disintegration of the Soviet Union have further reduced the receptiveness of island governments to these arguments.

The island governments have been encouraged in their opposition to French nuclear testing by regional and international lobby groups, and by strong anti-nuclear sentiments in New Zealand and, to a lesser extent, in Australia. French conduct has at times sharpened opposition: the island governments reacted angrily when they learnt that French agents had been responsible for an act of state terrorism in the form of the sinking of the Greenpeace vessel, *Rainbow Warrior*, causing one death, in Auckland harbour in 1985.

From the late 1960s regional lobby groups and governments have protested vigorously against French atmospheric testing. In 1973 Australia, Fiji and New Zealand took France before the International Court of Justice in the Hague over this question. In addition a New

Zealand frigate, supported by an Australian supply ship, cruised near the testing zones during the 1973 testing programme, in order to express opposition to, and to monitor, the tests. In 1974 France announced that it would be shifting from atmospheric to underground testing, so the International Court proceedings were not pursued.

Criticism of the tests declined somewhat for some years after the French testing programme 'went underground' from 1975, because underground testing was regarded as much safer than atmospheric testing. But it gathered new momentum in the 1980s, in part because of concerns over the potential long-term dangers of underground testing. In December 1980 the late Francis Bugotu, the (then) Solomon Islands Secretary for Foreign Affairs, complained about the holding of another French test, commenting that the Solomon Islands did not 'under any circumstances condone any form of nuclear activity in the Pacific'.[19] In response to the publication of the Atkinson mission's report in 1984, the (then) Solomons Prime Minister Mamaloni announced that his government would continue to deplore French nuclear testing and be convinced of its adverse effects. Similarly Tony Bais, Papua New Guinea's (then) acting Minister for Foreign Affairs and Trade, questioned the findings of the Atkinson mission. He said that: 'Papua New Guinea appreciates the report but is unmoved by the conclusions because the danger is there and must be stopped now.... we take the findings as "purely scientific in nature". The political and moral aspects are far more important than the scientific aspect.'[20]

In a similar vein, Vanuatu Prime Minister Father Walter Lini commented on the Atkinson report as follows:

> Our position ... still is, that we oppose the French nuclear tests on moral grounds and not necessarily on the premise that the tests are scientifically dangerous. Obviously if the French government thinks the tests are safe, why does it not experiment with them in France? The fact that the French government continues to carry out its nuclear tests in the South Pacific thousands of kilometres from France is itself morally wrong and no scientist can convince us otherwise.[21]

Although the 'Melanesian Spearhead' states of Papua New Guinea, Solomon Islands and Vanuatu have been especially outspoken in their criticism of French nuclear testing, other states also have expressed strong concerns. In November 1983, the Cook Islands Prime Minister, Sir Thomas Davis, said that he accepted, on the basis of the Atkinson mission's findings, that French testing did not threaten the Cook Islands with nuclear radiation, but queried: 'if it's safe why do it in our backyard?'[22] Similarly the Fiji representative told the UN General Assembly in

October 1988 that the tests should be shifted to France. He argued that if, as France maintained, the testing were safe and posed no danger to human or marine life, then France should have no fears about conducting them in its home territory.[23]

As these statements by island leaders illustrate, the opposition to testing from the governments and communities of the region has had health, environmental, philosophical and anti-colonial aspects. These aspects are interwoven in practice, though they can be separated for the purposes of analysis.

French spokespersons have been adamant that neither atmospheric nor underground testing has caused health risks, and that testing has caused only highly localised damage to the environment. But the critics of French testing have raised a variety of concerns, relating both to possible present-day and to potential longer-term implications. Feelings run high on nuclear testing, and the debate has often generated more heat than light. Yet although some criticisms and claims have been exaggerated or incorrect, the critics of testing have succeeded in identifying areas in which further comprehensive and independent research *is* necessary.

The French contend that the atmospheric tests held from 1966 to 1975 posed no general health risks because the mainly oceanic region in which the tests took place is very sparsely populated, and because the wind conditions prevailing at the time of the great majority of the tests ensured that fall-out was carried eastwards in the direction of South America and was dispersed harmlessly over a vast area of open ocean.[24] They contend that the tests added only a tiny amount to the already low level of natural radiation in French Polynesia, which is at roughly half the level in metropolitan France. The Atkinson mission's report concluded that: 'The radiation doses due to natural radioactivity and to radioactive fallout to which the populations of French Polynesia are exposed are below the world average, and they not give grounds for expecting radiation sickness to occur.'

Yet while it has not been proven that radioactivity from the atmospheric tests has harmed the health of the general population of French Polynesia, there are indications of grave effects on the health of some of those who worked on the atmospheric testing programme, and on that of members of the local populations on islands relatively close to the atmospheric testing sites.[25] The French authorities deny the validity of such claims, although they acknowledge non-radiological damage from minor industrial accidents. There is a need for further independent research on the question of risks to workers on the programme and to populations resident relatively close to the testing sites.

There are also some indirect linkages between the testing programme and public health in French Polynesia. One definite connection is with the new lifestyles and consumption patterns resulting from the new wealth and the socio-economic changes associated – although by no means exclusively – with the implementation of the testing programme. These new lifestyles and consumption patterns, along with improved health services, have greatly reduced those health problems, characteristic of a developing state or territory, which formerly existed in French Polynesia. On the other hand, the incidence, in the territory of the conditions and diseases associated with modernity have increased. These 'modern' ailments include lung and upper respiratory tract cancers and other conditions associated with cigarette smoking, as well as heart disease, dental caries, and other problems associated with alcohol abuse and/or an unbalanced and unhealthy diet. Similar changes have occurred in some measure in some of the other states and territories of the region, notably in Nauru, in the absence of any evidence of radiological damage, but in association with increased wealth and changing lifestyles and consumption patterns.[26]

There is also a connection between localised ecological disruption through construction works associated with the testing programme and the incidence of ciguatera fish-poisoning in the particular islands concerned.[27] Ciguatera is a disease which results from eating tropical fish which contain toxins produced by several coral reef plankton species. Herbivorous fish ingest the planktons and accumulate the toxins, and are in turn eaten by predatory fish. The toxins are concentrated as they move up the food chain. The fish themselves do not become ill from the presence of the toxins. But humans can become ill, in rare instances fatally, if they eat the affected fish.

Ciguatera was first recorded by Europeans in the sixteenth century. It is found wherever there are coral reefs, and is the commonest type of marine fish poisoning. Its incidence reflects damage to the ecology of reef systems, as a result of which toxic planktons proliferate and/or their toxin production increases. This damage can be caused naturally by storms and cyclones, or by human intervention in the form of port construction, dredging, and pollution.

The connections made in some accounts between ciguatera and the testing programme have been exaggerated. Even had French testing never taken place, ciguatera would still be present in French Polynesia because of natural and human disruptions to reef systems. Nonetheless, construction supporting the testing programme has sharply increased the local incidence of ciguatera in French Polynesia, notably near Hao and Mangareva but also around the formerly uninhabited islands of Moruroa and Fangataufa. Subsidence and fissuring directly resulting from nuclear tests may also contribute to ecological disruption, but this contribution is very small compared with the damage caused by construction work associated with the testing programme.

Critics of the testing programme have also expressed concern over damage to the geological structures of Moruroa and Fangataufa atolls and the resulting potential for the longer-term leaching into the sea of radioactive elements. These elements conceivably could find their way into the food chain. The Atkinson mission concluded that such leaching could take place in between 500 to 1000 years. But these findings have been challenged. In the mid-1980s two University of Auckland scientists, Manfred Hochstein and Michael O'Sullivan, developed a computer model which predicted that leaching would occur within ten to one hundred years.[28] Other researchers, including some associated with Greenpeace, have claimed that leaching, admittedly at infinitesimal levels, is already occurring.[29] This however is yet to be proven.

Some authorities have argued that it is most unlikely that the cesium-134 reported to have been detected reached the lagoon by leaching. This is because, for geochemical reasons, other radionuclides – for example, iodine and technetium isotopes – would be transported by groundwater a thousand times times faster than cesium isotopes. Another possibility is that minute quantities of radioactive materials could be released by the re-entry bores which on occassion are drilled into the glass-like material formed in the explosion cavity after detonation. The drilling sand could gather up material contaminated with elements associated with and produced by the nuclear explosion. At the drilling site small quantitles of drilling sand are discharged, and it is by this means that minute radioactive traces could find their way into lagoon sediments.[30]

The French authorities have argued that in any case, because the leached elements would be in very small quantities, with their toxicity reduced over time, they would pose absolutely no health or environmental risks.[31] The Cousteau mission, which visited Moruroa in June 1987, found that any pollution would be localised to the immediate area. But this mission also commented that Moruroa atoll was 'a very bad site for the storage of radioactive wastes', because of the proximity of water to the locations deep underground at which the nuclear explosions were detonated, and because of the fissuring of rock and coral by the explosions.[32] The Cousteau mission concluded that the short-term and medium-term risks of radiological pollution were negligible, but that the long-term risks were more difficult to evaluate on the basis of the information with which it had been provided.

In April 1991, during a visit to New Zealand, Prime Minister Rocard repeated apologies for the sinking of the *Rainbow Warrior*, and reaffirmed the French position that the underground tests entailed no health or environmental risks. Murray Matthews, the head of the radioactivity section of the New Zealand National Radiation Laboratory, reportedly said that there would be little if any danger to marine or human life if all the radioactivity from French nuclear tests in Moruroa were released into the Pacific. He was quoted as saying that: 'The effect of any dispersion from Moruroa would be very small and probably unmeasurable in the longer term, and certainly not measurable at New Zealand and other island sites remote from Moruroa.'[33] But spokespersons for Greenpeace and other organisations contested these views.

Some of the claims made by some anti-nuclear campaigners have been exaggerated, and at times alarmist.[34] But the question of longer-term leaching at the testing sites and its possible health and environmental implications requires further comprehensive and independent investigation. In my view the South Pacific Forum, as the regional organisation of the island states, should be involved. In 1991 the United States established a precedent by welcoming a Forum scientific mission to inspect its chemical weapon destruction facilities on Johnston atoll (see below).[35]

THE SOUTH PACIFIC NUCLEAR FREE ZONE TREATY

Regional opposition to nuclear testing and to the prospect of nuclear waste dumping has been expressed in the Treaty of Rarotonga (also known as the South Pacific Nuclear Free Zone Treaty). The idea of such a treaty had originally been raised in the early-1970s by a New Zealand Labour government. The treaty was signed by most members of the Forum at the August 1985 meeting on Rarotonga, the main island of the Cook Islands. It entered into force in December 1986, following its ratification by eight of the signatories.

The island governments regarded the treaty as a means to help prevent the region from becoming, during the Cold War, a setting for rivalry between the superpowers. They also saw it as a means to help protect the environment from current or potential risks, including by putting additional pressure on France to stop testing. The treaty prohibited the manufacture, stationing or testing of any nuclear explosive device in the treaty area, as well as the dumping of nuclear waste at sea in the area.[36]

The treaty also included protocols, intended for signature by the nuclear-testing powers. Protocol One embodied a commitment by nuclear powers with territories in the treaty area to not conduct nuclear tests in the area. Protocols Two and Three permitted other nuclear weapons states to agree not to use or threaten to use nuclear weapons against the parties to the treaty, or against dependent territories within the treaty area. France declined to sign Protocol One, because of its intention to continue testing in the region. Embarassingly for Australia, the United States and the United Kingdom declined to support the treaty and in particular to sign the first protocol. In contrast, the Soviet Union and the People's Republic of China had promptly agreed to sign the second and third protocols. Under Cold War circumstances, the United States and the United Kingdom were concerned about creating a precedent for nuclear free zones elsewhere, because other such zones might be constructed in a fashion which disadvantaged Western strategic interests. They also regarded their relations with France, a major if at times cantakerous ally, as taking precedence on this issue over their relations with Australia and New Zealand and with the Pacific island states.

The treaty area included Australia to the west, adjoined the Antarctic treaty zone to the south, adjoined the Latin American Treaty of Tlatelolco area to the east, and extended to the equator to the north (Map 7). By 1989, eleven of the Forum's members were parties to the treaty. They comprised Australia and New Zealand and nine of the island states, namely the Cook Islands, Fiji, Kiribati, Nauru, Niue, Papua New Guinea, Solomon Islands, Tuvalu, and Western Samoa. But Vanuatu and Tonga had declined to become parties to it.

Meanwhile the treaty area did not extend to include the two 'Compact' states of the Republic of the Marshall Islands and the Federated States of Micronesia. These states had not emerged as more or less sovereign entities until after the treaty had been signed at the 1985 Forum. They could possibly adhere to the treaty, thus extending its area of coverage. Their governments have given the matter some consideration, but without any sense of urgency. During the Cold War period, they were inhibited in pursuing the possibility of becoming parties to the treaty because of the negative attitude of the United States government. Neither does the treaty extend to cover Palau, which entered into a free association compact with the United States in October 1994. Palau may also in due course look into the possibility of becoming a party to the treaty.

Following the election of Bill Clinton to the presidency in November 1992, and in view of post-Cold War circumstances, the United States government has reaffirmed that the provisions of the treaty do not conflict with its essential strategic and defence interests in the region, and has undertaken to review its policy on the treaty. Should the United States decide at some stage to adhere to the protocols of the treaty, its extension to the Compact states would be facilitated. But this question, like other matters relating to the islands region, is not regarded by the United States government as having, under present circumstances, any particular import-ance or priority, so any policy change may be subject to a long delay.

The Australian government had done much to tailor the Treaty of Rarotonga to reflect a regional consensus which was not in conflict with what it saw as essential United States and broader Western interests. The treaty did not restrict the freedom of navigation through the region by nuclear-powered or nuclear-armed ships, and gave the parties to the treaty discretion to allow these vessels to visit their ports. Neither did it mention Australian exports of uranium. Some commentators thought that the treaty was insufficiently inclusive. In response the Australian government, in an effort to sidestep criticisms that the treaty failed to establish a fully com-prehensive range of anti-nuclear provisions, advised its diplomats in the mid-1980s that they should routinely refer to the treaty as the 'Treaty of Rarotonga', rather than as the 'South Pacific Nuclear Free Zone Treaty'.

In a 1990 study Michael Hamel-Green has offered a detailed critique of the treaty.[37] In my view he underestimates the extent to which support for the treaty formed part of the extensive programme of moderate disarma-ment measures pursued by the Australian Labor government from 1983 onwards, but exaggerates the extent to which Australia negotiated the treaty in order to head off radical domestic and regional anti-nuclear pres-sures, and help 'legitimize US and ANZUS nuclear activities and pol-icies'.[38] These pressures were present, but were by no means overwhelming. The treaty would not have come into operation had it not been for substantial administrative and diplomatic effort by the Australian government; it would have been easier for that government to sit on its hands.

The Melanesian governments, and especially that of Vanuatu during the 1980s, thought that the treaty did not go far enough. Vanuatu declined to become a party to the treaty. While under a *Vanua'aku Pati* government, Vanuatu regarded the treaty as insufficiently radical and comprehensive. In the early 1990s, in contrast, the coalition government in Vanuatu, in which the major party is the Francopone-based Union of Moderate Parties, indicated that it would review Vanuatu's policy on the treaty, but has not given this matter much priority. The coalition government, as noted earlier, has expressed opposition to nuclear testing, but presumably would not wish to create tensions in relations with France by becoming a party to the treaty. For their part, Papua New Guinea and the Solomon Islands delayed ratifying the treaty until 1989, whereas most other parties to the treaty ratified it in 1985 or 1986. Meanwhile Nauru also had reservations about the treaty, though it became a party to it. At the drafting stage the

Nauruan government had argued that the treaty should include a prohibition on missile testing in the region, and should embody stronger controls over radioactive waste-dumping in the high seas.[39] But other island governments, notably that of Tonga and in some measure that of the Cook Islands, were concerned about whether the treaty would be consistent with broad Western interests, especially given American reservations.

Since the treaty's ratification, some island opinion leaders have been disappointed with 'the energy expended, the concessions made and [its] embarrassingly poor results'.[40] These regrets focus on the refusal of the United States and the United Kingdom to endorse the treaty and on the failure of the treaty to change France's view that it has the right to conduct underground nuclear tests in French Polynesia.

The possible implications of non-defence uses of nuclear power have also been a source of concern. Some island governments and several regional lobby groups, especially the Nuclear Free and Independent Pacific movement, have been critical of Australian uranium exports to France. They have argued that no assistance should be given to any branch of the nuclear industry, because of health and environmental risks. They have also claimed that the safeguards against diversion of the uranium to military uses are inadequate, and have pointed out that the links between the defence and civil sectors of the nuclear industry are often close, especially in France. Several island governments and lobby groups have also protested against a plutonium shipment to Japan which passed through the Pacific islands region in late 1992/early 1993, and against plans to make further shipments. The Japanese government has responded with reassurances. The risks of an accident are very slight, but the island governments are concerned that such a contingency could have grave health and environmental implications.

NUCLEAR, CHEMICAL AND OTHER WASTE ISSUES

Through their support of the establishment of a nuclear free zone over much of their region, the island governments reaffirmed their opposition to the dumping of nuclear wastes in the region. They have also strongly opposed the dumping of other toxic wastes. In the 1960s and 1970s United States and Japanese officials suggested the dumping of nuclear and other toxic waste in deep-ocean areas in and near the region. In addition, United States officials raised the possibility of scuttling outmoded nuclear-powered submarines in these areas. In 1978 the United States proposed using an uninhabited island in the region to store spent nuclear fuel. In the

1980s Japan proposed the dumping of nuclear waste in the deep Marianas trench near the Northern Mariana Islands.[41] Because of protests from the island governments, complemented by protests from other governments in the Asia-Pacific region and from non-governmental groups, these various plans were not pursued.

But the issue remains alive. At the Forum in Brisbane in July/August 1994, Amata Kabua, the President of the Marshall Islands, advised that his government was been considering the possibility of establishing an international facility for destroying and disposing of nuclear waste in the Marshall Islands. He explained that the Marshall Islands lacked the resources to clean up the contaminated areas left by American nuclear testing. Some of these areas could be used for dumping. In addition, the returns from operating such a facility could be used to rehabilitate some of the contaminated areas.

In response to President Kabua's remarks, island leaders expressed reservations about the possible use of part of the Pacific islands region for toxic waste dumping. But they were also conscious that the Marshall Islands, because its resource base is so limited, could not afford to reject any potential source of external income without careful consideration of the costs, risks and benefits involved. The idea of using some already-contaminated islands in the Marshalls group for nuclear waste dumping had been raised on several earlier occasions. Meanwhile, critics of the French testing programme have warned of the possibility that France may seek to use its testing sites in French Polynesia for this purpose.

Should the Marshall Islands government pursue the matter further, other island governments and several non-government groups would be anxious lest a precedent be established for extensive nuclear and other toxic waste dumping in the islands region. They would also argue that atolls are not suitable locations for the dumping of dangerous wastes, since storm damage or, in the longer term, inundation as a result of global warming, could result in the wastes coming into direct contact with the marine environment.

The island governments have also expressed strong concern over the destruction of chemical weapons in the region. This issue arose shortly before the meeting of the South Pacific Forum in Port Vila in mid-1990, because of American plans to destroy chemical weapons on Johnston Atoll, an uninhabited American island roughly halfway between the Marshall Islands and the Hawaiian Islands. Most of the weapons concerned had been stationed in Germany, but they included stocks of chemical shells which had been held in the Solomon Islands since the Second World War.[42]

Island leaders were concerned about the potential environmental and health risks involved in shipping these weapons, and in their destruction in a high temperature furnace on Johnston Atoll. Greenpeace and other lobby groups also expressed strong concern, and called for the development of cleaner methods of disposal. The Pacific Conference of Churches declared that the planned incineration would 'continue the misuse of the Pacific as a dumping site for nuclear and chemical wastes', while the Australian Conservation Foundation said that the weapons should be destroyed on the United States mainland, rather than being sent 'to a tiny US island in someone else's backyard'.[43]

The United States had failed to offer adequate explanations and reassurance to island governments in advance of the Forum meeting. At the meeting the Australian government supported the planned destruction of the chemical weapons, in part out of loyalty to its great and powerful ally and in part because it saw the destruction of these weapons as a contribution to global disarmament measures. The island leaders reacted against the brow-beating style of Australian Prime Minister Hawke. They also complained that scientific assessments of the possible risks, supplied by Australia, only arrived when the meeting was underway. For its part, New Zealand took an ambivalent line. It expressed some support for the Australian stance but also confirmed its sympathy with island government concerns.

Even when concerns about the potential health and environmental risks had been assuaged, at least in part, island leaders remained irritated by what they saw as a colonialist assumption that the Pacific region was a suitable place to dump and destroy noxious chemicals. The (then) Fiji Prime Minister, Ratu Sir Kamisese Mara, asked why, if the destruction process was perfectly safe, it wasn't being carried out in Europe rather than in the Pacific. He thus echoed the argument frequently raised, including by Australian governments, concerning French nuclear testing.

The controversy helped motivate the American government to arrange, during a visit by President Bush to Honolulu in October 1990, a meeting between him and island heads of government. The Johnston Atoll issue was the key item on the agenda. President Bush reaffirmed American assurances about the absence of risks from the weapons destruction process. He also confirmed that Johnston Atoll would be used on a once only basis to destroy the chemical weapons stocks from Germany and the Solomon Islands, and noted that earlier plans to continue using the atoll as a destruction site for chemical weapons stored on the United States mainland had been shelved. President Bush also won island government sympathies by proposing measures to improve American commercial and investment links with the region, including by means of a Joint Commercial Commission. This meeting reassured island leaders that their concerns over environmental and other issues had been registered at the highest level in the United States.

Despite their concerns, however, the United States had implemented its plans to destroy chemical weapons on Johnston Atoll. To help provide further reassurance, in due course the United States government permitted an inspection of the facilities on the island by a Forum scientific mission, which reported that safety and pollution control guidelines and requirements had been rigorously followed.

CONCLUSION

In their stance on environmental and related issues island governments have been encouraged and supported by the increased public and political awareness of threats to the environment evident in much of the world since the mid-1980s. The island governments are conscious that their protests, complemented by those of lobby groups, apparently contributed to France's shift to underground nuclear testing; have helped avert, at least so far, the use of the region for nuclear and other toxic waste dumping; and have helped ensure, at least for the time being, that chemical weapons destruction in the region has not been implemented on a continuing basis.

Regional protests have been less successful in getting France to renounce its underground testing programme: President Mitterrand's suspension of these tests in April 1992 was essentially a response to trends in French domestic politics rather than to external protests. The French government is, however, aware that a resumption of testing would unleash a storm of criticism in the Pacific islands region and in the wider world. The communiqué of the 1994 Forum noted that: 'if France were to cease testing permanently, this would contribute significantly to improving further the relations between France and the Forum countries.' On the other hand, 'Any resumption of testing would be a major setback to the current positive trend in relations between France and the region.'[44]

In the years ahead continued pressure on the French government will be required to ensure the attainment of three objectives: that the testing programme is brought to a definitive end; that an impartial and comprehensive international enquiry is held into the health and environmental implications of a quarter-century of French testing; and that prompt and generous compensation is paid to any persons and communities shown to have suffered. If the French government is correct in its claim that in fact the tests have been completely innocuous, except for some very localised effects, it should have nothing to fear from, and should indeed welcome, international scrutiny. An international enquiry of the type envisaged should ideally go ahead under the auspices of the South Pacific Forum, in association with the United Nations and reputable international scientific organisations.

The island governments are likely to continue to show strong interest in a range of environmental and resources issues. The handling of some dimensions of these issues will require regional cooperation, as well as cooperation between the region and the wider international community. Other dimensions of them however must be handled at the level of the individual state. At this level, nonetheless, island governments can benefit greatly from regional liaison and information exchange.

The island governments have expressed strong concerns about the dangers actually or potentially associated with nuclear testing and nuclear and other toxic waste disposal, and about the threats which appear to be posed by global warning. Since the late 1980s these governments have also shown an increasing awareness of the risks and challenges posed by irresponsible resource exploitation. In the years ahead, their moral and diplomatic position on environmental, resource and nuclear issues is likely to be strengthened to the extent to which they combine international advocacy on these issues with the implementation, within their own jurisdictions, of effective measures to protect the environment and promote responsible resource exploitation.

6 External Actors: The Trend to Diversification

Over the last thirty-five years, the political map of the Pacific islands region has changed dramatically. During this period, Australia, New Zealand and the United Kingdom relinquished control over almost all of their colonies. The Netherlands came to terms with Indonesia's acquisition of Irian Jaya, and ceased to take part in Pacific islands affairs. The United States negotiated free association arrangements for some of its Pacific entities, while maintaining its sovereignty over others. France reluctantly accepted the transition of the New Hebrides to independence, but maintained control over three other entities, and from the late-1980s established itself as a significant player in regional affairs.

The strongest external connections of the island states have generally been with their former colonial administrators, because of institutional legacies and financial and technical assistance. In this chapter, I examine the interests and activities of the United States, France and the United Kingdom in the region, especially over the last decade. I do not consider Australia and New Zealand, discussing them instead in the next chapter. Since around 1980 several other powers, most of which have few traditional links with the islands region, have shown some increased interest, so I also examine their aims and involvement (see Table 6.1). And I review the involvement of a range of non-government actors. Some of these non-government actors are based outside the region, while the others have strong connections outside the region and/or outside any particular island state.

THE UNITED STATES

The United States dominates most of Micronesia, and maintains a modest involvement in the rest of the region. American contacts with the Pacific islands date from the late eighteenth century: whalers, missionaries, traders, beachcombers and planters paved the way for official involvement. In 1898 the United States annexed the northernmost part of the Polynesian cultural world, the Hawaiian islands, and acquired Guam as a spoil of the Spanish–American War. Hawaii became a United States territory in 1900, and the fiftieth state in 1950. Another Polynesian entity, the

Table 6.1   Pacific islands region – external connections, 1994

External powers	Territorial presence	Associated states	Diplomatic posts	Defence links[a]
Australia	0	0	10	8
New Zealand	1 (Tokelau)	2	· 10	5
United States	3[b]	2	6	4
France	3[c]	0	3	3
United Kingdom	0[d]	0	6	0
Japan	0	0	4	0
China	0	0	4	0
Taiwan	0	0	4 (includes two 'trade' posts)	0
Indonesia	1 (Irian Jaya)	0	3	1
Malaysia	0	0	1	1
Israel	0	0	1	0
Russia	0	0	0	0

Notes:
[a] The military links indicated mainly involve training.
[b] The United States territorial presence indicated here consists of Guam, the Commonwealth of the Northern Mariana Islands, and American Samoa.
[c] The French presence comprises New Caledonia, Wallis and Futuna, and French Polynesia.
[d] This table does not take account of the Pitcairn Islands (UK), the Hawaiian islands (USA), the Torres Strait Islands (Australia) and Easter Island (Chile), for the reasons given in the preface.
Source: adapted from Hoadley, *South Pacific Handbook*, p. 35.

eastern islands of the Samoan group, became an American protectorate from 1900, and an unincorporated territory in 1960. Following victory in the Second World War, the United States acquired control of the formerly Japanese possessions in Micronesia.

United States interest in the region has been primarily strategic.[1] It was pleased to acquire Guam because of Guam's excellent harbour facilities. The Hawaiian islands were important because of their location in the north east Pacific. The United States was attracted to American Samoa because of the harbour at Pago Pago. America has regarded the islands of American Micronesia as vital to the security of its trans-Pacific lines of communication. In addition, the Marshall Islands provided sites for nuclear testing, and a zone for intercontinental ballistic missile-testing.

Yet despite long association and a territorial presence, the islands region has generally been very low on the agenda of the United States government. American interest rose sharply however during the Second World War, when the Japanese onslaught and the American and allied counterattacks swept across a substantial part of the region. Some islands became battlefields, with tragic results for the local people. Others, while escaping direct involvement in the hostilities, became supply bases and staging posts. The generosity of American personnel and the great material wealth of the United States left a favourable impression, reflected in the attitudes of the island governments in the 1960s and 1970s. Nonetheless, positive attitudes towards the United States were tempered by concern over the tragic human and environmental costs and legacies of United States nuclear testing in the Marshall Islands from the late 1940s to the early 1960s, and by irritation with the often cavalier attitude of the United States to the rights and interests of small states.

In the early 1980s the island states became strongly concerned over American resources piracy, in the form of the operations of American tuna boats in the region. The declaration by the United Nations of the Law of the Sea in 1982 greatly enlarged the maritime territory of the island states. Whereas previously they had owned only the area up to 12 nautical miles out to sea from their coasts, they could now claim exclusive economic zones up to 200 nautical miles offshore. The United States however refused for several years to accept the application of the Law of the Sea. It also regarded the tuna which were the main deep-water fisheries resource as a highly-migratory species, to which, it argued, no particular state could lay claim.

In the mid-1980s United States policy-makers concluded that they could no longer take the region for granted, in view of Soviet and Libyan soundings, increased island government assertiveness and New Zealand's anti-nuclear policies, which had led to the suspension of the United States/New Zealand leg of the formerly trilateral ANZUS (Australia/New Zealand/United States) security treaty (see Chapter 7). Under American leadership the Western powers had developed a policy favouring the strategic denial of the region to powers which were likely to act against broad Western interests.[2] In part this approach reflected memories of the bitter campaigns in the region during the Second World War: the United States had decided that 'never again' would the islands be allowed to support a possible threat to United States interests. Strategic denial was expressed in efforts to keep the Soviet Union and its associates and also Libya from developing a presence in the region. From the mid-1980s the United States reaffirmed this policy and sought to reduce tensions with the island states.

Increased United States interest in and sensitivity to the region was demonstrated by the negotiation in 1986 of a multilateral fisheries deal with the island states, which did much to allay concerns about the operations of the American fishing fleet. This deal has subsequently been renewed, helping maintain positive attitudes to the United States. A measure of high-level American interest in trends in the region was reaffirmed at President Bush's summit with Pacific island leaders in Honolulu in October 1990. President Bush addressed concerns over the destruction of chemical weapons on Johnston Atoll and announced economic development initiatives, focusing on the development of a Joint Commercial Commission to foster private sector links.

But since then American interest has waned, reflecting the reduced strategic relevance of the islands region to the United States in the post-Cold War environment, the domestic preoccupations and budgetary problems of the American government, and pressing concerns in other parts of the world. In late 1993 the United States closed down its embassy in Honiara, Solomon Islands, considered but then decided against closing its embassy in Apia, Western Samoa, and announced the impending closure of the US Aid Office in Suva.[3] Washington did not even bother to tell the American Ambassador in Port Moresby in advance that his sub-post in Honiara was to be closed. As of late 1994 the Joint Commercial Commission had failed to gather momentum, and its prospects were uncertain. Its inaugural working meeting was not held until October 1993, and almost a year later further preparatory work remained to be done.[4] Following the victory of Bill Clinton in the presidential elections in November 1992, the American Ambassador to Fiji, a Republican-appointee, stepped down from her post and returned to the United States. The new administration took more than eighteen months to appoint her replacement.

In the circumstances of the post-Cold War period, President Clinton's administration has shown virtually no interest in the islands region. This is true even with respect to the American territories and associated states. Some educational, aid and defence cooperation links have continued to operate. On present indications, however, United States involvement in regional affairs and in bilateral relations with particular island states, other than with its 'free association' states, is likely to continue to be at a minimal level.

THE SOVIET UNION/RUSSIA AND LIBYA

In the nineteenth century Russian navigators, traders and scientists visited the region, but these contacts were not sustained. The Soviet Union began to show a modest interest as the Pacific island colonies became independent. It wished to assert what it saw as its right, as the other and rival superpower, to establish a presence anywhere in the world, and hoped for diplomatic and propaganda advantages.[5] It was also interested in the fisheries resources of the region, and in gathering intelligence.[6] In a totalitarian state these various aims and interests were closely connected for both ideological and institutional reasons. Thus, for example, its fishing fleet operated as an auxiliary unit of the Soviet navy.

In 1976 the Soviet Union approached Tonga about port access for Soviet fishing vessels in return for aid. It is not clear how far Tonga was interested in the proposal, but Australia reacted by sharply increasing its aid to Tonga and to the region, and headed off the Soviet offer. In 1980 the Soviet Union offered to undertake a five-year research project on maritime mineral resources in the region, in support of the activities of a regional intergovernmental body, the Committee for the Coordination of Joint Prospecting for Mineral Resources in South Pacific Offshore Areas (CCOP/SOPAC, nowadays known as SOPAC). Initial island government interest was countered by Australia, New Zealand and the United States, which offered an alternative project. The move blocked Soviet involvement in the area of research, preventing the Soviet Union from thus gaining increased access to the region.[7]

The attitudes of the island governments to the Soviet Union, which had already been negative, hardened after the Soviet invasion of Afghanistan in 1979. The island governments also condemned the shooting down by a Soviet fighter of Korean airliner KAL OO7 in 1983. The Western powers encouraged these responses. But in the mid-1980s, as concern with the Afghanistan conflict faded, and in response to their economic problems, first Kiribati and then Vanuatu reached fishing agreements with the Soviet Union. They did this despite warnings about the dangers of Soviet involvement and destabilisation. These warnings were based on the history of Soviet dealings with other developing states, reinforced by concern that the small scale of the Pacific island states could enable an external power to gain significant leverage, and have a destabilising influence, in return for a small investment of energy and resources. According to Richard Baker, a former American diplomat, and his co-authors, 'The example of Grenada, a tiny Caribbean nation that had fallen under Cuban influence, had a particularly strong influence on American thinking.'[8]

Both Kiribati and Vanuatu had confidence in their ability to deal sensibly with the Soviet Union. They also resented what they saw as a double standard whereby their links with the Soviet Union were criticised, while at the same time both Australia and New Zealand traded with the Soviet

Union. In addition, New Zealand had operated a fishing deal with the Soviets since 1978. The agreements between the Soviet Union and both Kirabati and Vanuatu only lasted one year. At renewal time the Soviet Union did not again offer the highly favourable terms of the initial agreements, and in each case the island government concerned declined to renew them. Overall, the Soviet Union failed during the 1980s to establish significant links with the island states.

During the 1980s Libya also made soundings in the islands region. Libyan interest reflected sympathy for revolutionary and 'liberation' movements, along with a wish to irritate the United States and France. Libya was at odds with France because during the 1980s France had countered its intervention in the central African state of Chad. From 1984 Libya provided encouragement, complemented by ideological and, in some instances, 'security' training, to elements in the Kanak nationalist movement in New Caledonia; to *Organisasi Papua Merdeka* (OPM) exiles resident in Vanuatu; and to elements in the ruling *Vanua'aku Pati* in Vanuatu associated with the (then) party Secretary-General Barak Sope. It also established links with some radical elements in the Australian Aboriginal community, and made contact with fringe groups among Tahitian nationalists in French Polynesia.[9]

In early 1987 Libya considered opening a diplomatic post in Vanuatu, but Vanuatu did not proceed with the proposal. The decision not to accept a diplomatic post resulted in large part from Libya's failure to pledge substantial aid. Other influences on the decision included church and other domestic opposition, and Australian diplomatic pressure, including warnings about Libya's record as a sponsor of terrorism. Australia also closed down the Libyan People's Bureau (that is, diplomatic post) in Canberra. This nullified the 'double standard' criticism, which had struck a chord with the island governments, that Australia was hypocritical in engaging in links with Libya while at the same time condemning connections between Libya and the island states.

THE MODIFICATION OF STRATEGIC DENIAL

From around 1988 Western policy towards the region changed. Greater emphasis was put on constructive bilateral and multilateral relations with the island states. The strategic denial approach was in large part suspended. This suspension took place because of the changes in Soviet policy during President Gorbachev's era, because of the disappearance of

Libyan interest, and because the island governments had become less amenable to advice on their external affairs.

In March 1990 the Soviet Union opened an embassy in Port Moresby. This was its first diplomatic post in any of the island states. It seems that Papua New Guinea caught the Soviet Union by surprise when it announced in 1989 that it would agree to a long-standing Soviet proposal that an embassy be opened. Port Moresby's decision on this question mainly reflected a wish to assert independence from Australia rather than any sudden enthusiasm for closer links with the Soviet Union. But changing Papua New Guinea perceptions of the Soviet Union in response to Gorbachev's reform initiatives were probably also influential. The Soviets also discussed a fishing deal with Papua New Guinea. An 'in-principle' agreement was reached, but the negotiations were not carried through. Some Papua New Guinea politicians and officials had suspicions about Soviet intentions. Meanwhile the Soviet government had preoccupations at home. Following the collapse of the Soviet Union, the post became a Russian embassy. The Russian government closed it down in April 1992, as an economy measure. Since around 1990, because of domestic preoccupations, Russian interest in the region has been minimal.

The opening of a Soviet embassy in Port Moresby had attracted scant media and political attention in the island states and in Australia and New Zealand. A few years earlier an event of this kind would have stimulated lively discussion. The view now generally taken by Australia, New Zealand and most other Western countries is that Russia and other external powers are welcome to develop their links with the region provided they engage in constructive and mutually beneficial relations. The United States changed its approach more gradually, but eventually also adopted this view.

Strategic denial still operates inasmuch as the free association states in American Micronesia have treaty arrangements with the United States which prohibit the establishment of a military presence in their territory by another external power. In addition any effort by Libya to renew its activities in the region would be countered. Passing interest by North Korea in 1989 also attracted some attention from the Western powers.[10] Yet subject to these qualifications, in practical terms strategic denial is now at an end.

FRANCE AND THE UNITED KINGDOM

During the 1980s French spokespersons and commentators often emphasised Western concerns about soundings by the Soviet Union and other 'unwelcome' powers, and argued that the French presence in the region was a guarantor of stability. In fact, however, aspects of that presence were criticised by island governments, and many observers argued that French policies were a significant threat to regional stability and security. The island governments have often been inclined to view France as essentially an external power reluctant to give up the Pacific remnants of its former empire. The view of the French government, which it has promoted actively in the region, has been that the French Pacific territories are an integral part of the indivisible French Republic, and that the French presence in the region will endure indefinitely.[11]

In the late eighteenth and early nineteenth centuries French navigators helped open up the region to Western awareness. In the nineteenth century France competed with its traditional rival, Great Britain, for influence. Although preempted in New Zealand, France established colonies in New Caledonia and in Tahiti and neighbouring island groups. After the Second World War these colonies became French overseas territories, with a measure of local self-government. France had also established a protectorate over the small Polynesian islands of Wallis and Futuna, to the north of Fiji. In 1959 the people of these islands voted for Wallis and Futuna to become an overseas territory of France, which it did in 1961.

These surviving outposts of the once vast French Empire had generally been of only meagre importance to metropolitan France. From the late 1950s, however, French interest in them increased. From 1963 France relocated its nuclear testing sites in French Polynesia, following the loss of the Saharan testing locale as a result of the independence of Algeria (see Chapter 5). The remoteness of most of the Pacific islands from major centres of wealth and power has in most instances minimised their strategic significance to the major powers. But, as noted earlier, in this case the isolation of these two small islands gave them an unanticipated strategic importance to France. Successive French governments have regarded the French nuclear deterrent as essential both to France's independent defence posture and to France's standing as a great power. They have mostly ignored regional condemnation of the testing programme. And they have ensured, at times by devious means, that France has maintained its presence in French Polynesia.

In New Caledonia the French presence was challenged in the 1970s and 1980s by the emergence of a nationalist movement representing the indigenous Melanesian Kanaks (see Chapter 4). French governments have resisted calls for an early transition to independence for the territory. The territory has value because of its rich resources of nickel and other minerals. In addition France wishes to retain control of its ten remaining overseas possessions, which are located in the North Atlantic, the Caribbean, Latin America and the Indian Ocean as well as in the Pacific islands region. It believes that these various remnants of its former empire add to French prestige, help in the promotion of French language and culture, and provide potential economic and other opportunities in particular regions.[12] On several occasions during most of the 1980s the island governments and the governments of Australia and New Zealand expressed strong concern over France's handling of New Caledonia.

France's relations with the island governments improved however in the late 1980s and early 1990s, following the restoration of peaceful conditions in New Caledonia from mid-1988 under the Matignon Accords and the suspension from April 1992 of the nuclear testing programme. These relations had already benefited, however, from active French diplomacy from the mid-1980s onwards.

In particular the coups in Fiji in 1987 had provided an opportunity for France to consolidate its presence in the region. After the coups, Fiji's formerly close relations with Australia and New Zealand were strained. France gained credit with the new Fiji administration by avoiding comment on the coups and by offering bilateral aid which helped make up for the suspension of Australian and New Zealand aid. In early 1988 France and Fiji agreed on an aid package worth over A\$ 16 million. The package comprised A\$ 8.6 million in loan funds, at concessionary rates, and a grant of A\$ 8 million. In the late 1980s and early 1990s France also improved its relations with several other island states by skilful diplomacy and the judicious provision of aid.[13]

France defends its policies actively and spends substantial amounts to maintain its presence. Almost all of this money is allocated to its territories. But a small but well-targeted portion is also used to strengthen relations with the island states. In late 1994 the French Minister for Overseas Departments and Territories in the Balladur government, Dominique Perben, said that France was spending nearly US\$ 50 million per year in the islands region, outside its own territories. This amount included more than US\$ 21 million devoted to bilateral and multilateral aid to the island states, a roughly similar amount which was France's 20 per cent contribution to European Union funding to the region, and several million dollars spent on defence cooperation, including EEZ surveillance to assist some states, and emergency and disaster relief operations.[14] It seems that about US\$ 12 million per year of this spending was bilateral aid to island states.

In contrast to France, the United Kingdom has sought to play only a modest role in the region. In the 1960s the United Kingdom decided to divest itself of almost all of its remaining colonial possessions. Overriding indigenous Fijian concerns about competition from the more enterprising Indian community, the United Kingdom negotiated a constitution designed to balance the interests of the two main communities and granted independence to Fiji in 1970. In the same year Tonga ceased to be a British protectorate. The Solomon Islands and Tuvalu attained independence in 1978, as did Kiribati the following year. In the Anglo-French Condominium of the New Hebrides, the United Kingdom encouraged a transition to independence in 1980, despite the reservations and obstruction of its French partner. The United Kingdom has maintained control only over Pitcairn and nearby islands. Pitcairn, the only inhabited island in the group, has a population of less than a hundred, so the group could not be expected to function as an independent entity.

There has been a long-term continuity in the British approach. In the colonial period Britain was often reluctant to expand its domains in the region; when it did acquire territory it was inclined to a policy of benign neglect. Funds to run the far-flung British Empire were sparse, and the islands had few resources justifying substantial investment. Britain minimised administrative costs and shared authority with local chiefs and notables and the Anglican and other Protestant churches. Local commercial activity was often mainly pursued by Australian, New Zealand, Chinese and (in Fiji) Indian enterprises. The lack of intense direct British involvement in island affairs eased subsequent withdrawal.

The United Kingdom provides aid to its former colonies and also contributes to multilateral programmes, especially via the European Union. It has chosen however to keep its aid spending and its general profile in the region at a modest level. Personal, educational and business links, and the Commonwealth connection, provide the United Kingdom with some influence, but this is exercised in a discreet, low-key way. Especially under successive conservative governments, and in accordance with its essential interests, the United Kingdom has given its connections with the United States and Europe much higher priority than those with the island states. Thus the United Kingdom has avoided taking a public stand on the at times controversial issues relating to the French presence in the region, and has joined with the United States and France in declining to sign the protocols of the Treaty of Rarotonga (see Chapter 5). The already modest level of British interest and involvement in the region seems likely to decline further over the next few years. One indication of this trend was the United Kingdom's decision, announced in October 1993, to withdraw from participation in, and funding of, the South Pacific Commission.

JAPAN

During the 1980s, and while strategic denial was still the central theme of western policy for the islands region, Japan began to show greater interest. Soviet and Libyan efforts to develop contacts with the island states, combined with conflict in New Caledonia and the coups in Fiji, as well as tensions elsewhere in the region, encouraged Japanese policy-makers to believe that what they regarded as Japan's southern flank was becoming a less benign security environment.[15] To some extent Japan lost confidence that the other Western and associated powers could be relied upon to ensure that regional stability was maintained. Meanwhile the United States was encouraging Japan to engage in more 'burden-sharing' on behalf of the Western association of states, in part by increasing sharply its spending on overseas development aid, including in the Pacific island states. Increased Japanese involvement was also part of a process whereby its economic dynamism resulted in the consolidation and expansion of its links with many Asian and Pacific countries.

The shift in Japanese policy towards somewhat greater involvement was marked by a speech given by Foreign Minister Kuranari in Fiji in early 1987 during a visit to the region. In what became known as the 'Kuranari doctrine' the Minister confirmed Japanese support for the independence and autonomy of the small island states, for the South Pacific Forum and regional stability, and for improved economic, aid, and cultural links between the region and Japan.[16]

For reasons of history and proximity, Japan has especially consolidated connections with the states and territories of American Micronesia. But its relations also began to develop significantly, from a low base, with the other parts of the Pacific islands region. Initially Japan took pains to consult closely with Australia, New Zealand and other powers with established links with the region. These powers responded favourably to increased Japanese involvement. As Japan's relations with the region developed, however, it began to act more independently, while maintaining consultation with other powers. In the five-year period from 1985, the amount per annum of Japanese aid spending in the region increased from US$ 24 million to US$ 98 million. This rate of expansion was more than 2.7 times the growth rate of Japanese aid on a world basis during the same period.[17] By 1990, with respect to most of the island states, Japan had displaced New Zealand as the second largest aid donor after Australia.[18] In addition Japan has consolidated its standing as a major market for raw materials from parts of the region, and Japanese investment in the region has risen sharply, with strong involvement in forestry and tourism. From the late 1980s Japan expressed guarded interest in the possibility of becoming a member of the South Pacific Commission, and has welcomed opportunities for bilateral and multilateral dialogue with Pacific island leaders.

Island governments have had mixed feelings about increased Japanese involvement in the region. Memories of the Second World War linger, complemented by anxiety about being swamped by Japanese aid and investment flows. Concerns have also arisen over the hard bargaining of Japanese investors and businessmen, which contrasts with the relaxed, easy-going Pacific islands style; over the highly-tied character of Japanese aid, which may result in a reduced priority for development criteria; over Japan's refusal to enter into a multilateral fisheries arrangement with the island states, because it finds it more profitable to deal with them separately; and over the repeated use by Japanese negotiators of aid as a lever with which to obtain concessional fishing rights.

Island governments have also reacted angrily against Japanese proposals to dump nuclear and other toxic wastes in the Pacific Ocean. They also condemned the shipment in late 1992/early 1993, via the islands region, of plutonium to Japan. In addition driftnet fishing by Japanese trawlers created bitterness, until it was banned by the Japanese government in 1990, a year in advance of the deadline established by the United Nations.[19] Concern has also arisen over increased activity by Japanese criminal elements in parts of the region, especially in American Micronesia.

Island government reservations about Japan's increasing profile in the region were expressed at the May 1991 meeting of the South Pacific Commission's Committee of Representatives of Governments and Administrations, during discussion of possible Japanese membership of the Commission. Some island delegates differentiated between 'the devils we know', that is, the existing donor country members of the Commission, and 'the devils we don't know', meaning Japan and the other external powers which had begun to develop their links with the region from the mid-1980s. The island delegates drew this distinction despite the prospect of increased Japanese aid if membership were granted, and despite a lack of in-principle opposition to Japanese membership. Their concern was that acceptance of Japanese membership, and of increased Japanese funding, could reduce the control of the island states and territories over the Commission. Yet the apprehensions of the island governments have been tempered by low-key and generally effective Japanese diplomacy, and they have been pleased to seek benefits from increased Japanese involvement. Indeed, in October 1993, at the annual meeting of the South Pacific

Commission, one island delegate responded to the United Kingdom's announcement that it intended to withdraw from the Commission by at once raising the question of possible Japanese membership.

In the early 1990s Japanese government interest in the region declined. The end of the Cold War and associated changes had brought an end to the perception that trends and developments in the islands region were potentially threatening to Japanese security interests. But by this stage Japanese involvement, both government and private, had attained some momentum, especially with respect to American Micronesia and, to some extent, Papua New Guinea. This was so even though the maintenance of this momentum was primarily a byproduct of the strength of the Japanese economy and of Japan's intention to assume a higher profile in the broader Asia-Pacific context.

OTHER EXTERNAL STATES

Since the early 1980s several other external states or groups of states have been engaged in establishing or consolidating connections with the region. They include Taiwan (the 'Republic of China'), the People's Republic of China, the ASEAN grouping, Indonesia, Malaysia, India, Israel, and the European Union.

During the nineteenth and early twentieth centuries Chinese labourers and traders established themselves in many of the Pacific islands. While remaining only a tiny minority, comprising at most only a few per cent of the populations concerned, they found a niche in commercial activity. Some of these communities provided support to the Chinese nationalist movement, and maintained contact with Taiwan following the Communist victory in 1949. As the island colonies became independent, Taiwan sought to establish connections with them. The presence of unobtrusive yet influential local communities of Chinese descent, as well as the anti-Communism associated with strong Christian traditions, facilitated this endeavour, and several island states developed links with Taiwan. In its diplomacy in the region Taiwan has pursued its rivalry with the People's Republic of China (PRC), has endeavoured to increase its international recognition and acceptance, and has sought to advance its fisheries and investment interests.

For its part the PRC has sought to counter Taiwan's efforts to consolidate connections with the region. It has established embassies in Papua New Guinea, Fiji and Western Samoa. Competition between the two powers has led to some frictions, notably in the Solomon Islands and Fiji.

In the late 1970s and early 1980s the PRC was also concerned by Soviet soundings in the region, in view of its wish to counter the threat of Soviet hegemonism and encirclement. The PRC has also been motivated to develop its links with the island states because of its standing and potential as a major Asia-Pacific power, because of its status as a developing country, even if on a far vaster scale than the island states, and because of the resource potential of some of the island states. While in Fiji during a visit to the region in 1985, the General Secretary of the Chinese Communist Party, Hu Yaobang, announced that China's policy towards the region embodied three principles: respect for the domestic and foreign policies of the island states, respect for the close relations between them, and respect for their treaty arrangements with the big powers.[20] In the late 1980s and early 1990s the PRC continued to consolidate its connections with the island states, albeit at a modest level, including by the provision of some aid, notably for building projects.

The ASEAN grouping, encouraged by Indonesia, has developed links with Papua New Guinea, which has special observer status at the annual ASEAN meetings. Among the ASEAN states, both Indonesia and Malaysia have been prominent in developing links with the states of the region. Indonesia has mainly focused on Papua New Guinea, seeking to regulate issues relating to their joint border and to OPM activities, and to develop investment and commercial links, but has also shown some interest in developing relations with the other island states.[21] Indonesia has generally been successful in managing the sources of tensions in its relations with Papua New Guinea, despite considerable sympathy in Papua New Guinea for the OPM. Indonesia maintains diplomatic posts in the region in Port Moresby and Suva and also in Noumea, New Caledonia, where there is a small resident Indonesian population descended from indentured workers brought in from the then Dutch East Indies up until the late 1940s.

Malaysian interest began in the early 1980s, and gathered momentum later in that decade. It has in part been commercial, with substantial Malaysian involvement in logging and other enterprises in Papua New Guinea and also in the Solomon Islands and Vanuatu. Corruption and environmental devastation has been associated with the activities of some Malaysian logging companies. Malaysian interest has also been political and diplomatic. Malaysia has tended to concentrate on Papua New Guinea, but has also developed some links with the Solomon Islands and Vanuatu.

Malaysia made a cautious but positive response to Fiji, following the coups in 1987, when the post-coups administration looked to Malaysia for sympathy and support. Malaysia has some similarities to Fiji. They both have a British colonial heritage, and an ethnically bipolar society in which politics are shaped by differences and rivalries between two broad groupings, one indigenous and the other non-indigenous. The Malaysian government, like its counterpart in Fiji, has given priority to the interests of indigenous nationals. One example of an attempt to develop the Malaysia–Fiji relationship followed Fiji's establishment of a state-owned company with an import monopoly on crude oil, which planned to import oil from Malaysia for domestic consumption as well as for resale to neighbouring island states. Previously, Fiji had depended on Australia and on ESSO in Singapore for the supply of its crude oil.[22] This initiative demonstrated Fiji's wish to diversify its external relations while reducing its links with Australia, especially as the new arrangements did not bring substantial cost advantages. In the event, however, this and other efforts to consolidate and diversify the Malaysia/Fiji relationship have had only limited success.

In 1987 the coups in Fiji drew India's attention to the region. The Indian government denounced the coups, and expressed concern about the well-being of the Fiji Indians. India would veto any moves for the return of Fiji to the Commonwealth, following its departure after the coups, and would increase diplomatic pressure on Fiji if conditions worsened sharply for the Fiji Indians. There were reportedly links between members of the Indian intelligence services and an attempt in 1988 to supply arms to the Fiji Indian community.[23]

Some commentators have suggested that India might consider direct intervention, should circumstances in Fiji deteriorate. They have pointed to India's developing blue water naval capability, and the history of Indian interventions in the island states in the Indian Ocean, including in Sri Lanka and the Maldives. But such assessments lack credibility, I believe. India is likely to be preoccupied for some years with internal economic and political problems and with relations with its immediate neighbours. It regards the Indian Ocean as part of its natural sphere of influence, but makes no such claim with respect to the Pacific islands region. Moreover links between the Fijian Indians and India have become tenuous. The main process of migration was completed by early in the twentieth century, and Indian attitudes to diaspora communities are often dismissive.

Another external state which has shown some interest in the region is Israel, though its level of involvement is modest. The Jewish communities in the region, where they are exist, are minuscule, and commercial links between Israel and the island states are very small. Israel has an embassy in Suva. In view of its vulnerable position, Israel has wished to put its case internationally, including with the governments of the developing states, among whom it has many critics, reflecting sympathy for the Palestinian cause. Israel may have slightly raised its profile in the region in the mid-1980s because of indications of interest by Libya, one of its leading adversaries. During the Cold War period Israel also actively pursued an anti-Communist agenda. Its modest aid to the region has included the provision of trade union and cooperative training.

Israel's links with Fiji have been developed through the involvement of Fijian forces in peacekeeping operations in Lebanon and elsewhere in the Middle East. Following the Fiji coups, when military and other links between Fiji and Australia and New Zealand were suspended, Australia cancelled the provision of patrol boats to Fiji. Israel stepped in and provided four patrol boats under credit arrangements.[24] Israel has also developed some links with Papua New Guinea, including through the sale of defence equipment. In August 1994 Israel and Papua New Guinea signed a defence cooperation agreement, though it was not immediately clear what this would involve. In the post-Cold War environment, and as the peace process in Israel gathers some momentum, Israel seems likely to continue its very modest level of involvement in the region, but does not aspire to become a significant player in regional affairs.

The European Union (formerly the European Community) has no political or strategic interests in the region, but has significant economic links with several island states. These links mostly operate within the context of the Lomé Convention, which operates between the Community and the ACP (Africa-Carribean-Pacific) countries, a group of developing countries which formerly were colonies of, or were otherwise associated with, one or other of the European powers. The first Lomé Convention was negotiated in 1974, in the African capital of that name, and subsequent conventions have been renegotiated since then. Under the conventions the ACP countries have guaranteed access to the European Union, at subsidized prices, for their agricultural produce. The Lomé Conventions have been particularly important for Fiji, which has been able to ensure access for the sale of sugar, its main product and export, in Europe at above world market prices. In addition, the European Union provides some aid to multilateral projects and to some island states.

The United Nations and the Commonwealth have also been involved in the region. The United Nations monitored the transition of most of the colonies in the region to self-government and independence, and welcomed several of the new states to its membership. Through its Committee of Twenty-Four on Decolonisation, and votes in the General Assembly, it has put diplomatic pressure on France to implement a process of decolonisation in New Caledonia. The United Nations also endorsed the incorporation of Irian Jaya into Indonesia and, less controversially, has oversighted the transition of some of the components of the United States Trust Territory of the Pacific Islands to free association status. The involvement of the Commonwealth has been more low-key, although Commonwealth meetings have provided a useful forum for island state members. In 1990 the Commonwealth Secretariat was involved in efforts to negotiate a settlement of the Bougainville dispute, though without success.

NON-GOVERNMENT ACTORS

With respect to security and sovereignty, the external relations of particular island states and, in some instances, the region as a whole have also been shaped in part by the involvement of a variety of non-government bodies and institutions. Their activities are many and various, and are often difficult to put into perspective. They help shape the climate within which decisions are made, help distinguish policy options and, at times, shift the balance in favour of a particular course of action. Some of these actors are based outside the region. Others among them have strong connections outside any particular island state, and/or outside the islands region.

The Christian churches have played a significant part in the region throughout and since the colonial period. Almost all Polynesians and Micronesians, and a large majority of Melanesians, are at least nominally christian; church organisations have contributed substantially to education and welfare; and many senior islander politicians and officials have strong church connections. Prime Minister Rabuka of Fiji, for example, is a former Methodist lay preacher; Father Walter Lini, an Anglican priest, led Vanuatu to independence, served as prime minister throughout the 1980s, and is still a prominent political figure. This heritage has contributed to strong suspicions of communism in the region, and to less support, compared with circumstances in some other parts of the developing world, for hard-line radical politics. Liberation theology on the Latin American model has had some sympathizers in the islands region, but overall church leaders have been fairly cautious in their approach.

On the other hand the Christian heritage has also encouraged a strongly moral, and at times moralistic, approach to contentious issues. Over several years, the Pacific Conference of Churches has championed reformist, radical and social justice causes in the region. In Vanuatu in the 1980s, the presence of several Anglican and Presbyterian ministers of religion in the cabinet, including Prime Minister Lini, helped shaped Vanuatu's distinctive attitudes to regional and international issues.

Since 1975 the NFIP (Nuclear Free and Independent Pacific) movement, a loose coalition of radical and reformist groupings, has undertaken anti-nuclear and anti-colonial campaigning.[25] The NFIP presents itself as embodying broad 'grass-roots' movements, but much of its impetus has come from small but active groups. It has denounced nuclear testing and dumping and port visits by nuclear-powered or armed ships, called for early independence for dependent territories, and criticised the ANZUS alliance and the United States role in the region. In association with local peace groups, churches and trade unions, it has contributed to sharpening concerns over some of these issues in several of the island states. But following the coups in Fiji in 1987 and a militant reassertion of indigenous rights there and elsewhere in the islands region, as well as in New Zealand and Australia, the NFIP's influence was weakened by internal tensions over how far indigenous rights should take precedence over other concerns.[26]

The NFIP's activities have won support from unions in some island states. In the 1980s leftwing unions in Australia and New Zealand supported the development of a regional union body, the South Pacific Trade Union Forum, which expressed views on several regional political and security issues, including nuclear and colonial questions. Some of the unionists involved had links with a Soviet front, the WFTU (World Federation of Trade Unions); others, though acting independently, pursued objectives that were in some respects convergent with those of the Soviet Union in the region, especially with respect to efforts to reduce the standing and influence of the United States.[27] Most of the unions in the region had links with the anti-Communist ICFTU (International Confederation of Free Trade Unions). In the 1980s ICFTU-affiliated unions in Australia and the United States developed their connections with South Pacific unions in order to counter the activities of the Pacific Trade Union Forum and of the WFTU. In doing so they received official American support.[28] In post-Cold War circumstances, however, efforts by external groupings to influence trade unions in the region have waned, though some training and liaison links have continued.

Greenpeace has also had considerable impact in the region, dramatising environmental and associated issues. By sending protest vessels to French Polynesia, and by other means, Greenpeace has helped develop concerns over the health and environmental implications of nuclear testing. In May 1985 the Greenpeace vessel *Rainbow Warrior* drew attention to the tragic legacies of American nuclear testing by transporting the inhabitants of Rongelap island, which had been contaminated by fallout from atmospheric testing in the 1950s, to a new home.[29] A few weeks later, in July

1985, the sinking by French agents of the *Rainbow Warrior* in Auckland Harbour heightened concerns over the French presence and the French testing programme. In the late 1980s Greenpeace campaigned vigorously against driftnet fishing in the region. In 1990 Greenpeace campaigned strongly against the destruction by the United States of chemical weapons on Johnston Island, contributing to the expression of strong island state concerns over this issue at that year's meeting of the South Pacific Forum. In the early 1990s Greenpeace and other environmental groups have campaigned against exploitative and environmentally irresponsible resource projects, and have denounced the industrial powers for failing to do more to limit the contribution of their economic activities to global warming.

International financial organisations have a substantial impact on the domestic and external affairs of the island states. They help shape the framework within which the island governments operate, and encourage certain policy choices. In Papua New Guinea from 1990 onwards, for example, the World Bank, the International Monetary Fund, and the Asian Development Bank assisted the (then) Namaliu government to implement a far-reaching programme of economic stabilisation and structural adjustment. The programme was at first reasonably successful, but lost momentum because of reduced fiscal discipline, especially following national elections in 1992. Under a new government led by Paias Wingti, public spending was undisciplined and the deficit rose to risky levels. After he replaced Wingti as prime minister in August 1994, however, Sir Julius Chan implemented austerity measures and indicated an intention to pursue the reform process.

Sometimes unintended consequences occur as a result of reform programmes, because tough government measures tend to sharpen social tensions. In the early 1980s the World Bank urged Fiji to adopt austerity measures. The Alliance government complied by initiating a wage freeze, in order to defend Fiji's reputation for responsible economic management and to ensure Fiji's continued attractiveness for loans and investments. The wage freeze contributed to the momentum gained by the Fiji Labour Party and hence to the defeat of the Alliance and the narrow victory of the coalition led by Dr Timoci Bavadra in the 1987 elections, helping in turn to create the context for the coup in May 1987.[30]

Multinational companies also have had a significant presence, especially with respect to resource and tourist development. Several of these companies operate on a scale, with respect to the size of their budgets and their numbers of personnel, larger than that of the governments of some of the smaller island states. Some big companies have engaged in transfer pricing to evade tax.[31] This has reduced the ability of island governments to earn reasonable returns from foreign business activity, frustrating the exercise of sovereignty and the development of national self-reliance. In particular, rapacious behaviour by several timber companies has caused environmental devastation, obstructing efforts to implement sustainable development, and has encouraged corruption and a weakening of the viability and credibility of the states concerned (see Chapter 5).

Other business groupings, and carpetbaggers and adventurers, also have had an influence. As noted earlier, tuna poaching by some American and other vessels in the 1970s and early 1980s sparked protests from island governments, and led to regional cooperation in fisheries management and maritime surveillance. In 1979 one businessman of uncertain reputation collected most of the savings of Tuvalu, amounting to over half a million Australian dollars, claiming that they would be invested to help establish a fishing industry. The scheme came to nothing, but it took several years for the funds to be recovered.[32]

In the late 1970s and in 1980 real estate speculators and libertarian adventurers encouraged abortive secessionist attempts on Espiritu Santo and other islands in Vanuatu. In late 1993 the Vanuatu Finance Minister, working through an Australian intermediary, approved a scheme intended to open a line of credit for Vanuatu, reportedly for up to two billion US dollars, for infrastructure and development projects. Vanuatu's recurrent budget is about US$ 50 million.[33] Some months later, although substantial commissions had been paid, it appeared that no loan arrangements had as yet come into operation. In the early 1990s the Nauru government reportedly lost millions of dollars through a 'con job' by an expatriate manager of the Nauru Phosphates Royalties Trust company.[34] This and other heavy losses through malpractice and/or mismanagement have reduced Nauru's ability to manage its affairs responsibly and to provide a secure future for its people. In September 1994 the Chief Ombudsman of Papua New Guinea, Sir Charles Mino, said in his independence day anniversary message that Papua New Guinea was saddled with crime, bribery and corruption because of the self-interest of its leaders. He called for the emergence of more honest leaders, in order to stop foreign adventurers and carpetbaggers from making fast money by exploiting ordinary Papua New Guineans.[35]

Involvement by international criminal groupings, engaged for example in money-laundering and drug smuggling, also has the potential to challenge the security and sovereignty of the island states. This is especially so because of their small scale, and because of the presence in two of them, namely Vanuatu and the Cook Islands, of tax havens. The activities of such groupings encourages corruption and threatens to disrupt fragile economies, and in certain circumstances could challenge constitutional rule. Circumstances in some of the Caribbean island states illustrate that these risks have substance. In American Micronesia the Japanese Yakusa gangs have established a presence, taking advantage of opportunities provided by high levels of Japanese tourism and investment, and may be able to expand their influence elsewhere. Here and elsewhere, drug-dealing has encouraged corruption.

From 1990 the South Pacific Forum began to put a high priority on information exchange and other measures to contain criminal activities. But serious problems have continued. The island governments lack skills and experience. Meanwhile bureaucratic rivalries and a lack of coordination have been present in Australia and other donor states. Australia's efforts to assist have been hampered in particular by its federal constitution, which fragments its legal and policing systems, adding to difficulties in liaison with the island governments.

CONCLUSION

The island states have generally maintained strong links with their former colonial powers, in considerable part because of their dependence on aid from these powers. But in the 1980s rising interest from other external powers both encouraged, and was encouraged by, an increased emphasis by several of the island governments on diversifying their external relations. This interest in diversification was not at first welcomed by the former colonial powers, at least in those few instances where it related to the Soviet Union and its allies and to Libya. The former colonial powers were more relaxed about increased involvement by other powers, and encouraged greater Japanese interest. Until the late 1980s, the former colonial powers sought to ensure the strategic denial of the region to powers which were likely to act against broad Western interests. From around 1988, however, their policy began to change, and the pace of change quickened as the Cold War came to an end. Henceforth the former colonial powers put greater emphasis on constructive bilateral and multilateral relations with the island states, and largely suspended the strategic denial approach.

Overall, then, the longer-term trend in the external affairs of the island states has been towards greater diversification and complexity, even though links with traditional partners mostly remain strong (Table 6.1). This trend seems likely to continue, though with gradual and cumulative rather than immediate implications. In particular Japan and several other

Asian countries have developed a somewhat increased profile in the region. The trend has been strengthened by the activities of a range of non-government actors.

In seeking to diversify their external contacts, the island governments have asserted their independence and explored a wider range of potential sources for aid and investment. Many island leaders have put particular emphasis on developing relations with the Asian countries. In late 1993 the Australian journalist Mary-Louise O'Callaghan described the 'Look North' policy of Paias Wingti, the (then) Prime Minister of Papua New Guinea, as involving a process of 'diversifying Papua New Guinea's trade, economic and security interests out of its Australian childhood saddle and harnessing them instead to the bucking Asian economic bronco.'[36]

But for Papua New Guinea, and for several of the other island countries, the results have been mixed. Some Asian companies have been cautious, because of the difficult investment environment in the island states. Others have been rapacious. According to a late 1994 report on trends in Papua New Guinea in the *Business Review Weekly*:

> Planeloads of businessmen, bureaucrats and politicians have flown off to the north and west, largely at taxpayer expense. Proposals have been received, feasibility studies commissioned. But cold hard cash? Very little, except in the timber sector, where a lack of policing and a prolif-eration of profits have provided strong incentives for Malaysian investors, and in fish canning and cement, where taxpayer-funded incentives have attracted Malaysian and South Korean money....Wayne Golding, president of the Papua New Guinea Chamber of Manufactures, says there is no doubt Asian businessmen have money to invest but that they are very cautious: 'When they do come here, there's a lot of talk but very little delivery. That has been evident in the past five or six years when investment by Malaysians has been massive in the logging industry but very small elsewhere. Out of Indonesia, where we have done a heap of lobbying, we have generated nothing. We have some Singaporean investment but it is mainly in real estate. So we have not had a broad spectrum of investment from the north.[37]

Meanwhile some commentators have expressed reservations about com-mercial links with the Asian region. In September 1994 Margaret Taylor, formerly Papua New Guinea Ambassador to Washington, warned that Papua New Guinea was a 'sitting target' for exploitation by some irre-sponsible Asian companies. She added that: 'There's a whole new wave of Asian colonialism that is coming into this country [that is, Papua New Guinea]. It's all based on extraction of resources.'[38]

The island governments recall the exploitation and injustices of the colonial period. They are also conscious that the former colonial powers have always acted in accordance with a healthy sense of their own self-interest, and that the interests of these powers and the island states do not in all cases converge.

Yet these former colonial powers also have traditions of open government and public accountability. Their policies and practices with respect to the island states are actually or potentially subject to scrutiny and pressure by the press and public opinion, both domestically and internationally. Their policy approaches nowadays take a long-term perspective, and are mainly directed towards encouraging and supporting economic and social development in the region. Island governments would be well advised to note that these influences favouring responsible behaviour are not always present in the external states which are newly active in the region. For similar reasons, their relations with several of the non-government groupings with an interest in the region also need to be handled cautiously.

7 The Limits on Power: Australia and New Zealand and the Region

Australia – and, to some extent, New Zealand – have often been seen as wielding the weight and influence of great powers in their relations with the Pacific island states. And their importance in relation to the islands region has often been contrasted with their more modest profile in world affairs.

Several commentators have expressed these views. From around 1970, according to the New Zealand political scientist Rod Alley, an increasingly prevalent view developed in New Zealand on 'the distinctive role open to New Zealand in the South Pacific'.[1] At this time a senior New Zealand diplomat, Paul Gabites, described the islands region as 'perhaps one area of the world where, in spite of our limited resources, we can make a substantial individual contribution'. The region, moreover, was one in which 'our contribution need not be dwarfed by that of larger powers'.[2] By the late 1970s the historian Mary Boyd said it was time to discard the 'myth' that New Zealand was 'the best friend and natural leader of Pacific [island] countries'.[3]

In the early 1980s the (then) Australian Foreign Minister, Bill Hayden, denounced France for continuing nuclear tests in what he described as 'our backyard'. In the mid-1980s Prime Minister Lini of Vanuatu described Australia and New Zealand as neo-colonial powers in the region because of their development of rapid reaction forces. In 1988 the New Zealand–based political scientist Steve Hoadley described Australia as 'the major actor [in the region] south of the equator, especially in the Melanesian sub-region'.[4] In assessing Australia's policy, announced in December 1989, of 'constructive commitment' in the Pacific Islands, Australian political scientist Greg Fry argued that this policy in fact amounted to a continuation of an Australian version of the Monroe doctrine, similar in some respects to that pursued by the United States with respect to Latin America, whereby Australia pursued regional hegemony.[5] Around 1990, the American analyst John Dorrance described Australia and New Zealand as 'the superpowers of the South Pacific'.[6] Reporting from the South Pacific Forum meeting in Honiara in July 1992, ABC South Pacific correspondent Jemima Garrett commented that at times Australia had difficulty in adjusting to the unaccustomed role of being a 'metropolitan power' in the region. Her colleague, Erinna Reddan, reporting from the 1994 Forum in Brisbane, described Australia as 'like a superpower'.

There can be no doubt of course that vast asymmetries in area, population, wealth, level of development and military power exist between Australia, especially, but also New Zealand on the one hand, and the island states on the other (see Table 1.1). Australia's land area is substantially greater than that of all the island states combined. New Zealand's land area is smaller than that of Papua New Guinea, but is far greater than that of any of the other island states. Some of the island states lay claim to extensive exclusive economic zones, but Australia and New Zealand have a much greater capability to police and to exploit directly their EEZ resources.

Australia's population of over 17 million is some three times larger than that of all fourteen of the Pacific island states combined. New Zealand's population is smaller than that of Papua New Guinea, but is several times greater than that of any of the other island states. In economic and military terms, Australia and New Zealand also dwarf their island neighbours. As developed countries, both Australia and New Zealand have per capita Gross Domestic Products several times greater than those of the island states. Phosphate-rich Nauru has been an exception. But as noted earlier, its prosperity is unlikely to last once the phosphate runs out, as will happen over the next decade or so. In any case, Nauru is too small an entity to play a major role in regional affairs. Among the island states, only Papua New Guinea, Fiji and Tonga have military forces, and these forces are in no way commensurate, in size, strength, quality of equipment and projection capability, to those of Australia and New Zealand.

There can also be no doubt that links between Australia and New Zealand and most of their island neighbours are extensive and close. Both Australia and New Zealand are important aid donors to several of the island states. Australia is overall the leading donor to the Melanesian states and Fiji, and to the Polynesian/Commonwealth Micronesian states. Since around 1990 New Zealand has ranked third overall behind Australia and Japan as an overall aid donor to most of these states,[7] but remains an important bilateral donor to some of them, and a major outlet for migration from the Polynesian states.

Australia's links with its former colony, Papua New Guinea, include the provision of substantial aid, amounting in the early 1990s to over 15 per cent of the Papua New Guinea government's revenue. In 1992/93 Australian aid to Papua New Guinea totalled A$ 334.4 million, with a further A$ 118 million going to the other island states. Australia is the leading donor to the South Pacific Commission and contributes to other regional organisations.[8] It assists the island states through defence cooperation, including by provision of training and equipment. Through RAAF and RAN patrols, Australia contributes to the aerial and naval surveillance of island state EEZs. To further assist the island states to monitor their EEZs, Australia has provided them with, at substantial expense and with mixed results, fifteen patrol boats, and is contributing to the crew training, maintenance and running costs of these vessels.[9]

New Zealand, in accordance with its smaller size, provides a smaller amount of aid overall. Nonetheless it is a significant donor, both multilaterally and bilaterally. In 1991/92, 70 per cent of its bilateral aid allocation of NZ $ 124 million was directed to the island states.[10] Its bilateral aid is directed particularly to its former colony of Western Samoa and to its freely associated states of the Cook Islands and Niue. It also assists its self-governing dependent territory, Tokelau. In addition New Zealand provides defence aid to the region through its Military Assistance Programme.

Because of the striking differences in scale, economic structure, wealth and military force between Australia and New Zealand and the island states, and because of their close links with several of these states, observers often jump to the conclusion that Australia and New Zealand dominate the affairs of the Pacific islands region.

But this conclusion is less soundly based than appearances would suggest. In this chapter, I challenge the widely-held assumption that Australia and New Zealand are indeed 'great powers' in relation to the Pacific island states and the islands region, and emphasise the limits on their power in that region. I first review the history of Australian and New Zealand relations with the region before examining the main present-day restraints and limits on the exercise of Australian and New Zealand influence and power, at the international, regional and domestic levels. I then consider some recent developments and issues to demonstrate that Australia and New Zealand have less power and influence in the islands region than is often assumed.

OVERVIEW: AUSTRALIA AND NEW ZEALAND AND THE PACIFIC ISLANDS

Australian and New Zealand interest in the islands region has been mainly strategic, although commercial and other motives have also been present. In the nineteenth century political and opinion leaders in the Australian colonies and in New Zealand were anxious about the activities of the great powers, other than Great Britain. They were anxious over possible threats to their territory and, as far as possible, wanted the islands region to be a 'British' preserve.

Australian and New Zealand agitation prompted a reluctant Britain to thwart French ambitions in the New Hebrides (now Vanuatu). Britain's involvement led eventually to the establishment of a joint Anglo-French Condominium over this archipelago in 1907. Australia prompted the establishment of a British protectorate over southeastern New Guinea in 1884, soon after Germany's establishment of a protectorate over the northeastern part of the island and neighbouring islands. At the outset of the First World War, Australian forces took over German New Guinea. From 1922 Australia administered the mandated territory of New Guinea as well as the territory of Papua (formerly British New Guinea) over which it had gained control in 1906. The two colonies were merged under a unified administration during the Second World War.

Australia's main interest during the late nineteenth and early twentieth centuries tended to be directed to Papua New Guinea and the New Hebrides, and to a lesser extent Fiji and New Caledonia. New Zealand's attention focused more on Fiji and on the Polynesian islands. Although Fiji was a British colony, New Zealand had a strong commercial and educational presence there. In 1901 New Zealand acquired the Cook Islands, some of which had been under a British protectorate since 1888. New Zealand took over German Samoa at the beginning of the First World War, and after the war was granted what became known as Western Samoa as a mandated territory. In the early twentieth century New Zealand also acquired Niue and Tokelau, and from 1919 shared formal responsibility for the former German possession of Nauru with Britain and Australia, though in practice Australia ran the administration of this island.

Since early in the twentieth century, Australia's, and in some measure New Zealand's, attention has focused from time to time on the implications for their welfare and security of the strength and ambitions of Japan. During the Second World War, the defence of the islands to the north of Australia and New Zealand from Japanese forces exacted a heavy human and material cost from all involved. After the American and allied victory, Australian interest in the region receded, although H. V. Evatt, Australia's Minister for External Affairs in the immediate post-war period, took a leading part in the formation of the South Pacific Commission.

Until the 1980s Australia's security concerns over its neighbouring regions mainly concentrated on Southeast and Northeast Asia. The Pacific islands region was largely ignored, although some effort was put into social and economic development in Papua New Guinea. New Zealand showed somewhat greater interest in the islands region, in particular because of its connections with some of the Polynesian islands, but overall its priorities remained elsewhere. Despite misgivings over Indonesia's acquisition of Dutch New Guinea, Australia acquiesced when it became clear that neither the United States nor the United Kingdom would support it in opposition to Indonesia over this issue.

But as the decolonisation of the island colonies got underway, the emergence of a variety of small states drew some increased Australian and New Zealand attention to the region. This interest was further encouraged by diplomatic probings by the Soviet Union from the late 1970s, and by the declaration of the Law of the Sea in 1982 which permitted island states to claim extensive exclusive economic zones.

Australian governments have been conscious of the vast land area and giant maritime zone of their island continent, along with its proximity to Southeast Asia, and thus of the enormous difficulties in defending what Ross Babbage has described as 'a coast too long'.[11] Only a major power could invade Australia. On present indications such an invasion seems highly unlikely. But regional powers could conceivably pressure Australia by raids on isolated settlements and facilities and by cutting lines of communication. None of Australia's neighbours is at present perceived as a threat. Yet decision-makers are conscious of the possibility of rapid change, in ways which could be harmful to Australian interests, in the large, diverse, and complex Asia/Pacific region.

Australian governments have emphasised the central importance of Australia's close alliance, expressed through the ANZUS treaty and in other ways, with the United States. The alliance acts in some measure as a guarantor of Australian security, gives Australia privileged access to senior levels of American leadership and to American intelligence and assessments, and contributes to Australia's international profile, albeit at the risk of being drawn too readily into wider conflicts.

Compared with Australia, New Zealand has a reduced sense of vulnerability. It is remote from centres of possible threat, is surrounded by vast areas of ocean, and has close and friendly links with its nearest large neighbour: Australia. New Zealand's relationship with the United States had traditionally been less close and less substantial than that of Australia, even before the ANZUS rift of the 1980s.

It was over ANZUS that the policy stances of Australia and New Zealand diverged somewhat in the mid-1980s. This was despite their many shared interests and their traditions of cooperation, including in the Pacific islands region. The key question was that of port visits by potentially nuclear-armed or nuclear-powered ships. In 1984 the newly-elected New Zealand Labour Government led by David Lange banned visits by such ships to New Zealand ports. The New Zealand intention to ascertain in advance whether a prospective visiting ship was nuclear-armed or -powered conflicted with the United States policy of neither confirming nor denying the presence of a nuclear capability.

United States naval visits to New Zealand were infrequent, and of small importance in themselves to US naval operations. But the Reagan (and subsequently the Bush) administrations were concerned about the possible consequences of acquiescing in New Zealand's changed policy for attitudes in states and regions of more direct importance to United States and Western strategic arrangements. They also believed that providing occasional port access should be regarded by New Zealand as a routine and uncontroversial contribution to common Western interests, especially since the main burden in defending those interests was borne by the United States. After conciliation efforts failed, those provisions of the ANZUS treaty relating to New Zealand ceased to operate, and New Zealand ceased to be an ally of the United States.

The differences between Australia and New Zealand over nuclear ship visits reflect the underlying contrasts between the two states. Henry Kissinger's reported remark that 'New Zealand is a dagger pointed at the heart of the Antarctic', underlines New Zealand's remoteness. This isolation from the potential centres of major conflict, and New Zealand's own relatively harmonious history in recent decades, despite some heightening of racial tensions since the early 1980s, has encouraged an idealistic and at times moralistic trend, with isolationist overtones, in foreign policy.

The policy on nuclear ship visits has been popular with the New Zealand electorate. In due course it drew attention away from the painful restructuring of the New Zealand economy undertaken by the Lange Government. In response to the electoral popularity of the policy, the New Zealand opposition National Party shifted its position in February 1990 to accept the ship visits ban, and continued this stance after winning government in October 1990.

In late 1991 the United States announced, as part of disarmament measures in response to the end of the Cold War, that henceforth tactical nuclear weapons would not be deployed on its naval vessels. The New Zealand National Government accordingly began examining whether the anti-nuclear ships policy could be revised, including by seeking to assuage concerns about conceivable risks, which are minimal, from port visits by nuclear-powered vessels. But the strength of anti-nuclear feeling in the electorate has limited the government's freedom of manoeuvre.

In the post-Cold War environment, with concerns over the Soviet Union no longer present, and no military threats evident to New Zealand security, the advantages of returning to ANZUS do not seem compelling to the New Zealand electorate. Meanwhile the United States government under President Clinton, as under his predecessors, has shown little inclination to accept a compromise formula over ANZUS. It insists that the anti-nuclear policy should be fully reversed before a reactivation of ANZUS as it relates to New Zealand can occur. With both sides maintaining their established positions, the return of New Zealand to full partnership in ANZUS remains blocked.

The ANZUS rift created some tensions between Australia and New Zealand, but their governments have worked to maintain the relationship. In late 1989 the New Zealand Government decided, despite lively domestic criticism, and after considerable Australian persuasion, to participate with Australia in a joint frigate building programme to increase its blue water naval capability. Australia saw this decision as confirmation that New Zealand intended to cooperate closely with Australia in pursuing shared security interests, especially in the Pacific islands region. Difficulties between Australia and New Zealand will recur, but they will continue to work together in the Pacific islands region.

LIMITS AND RESTRAINTS: INTERNATIONAL, REGIONAL AND DOMESTIC

The limits and restraints to which Australia and New Zealand are subject in their relations with the island states may for convenience be considered in three interrelated contexts, namely international, regional, and domestic. The context at the international level includes the norms and practices established by the international community since the end of the Second World War; the regional context includes both regional institutions and changing circumstances and attitudes; and the domestic context comprises perspectives and priorities, both governmental and popular, in Australia and New Zealand.

To appreciate the international context of Australia and New Zealand's relations with the island states, we need to put the emergence of the island states as sovereign entities – despite their lack of cohesion and/or their economic weakness – in historical perspective. As noted earlier (see Chapter 1), the transition of the Pacific island colonies and many colonies elsewhere to full independence generally resulted more from changes in international morality and international law than from internal pressures.

The states which emerged in the islands region from 1962 onwards appear to be weak and vulnerable, and thus readily influenced from outside. But despite their apparent vulnerability, their sovereignty is upheld by current international norms and practices. Both Australia and New Zealand have fully supported the process of decolonisation which has led to the emergence of these states, and of those elsewhere. They both also support the integrity and sovereignty of the island states. In the case of their own colonial possessions in the region, both Australia and New Zealand were positive about eventual decolonisation. Indeed, New Zealand took an active part in preparing Western Samoa and the other New Zealand colonies, other than tiny Tokelau, either for full independence or else for self-government and independence-in-association.

The conservative coalition governments which held power in Australia from 1949 to 1972 had doubts about Papua New Guinea's readiness for independence. They made only modest efforts to prepare this complex and fragmented entity for eventual decolonisation. But Andrew Peacock, the responsible minister in the last coalition government before the 1972 elections, encouraged an early move to independence. Under Prime Minister Gough Whitlam, the Labor governments which held power from 1972 to 1975 moved hastily to establish Papua New Guinea as an independent state, in the absence of any extensive Papua New Guinea support for a rapid move in this direction.

Limits and restraints on the exercise of Australian and New Zealand power also operate at the regional level. Some of these consist of the expression at the regional level of the international context discussed above. The various regional organisations operating in the islands region have been shaped by these international institutions, norms and attitudes. The role of the South Pacific Forum, the regional organisation comprising the island states and also Australia and New Zealand, is central, although other regional organisations have some significance. Australia and New Zealand have strongly and consistently supported these various bodies. These bodies not only provide means within which Australia and New Zealand can pursue particular national interests, but also establish restraints on the ways in which those interests are pursued. By acting as a supra-national body, the South Pacific Forum reinforces the legitimacy of even the smallest and weakest of island states, and provides a constraining framework on Australian and New Zealand involvement in regional affairs. If the Forum and other regional organisations were weaker or non-existent, then it would be easier for Australia and New Zealand to exert bilateral pressure and influence.

The regional-level restraints on the power and influence of Australia and New Zealand also include of course changing circumstances in the region since around 1985. These changes include greater assertiveness and independence-of-mind on the part of island governments, which have been reflected in efforts to diversify external connections, and to reduce reliance on Australia and New Zealand. Meanwhile various external states and organisations have shown interest in developing relations with the island states, helping expand and diversify the region's external links. Although the links of most of the island states with Australia and New Zealand remain important, these new linkages seem likely to develop considerable substance over time. This trend is increasing the complexity of the international environment in which the island states operate, and is adding somewhat to their freedom of manoeuvre.

The regional community has also become more diverse and complex as new states have emerged, with implications for the standing and influence of Australia and New Zealand. In the 1980s Vanuatu often adopted policy stances at odds with those favoured by Australia and New Zealand. In the late 1980s the Federated States of Micronesia and the Republic of the Marshall Islands became members of the South Pacific Forum, and will be joined there in due course by Palau. These states remain closely tied to their former administering power, the United States, and have only insubstantial links with Australia and New Zealand.

In addition, intractable problems of social and economic development have emerged in several island states, which neither Australia nor New Zealand can resolve unilaterally. This has encouraged the island governments to put increased emphasis on a wider range of external relationships, and has encouraged the Australian and New Zealand governments to emphasise that ultimately it is the island governments which must take responsibility for grappling with these problems.

This is particularly so with respect to Papua New Guinea, the largest and most populous island state. Developments in the late 1980s and early 1990s in Papua New Guinea have had particular implications for Australia's standing and relevance. Because of its resources wealth, Papua New Guinea has the potential to become economically self-reliant. Should all go well, the phasing out of Australian and other aid could conceivably be completed within ten to fifteen years, reducing the relevance of the Australian connection. But meanwhile Papua New Guinea has suffered increased and increasingly intractable internal problems, including the secessionist revolt on Bougainville, secessionist stirrings elsewhere, law and order problems, and uncertainties about the present and future role of the police and the army.

Australia is likely to continue to assist the Papua New Guinea government in managing these problems. But the colonial heritage has created ambivalence and bitterness in the attitudes of the Papua New Guinea élite to Australia. In recent years Papua New Guinea governments have shown a strong inclination to look for support, role models and advice elsewhere, and to seek to develop links with the booming economies of Asia. Accordingly, Australian influence on Papua New Guinea seems likely to diminish in the medium term, both because Papua New Guinea is fiercely independent and may become more economically self-reliant, and because of the limitations on Australia's ability to assist in the resolution of present problems.

Last, but certainly not least, the domestic context of Australia and New Zealand's relations with the island states requires consideration. Since European settlement, most Australians have lived on the eastern seaboard of their vast country. Australia would seem to look towards the Pacific islands. But the national orientation has mostly been further afield. Towards Britain until the Second World War, and since then, also and increasingly towards the United States, Europe and Northeast and Southeast Asia. For most Australians, the Pacific island states and territories are possible tourist destinations, but little more. For Australian governments, interest in the region has been episodic, although, as noted earlier, attention heightened in the middle and late 1980s.

Few in Australia think of Australia as being a Pacific islands state, although many would accept that, in strategic terms, Australia is linked to the islands region. The cliché is that Australia is geographically a close neighbour or even 'part of' Asia, while historically and culturally mainly European. Since the mid-1980s Australian opinion leaders have urged their compatriots to expand their economic and cultural links with the economically dynamic countries of Northeast and Southeast Asia. Australia's economic orientation to Japan, the European Community and the United States is complemented by its military/strategic links with the United States, especially through ANZUS, and by cultural and family links to Europe.

Yet despite public indifference, the Pacific islands region is inescapably relevant to Australian security and political interests, if only because the Pacific islands are where they are. These islands are adjacent to important lines of communication between Australia and the countries of Northeast Asia, its major economic partners, and the United States, its major ally. The region is also of some political importance. It includes resource-rich but troubled Papua New Guinea, Australia's former colony. In an increasingly interdependent world, in which multilateral diplomacy has considerable importance, it is in Australia's interest that its small but relatively numerous neighbours to the north and northeast be at least neutral or, better still, positively disposed towards it.

New Zealand, too, is able to benefit from cordial links with the island states. In the early 1990s, for example, New Zealand was assisted in its successful bid to gain one of the non-permanent seats on the United Nations Security Council by support from the island states. This support encouraged other developing countries to favour New Zealand's bid.

New Zealand's stance has been shaped by its location in the Pacific islands region, by the fact that about 12 per cent of·its population is of either indigenous Maori or immigrant Polynesian stock, and by the attenuation of its links with the United Kingdom since that country joined the European Community. Many New Zealanders have come to regard New Zealand as in some respects a 'South Pacific country'. In October 1987 Prime Minister Lange declared: 'We not only accept but celebrate what the map tells us – that we are a South Pacific nation'.[12] But this standpoint has attracted criticism in New Zealand, from those who stress New Zealand's links with the United Kingdom, in particular, and with Europe, North America, Asia and the wider world. Neither is it endorsed by island leaders. They consider New Zealand, along with Australia, as external to the inner circle of Pacific island states, even if they also think of New Zealand as less overwhelming and less potentially overbearing than Australia.

The debate in New Zealand over whether and if so in what ways New Zealand is a Pacific island country has been part of an examination of what New Zealand's identity is and should be. In this respect this debate parallels that in Australia about how far and in what ways Australia should redefine its identity, endeavour to reach a lasting accommodation with its gravely disadvantaged indigenous communities, and more closely associate itself with Asia.

In Australia and New Zealand, both at government level and in their respective electorates, there is of course a willingness to maintain extensive relations with the island states and to play an active role in the South Pacific Forum. What *is* in doubt, however, is whether either Australia or New Zealand nowadays aspires to play a dominant role in the Pacific islands region. The reason why neither country aspires to such a role, I would argue, is that neither of them has compelling economic or strategic interests in the region.

For Australia and New Zealand, the island states are overall too small and too poor to be major economic partners. Australia's main economic relationships lie elsewhere, and its trade with most of the states of region is minimal. Australia and New Zealand's bilateral relationship, under the Closer Economic Relations (CER) arrangements, is far more important to both of them than any of their economic relations with the island states. In a typical year in the late 1980s, for example, Australian exports to the Pacific island states and territories amounted to less than 3 per cent of its total exports, while Australia's imports from these entities comprised less than 0.6 per cent of its total imports.[13] New Zealand's trading links with the region have been similarly modest. In 1990, New Zealand's exports to the Pacific island states and territories comprised 3.2 per cent of New Zealand's total exports, while its imports from the region comprised less than one per cent of its total imports.[14]

The future of both Australia and New Zealand lies in consolidating and developing their trade and investment links with the wider world, and notably with Europe, North America and, especially, Asia. Australia's economic links with Papua New Guinea would seem to be a partial exception. Australia has significant trading and investment links there. Investment in Papua New Guinea may increase further as major oil and mineral projects come on stream, provided that thorny land control, compensation and environmental problems can be resolved. But Australian economic involvement and prospects in Papua New Guinea is essentially relevant to bilateral relations between these two states rather than to Australia's overall connections with the islands region. And in any case, they are dwarfed by Australia's economic relations with the Asian states and with the wider world.

Strategically, the island states and territories will always have some importance for Australia and New Zealand, for obvious reasons of relative proximity. For Australia this is especially so with respect to Papua New Guinea. But the relative strategic importance of the island states and territories in relation to Australia and New Zealand is, under present circumstances, modest.

The question of the region's strategic relevance to Australia and New Zealand should be put into historical perspective. During 1992 several commemorations took place to mark the fiftieth anniversaries of some of the major campaigns and battles in the Pacific war. These included the Battle of the Coral Sea, the Papua New Guinea campaign, and the struggle for Guadalcanal and the Solomons Islands. A consideration of these dramatic events of over half a century ago helps highlight the great differences in the strategic outlook of Australian and New Zealand concerning the Pacific islands region between then and now.

Japan, then a determined and powerful military aggressor, is now a leading economic partner for both Australia and New Zealand. Territorial, ethnic and other tensions in the wider Asia–Pacific region are not lacking, but there is no power or combination of powers, there or elsewhere, which seems likely to pursue its ambitions by using the Pacific islands as 'stepping stones' to threaten Australia and New Zealand militarily. So no military threat to Australia and New Zealand exists – or seems likely to develop in the foreseeable future – from or through the Pacific islands region. Moreover the importance of strategically-located stepping stones has been reduced – though not entirely removed – by advances in transport and communications.

It is conceivable that military conflict between Indonesia and Papua New Guinea could develop along their common border over the activities of the OPM (*Organisasi Papua Merdeka*), and that in certain circumstances Australia could be drawn into the conflict (see Chapter 2). At present, however, this conflict is in abeyance, because of the OPM's internal divisions and its inability to mount a major challenge to Indonesian rule and because the governments of both Papua New Guinea and Indonesia have demonstrated a strong commitment to joint management of their bilateral tensions. Should tensions sharpen, it seems unlikely that this conflict could spark major hostilities between Indonesia and Australia, unless the stance and ambitions of the Indonesian government changes dramatically and unexpectedly in a more bellicose and expansionist direction.

Since the mid-1980s Australia, and to some extent New Zealand, have put increased emphasis on military self-reliance and on the effective defence of their land and sea territory, reducing the emphasis on long-distance deployments. One result of this process of reassessment has been that, as a result of an increased emphasis on territorial defence, the relative strategic importance of the island states and territories to Australia and New Zealand has been downgraded. Meanwhile defence planners have become increasingly conscious that in the scenario of a military onslaught on Australia, an attacking power with the capabilities to take on such a task would probably possess sufficient force mobility to be able to penetrate rapidly or else by pass altogether the islands to the north and northeast of Australia.

Australian governments were formerly inclined to regard Papua New Guinea as Australia's 'first line of defence' – to be defended of course with the aid of a great and powerful ally, namely the United States. Nowadays Australian policymakers appear to be increasingly inclined to regard Papua New Guinea as a 'strategic quicksand' which, in the event of a major onslaught on Australia via Papua New Guinea, could absorb massive Australian defence resources to little purpose with respect to the defence of Australia. In most scenarios Australia would seek to assist Papua New Guinea against attack. But it probably would do so by the use of air and sea power rather than by the deployment of ground forces.

Ground forces could be rapidly swallowed up and would be difficult to disengage, and their deployment would weaken the defence of Australia's own territory.

The strategic relevance of the island states to Australia and New Zealand has also been reduced by the end of the Cold War and the disintegration of the Soviet Union. During the era of superpower competition, Soviet efforts to develop relations with the island states attracted suspicion and counter-measures from Australia and New Zealand, because these efforts were seen as impinging upon a Western sphere of influence. Such concerns are now a thing of the past. Libya's efforts in the mid-1980s to develop links in the region also attracted hostility, but its initiatives were not sustained. Nowadays both Australia and New Zealand are generally relaxed about efforts by the island states to expand and diversify their external connections, and about interest in the region from a variety of external players.

Australian and New Zealand perspectives on the islands region have also been modified because with the end of the Cold War, and with urgent environmental, economic and other problems demanding attention, the security agenda has been expanded beyond traditional military and strategic concerns. These sorts of problems are of course relevant to the island states, but their assessment and amelioration often requires much policy attention to be directed mainly to the global or at least wider Asia–Pacific regional level, rather than particularly towards the Pacific islands region.

Australian and New Zealand interest in the region has also been reduced since 1988 onwards by an improvement in their relations with France. This improvement followed France's establishment of an interim settlement in New Caledonia and its suspension of its nuclear testing program. It has been reinforced by the eventual successful negotiation of the GATT round in 1993 and by efforts to reestablish cordial relations from both the French and the Australian/New Zealand sides. Relations with France could again worsen. But while they remain positive, both governments have less reason than otherwise to focus sharply on the islands region.

Thus far I have mainly examined government-level attitudes to the islands region in Australia and New Zealand. But these attitudes also reflect those in the respective communities. In the nineteenth and early twentieth centuries proponents of an Australian or Australasian 'Monroe doctrine' for much of the region attracted significant community interest and support. Nowadays, in contrast, the level of overall interest in and awareness of the Pacific islands at other than a superficial level is low in both countries, perhaps especially in Australia, and may be in decline. In both Australia and New Zealand, moreover, many of those members of that small section of the public which does have a high level of interest in the region are associated with various non-government organisations, including political, environmental and development aid groups. These people and groups compromise an informal lobby. They tend to see themselves as champions of Pacific islander interests and to be critical of government policies which involve or appear to involve 'neo-colonialism,' thus discouraging the insensitive exercise of power and influence.

In sum, neither at the élite nor the popular level in either Australia or New Zealand is there a predisposition favouring the assumption of a dominant role in the Pacific islands region. In both countries present preoccupations are either domestic, especially in a time of economic restructuring, or else are directed to the wider world. New Zealand, for ethnic, historical and geographical reasons, is closely associated with the region, and its government is conscious of its responsibilities to the island states. But New Zealand's main interest is in Polynesia and to some extent in Fiji. Even in this part of the islands region, however, although its influence is strong, it does not seek to play a dominating part.

A redefinition of Australian government perspectives on the Pacific islands region in the post-Cold War environment was expressed by the creation in early 1993, by the newly-elected Keating Labor government, of a minister for development cooperation and Pacific island affairs. A former diplomat, Mr Gordon Bilney, was appointed to the position. By establishing this junior ministry, the government confirmed Australia's continuing interest in the region, and in some respects gave the region a special status. But the creation of the position also indicated that the details of Australia's relations with the island states would henceforth be of reduced concern for the senior minister in the external affairs area, Senator Gareth Evans. Earlier, the island governments had responded favourably to the efforts of Senator Evans to develop contacts in the region. Most island leaders welcomed the establishment of the junior ministry, and responded well in due course to Gordon Bilney's active fulfillment of his responsibilities. But some island leaders, notably in Papua New Guinea, contended that the new arrangement reflected a downgrading of the relative importance of the island states to Australia.

In the early 1990s both Australia and New Zealand have encouraged the island states to become more self-reliant, in order to reduce their dependence on donor countries. At the meeting of the South Pacific Forum in Brisbane in July/August 1994, for example, both governments endorsed the opening by the Forum island governments of a trade office in Japan, in order to assist the island states to develop their economic links with that country. Australia has also supported moves to give the South Pacific

Forum, as a regional grouping, observer status at the United Nations. This would help foster greater international awareness and confidence amongst the island states, increasing their ability to pursue their national and regional interests in international forums.

Australia, and to some extent New Zealand, have also emphasised that the island governments themselves must assume the major responsibility for responding effectively to the serious economic, developmental and environmental problems which they face. In an speech delivered on 15 June 1994, which was telecast directly to the region, Gordon Bilney, Minister for Development Cooperation and Pacific Island Affairs, warned that: 'At this time of far-reaching international change, it is essential that countries of the region realise that the level of interest of foreign investors or donor countries in the South Pacific will depend to a large extent on the implementation of sound and sustainable policies by national governments.'[15]

Overall, therefore, the domestic characteristics and attitudes of Australia and New Zealand, in combination with the regional and international aspects discussed earlier, provide limits and restraints on the exercise of power and influence by Australia and New Zealand in the Pacific islands region. Next, I will consider some recent incidents, relating to Fiji, Bougainville, Vanuatu, Nauru and the South Pacific Commission, which provide examples of the operation of these limits and restraints.

SOME RECENT INCIDENTS

The initial responses of the Australian and New Zealand governments to the first Fiji coup in May 1987 were strongly critical. Within weeks however both governments had moderated their positions. They realized that Rabuka had broad support within the indigenous Fijian community, and that the attitude of most of the Pacific island governments towards the coup was more sympathetic than critical. Both governments soon decided that continuing pressure on Fiji would be counter-productive, in relation both to the resolution of Fiji's internal conflicts and to the regional standing of Australia and New Zealand. In due course they sought to place relations with Fiji on a more normal footing, while encouraging Fiji to return to constitutional rule. Australia resumed its aid programme from late 1988, and its defence aid following the May 1992 elections in Fiji.

The enactment of a new constitution in Fiji, and the subsequent elections in May 1992, had involved a return to constitutional rule. Yet the election results and Rabuka's appointment as Prime Minister also endorsed the assertion of indigenous rights and interests which had helped motivate the two coups he led in 1987. This assertion was embodied in the post-coups constitution, notably in provisions giving ethnic Fijians dispro- portionately large representation in parliament, and in the electoral system, under which Indian and urban voters, including ethnic Fijians, are disadvantaged.

The outcome overall was a victory for Rabuka, who had left the military only in 1991, with the rank of Major-General, to devote himself to pol- itics. There are some prospects for further constitutional and political change, which may reduce the political and other disadvantages experi- enced by non-indigenous Fijians. But such change seems unlikely to be either rapid or substantial. Both Australia and New Zealand have been obliged to accept the new conditions established by the 1987 coups, although their stance after the coups did at least contribute in some measure to an eventual return to constitutional rule.

The limits on Australian influence in the Pacific islands region have also been evident during the Bougainville conflict (see also Chapters 2 and 8). The conflict created two security issues for Australia. First, there was the possible need to evacuate several hundred Australian citizens from the island. In 1989–90 the Australian government took some preliminary steps in case intervention was required. But in response to a diplomatic warning and press reports, and with the situation continuing to deteriorate, most Australians in due course used civil transport to depart.

Second, the question arose of how far Australia should assist the Papua New Guinea Defence Force (PNGDF), given Australia's close strategic ties with Papua New Guinea and the background of the substantial defence assistance Australia had provided since independence in 1975, including loan and advisory personnel in key operational support areas. The Australian government wished to assist PNGDF operations. But it also wished to avoid complications, including the potential for political back- lash, especially in Australia but also in Papua New Guinea, against direct involvement by Australian servicemen. Its solution was to preclude Australian Defence Force personnel and units from the operational area around Bougainville while facilitating the provision of supplies and support to the PNGDF. Australia supplied arms and ammunition, under arrangements in place since 1977; provided training for reconnaissance forces; and transferred four UH-IH (Iroquois) helicopters to the PNGDF for transportation and surveillance. But the PNGDF used these helicopters in combat, after fitting them with machine guns, and for dumping bodies at sea. In using the helicopters in these ways it contravened the end use con- ditions earlier agreed on, and sharpened concerns in Australia over human rights abuses, undermining the Australian government's attempt to limit Australian involvement and to avoid controversy.[16]

Overall, Australia has kept its involvement to a modest level, has been conscious of Papua New Guinea's sovereign rights and responsibilities, and has argued that the problem is essentially an internal matter for Papua New Guinea to resolve. Australian training and supplies have assisted the Papua New Guinea army and police, but the Australian government has kept this support to the minimum level consistent with what it sees as Australia's obligations to its ex-colony and close neighbour. The Australian government could conceivably have done much more, with considerable impact but with minimum risk of Australian casualties, for example by providing naval and air support to the Papua New Guinea forces. But the Australian government has shown no inclination to take this course of action. If, on the other hand, the Australian government had declined to provide military assistance to help in the containment of the conflict, the Papua New Guinea government would presumably have looked to other prospective defence partners, including in Southeast Asia, reducing Australia's longer-term strategic access.

The Australian government has also repeatedly urged the need for a political solution to the conflict, and has raised human rights concerns with the Papua New Guinea government. This stance has had bipartisan support. The Australian government has been embarrassed by the indiscipline of the Papua New Guinea forces and by their use, in contravention of their government's agreement, of the transport helicopters in combat roles. Because of suspicions and anxieties on both sides of the conflict, Australia has found it difficult to play a mediating role. New Zealand, by comparison, did not have the same strategic, personnel or economic involvement in Papua New Guinea. It was able to present itself as a more impartial intermediary between the Bougainville Revolutionary Army and the Papua New Guinea Government. From 29 July to 5 August 1990 talks aimed at resolving the dispute were conducted on HMNZ *Endeavour*, New Zealand's supply ship, off Bougainville. But these negotiations did not bear fruit, and subsequently New Zealand has not been significantly involved.

It is instructive to consider Australia's response to the conflict with respect to the three contexts – international, regional, and domestic – discussed earlier. In the international context Australia has upheld Papua New Guinea's position as the legitimate post-colonial successor state, with the right to maintain its territorial integrity. In the regional context, Australia has recognised the changing circumstances in which Papua New Guinea is determined to play a more assertive role, and has accommodated itself to tensions and difficulties in their relationship. In its domestic context, despite an active campaign by supporters of the Bougainville secessionists, Australia has not experienced a groundswell of opinion urging the development of a different approach. Though Australia has provided some assistance to Papua New Guinea in the handling of the revolt, it has not sought to play a decisive role in resolving the crisis.

Neither, in a different set of circumstances, has Australian influence gone unchallenged in Vanuatu during recent years. In early July 1992 the Vanuatu government expelled James Pearson, the acting Australian High Commissioner to Vanuatu. It claimed that he had interfered improperly in Vanuatu's internal affairs by speaking strongly at a Union of Moderate Parties meeting, at which he was present as an observer, about the negative implications for business confidence of proposed legislation giving the government summary powers to revoke commercial licenses.

The diplomat may have been outspoken, even abrasive. Yet the Australian government believed that the expulsion order was an overreaction. Some observers thought that the expulsion was partly motivated by the animosity of some members of the mainly Francophone Union of Moderate Parties (UMP), the main party in the coalition government, towards Australia. This animosity reflects their memories of Australian diplomatic support for the Anglophone nationalist movement in the lead-up to independence in 1980, and of Australian assistance in quelling the secessionist revolt on Espiritu Santo in August/September 1980. Australian Foreign Minister Gareth Evans sought to resolve the question in discussions with Vanuatu Prime Minister Maxime Carlot Korman at the South Pacific Forum held in Honiara, the capital of the Solomon Islands, later in July 1992. But he failed to do so, in part, according to the Vanuatu government, because of his undiplomatic use of language.

Australia retaliated by cancelling a planned Australian Navy visit, at an estimated loss to the Vanuatuan economy of several hundred thousand dollars, and by suspending other official visits until the end of 1992. Relations between the two countries remained cool for several months. Routine port calls continued, however, as did the provision of Australian aid, and relations returned to normal in due course.

Bilateral tensions resurfaced, however, albeit briefly, in October 1992 over the election of George Ati Sokamanu, a former President of Vanuatu, as Secretary General of the South Pacific Commission. The Australian government held strong reservations about his appointment. It thought that despite his experience he lacked the modern management skills and expertise required to update and reform the Commission's administration. Doubts also existed about his judgement. He had been involved while serving as Vanuatu's President in an abortive constitutional coup attempt in December 1988, during which he had attempted to install his custom nephew Barak Sope as prime minister. The selection process was also contentious: Sokamanu had been left as the sole candidate after the surprise withdrawal, at the last minute, of the alternative candidate, Jioji Kotobalavu of Fiji. Kotobalavu had been strongly favoured, especially by donor governments who wished to see the administration of the Commission updated and improved. An Australian attempt to postpone the vote until additional candidates could be found was not supported by the island state and territory delegates. An islander delegate from one of the French territories quipped that the process reminded him of procedures for the election of the President in the former Soviet Union.

Kotobalavu's withdrawal appeared to result from behind-the-scenes negotiations between the Vanuatu and Fiji governments, with the assent of other island governments. Sokamanu is well liked in Fiji, where he spent several years in the pre-independence era on secondment from the British administrative service in the (then) New Hebrides. The island governments apparently thought that as an ex-head of state, and given his seniority, he should be found a suitable job. Some Vanuatu leaders reportedly believed that Australia's opposition to Sokomanu's candidature was 'payback' for the expulsion of Pearson the previous July, though this does not seem to have been the case. For his part, the newly-appointed Secretary-General publicly accused Australia in particular, as well as other donor states, of having a 'colonial club' mentality.[17]

These incidents relating to Vanuatu and the South Pacific Commission are minor, compared with the Fiji and Bougainville cases. Yet they do show that despite the apparent leverage at its command, the Australian government does not always prevail. In the first case, it failed to prevail on the Vanuatu government to change its decision on, or at least publicly apologize for, the expulsion of Pearson. In the second, despite its role as the leading donor and key supporter of the South Pacific Commission, and despite its strongly expressed wish for major reforms in the Commission's operations, Australia was obliged to accept an appointee about whom it had strong reservations.

A further example of the limits on Australia's ability to dominate the island states, and its need to negotiate compromise settlements of contentious matters, relates to its dispute with Nauru over damage from phosphate mining. Just before the 1993 meeting of the South Pacific Forum, which was held in Nauru, the Australian and Nauruan governments reached an out of court settlement comprising A\$ 107 million of their dispute over compensation and restoration costs for the massive environmental damage to the island by phosphate mining during the colonial period. Gordon Bilney, Australia's Minister for Development Cooperation and Pacific Island Affairs, had played a leading part in the negotiations.

Under the settlement Nauru did not proceed with the case which earlier it had brought before the International Court of Justice. The two governments also signed a joint declaration of principles to govern their future relations. Nauru had found the Australian offer persuasive: there was no guarantee that its court case would succeed. Moreover, such a court victory would be Pyrrhic: Australia would henceforth be unlikely to cooperate on aviation, health, educational and other matters of importance to Nauru.

For its part, the Australian government, though it denied any Australian culpability, had felt obliged to reach a settlement. It had not wished to suffer the opprobrium which would inevitably be associated with the court case, whatever the final outcome. The Nauru government appeared to have a strong case on moral grounds, whatever the legal technicalities. And the Australian government had been conscious that, unless a settlement was reached in advance of the Nauru Forum, the dispute would be discussed informally at that meeting, attracting much negative press and international attention.

The disequilibrium in size and influence between Australia and the island states can of course on occasion work in favour of Australian goals. With respect to Vanuatu, for example, Australian government statements in 1987 critical of Vanuatu's contacts at that time with Libya, together with Australian press coverage, had an immediate impact on Australian tourist arrivals in Vanuatu, thus operating as a *de facto* economic sanction. But this was an unintended consequence rather than the result of calculated policy. In the dispute over the Pearson expulsion, however, the use of diplomatic means failed to encourage the Vanuatu government to reconsider its position.

On occasion the asymmetry that apparently works in Australia's favour in fact works in part in the opposite direction. This is because the use of strong pressures can be seen as bullying by the island states, with negative effects for Australia's standing. Thus when the Australian government has been able to get its way on contentious issues, including by bullying, this outcome at times has been soured by a legacy of island government resentment. According to David Lange, the former New Zealand prime minister, the (then) Australian Prime Minister Bob Hawke offended particular island leaders on two occasions at Forum meetings. The offence given may have complicated later relations. He comments that:

At the South Pacific Forum in Tuvalu in 1984, I saw Hawke give unnecessary and enduring offence to the president of Nauru. Impatient at being asked the same question four times, Hawke lapsed into foul-mouthed rebuke. In 1985 on Rarotonga in the Cook Islands, Vanuatu's Walter Lini was unwise enough to mention Australian uranium mining [which had been criticised by anti-nuclear campaigners] in open session. Hawke went into meltdown, screaming obscenities at Lini across the floor. With some difficulty, Lini was then persuaded to agree to the forum communiqué, which announced the conclusion of the South Pacific Nuclear Weapons Free Zone Treaty. He was still seething. Not long after the communiqué was released, Lini publicly repudiated it.[18]

Indeed, the Vanuatu government declined to become a party to the treaty, and for several years criticised it stridently. Of course Vanuatu's policy on the treaty was shaped by several influences, but Hawke's comments may have strengthened Lini's reservations.

CONCLUSION

In this chapter I have argued that the power and influence of Australia and New Zealand in the Pacific islands region is limited and restrained in several ways. So, although they remain important players in regional affairs, they are not in a position to play a dominant role. These various limits and restraints include the presence of international norms and attitudes concerning the sovereignty of the states which have emerged from former colonies and protectorates; the legitimacy established by the South Pacific Forum and other regional bodies and institutions; the increased assertiveness of the island leaderships; the modest and sporadic interest in the region at both the élite and popular levels in Australia and New Zealand; and a related absence of compelling Australian and New Zealand interests – whether economic or strategic – in the islands region. Certainly neither power wishes to assume, or sees merit in assuming, a role as 'regional policeman'.

In the early 1980s Australia exercised a largely unchallenged position of leadership with respect to most of the Pacific island states. A decade later that status has come under question.[19] Australia's importance and influence remains strong, but is in relative decline. Australia will need to engage in active and skilful diplomacy to promote its national interests. The pursuit of these interests will continue to require a delicate balancing of competing imperatives. In response to the Bougainville conflict, for example, Australia has assisted its former colony, Papua New Guinea, but only in a relatively modest fashion. Limits on resources and preoccupations elsewhere may also in due course require a sharper focus in Australia's approach to the region. That focus would be on the entities most strategically and economically relevant to Australia, namely Papua New Guinea, Solomon Islands, Vanuatu, New Caledonia and Fiji.

For its part, New Zealand wishes to make an active and constructive contribution to Pacific islands affairs, especially with respect to its links with some of the Polynesian states. But like Australia it has other domestic and international preoccupations. It similarly seeks to be a helpful partner rather than a dominant presence.

8 Intervention Contingencies: A Gap between Ends and Means?[1]

The constraints on Australian and New Zealand influence in the Pacific islands region have also been reflected in the development of their attitudes to, and policies on possible military intervention in, the island states. On several occasions since 1980 Australian or New Zealand forces have stood ready to intervene or have intervened in parts of the region. In August-September 1980 Australia provided logistical and communications support, including the provision of twenty loan personnel, to assist the Papua New Guinea defence force, which was acting on behalf of the government of newly-independent Vanuatu, to quell a secessionist revolt on the island of Espiritu Santo.[2] Later in the decade the question of intervention again arose in response to the Fiji coup in May 1987, to disturbances in Vanuatu in May 1988, and to the revolt in Bougainville from 1988 onwards. In late 1994 Australia and also New Zealand provided assistance to a multilateral Pacific islands peacekeeping force, which was tasked with maintaining order on Bougainville during peace talks.

The first Fiji coup in May 1987 jolted Australia and New Zealand from their previously complacent outlook on internal security issues in the region. Apart from the assistance given to Vanuatu in 1980, Australian and New Zealand security cooperation with the island states had hitherto focused primarily on development and infrastructure tasks. Australia and New Zealand had also sought to assist the island states to police and manage the extensive marine and seabed resources provided for in the 1982 Law of the Sea Convention, notably through the provision by Australia of patrol boats to the island states and through aerial surveillance by the RAAF and RNZAF.

With the Fiji coup, a whole range of new or else largely forgotten security considerations became apparent. How could Australia and New Zealand effectively protect their national interests, especially the safety of their citizens resident in or visiting a particular island state? In what circumstances, if any, should Australia and New Zealand become involved militarily? Did they have the relevant capabilities to do so effectively? To what extent, if any, should these possible tasks help shape their force structures? Would direct involvement in the island states enmesh

137

Australia and New Zealand in internal political wrangles, possibly jeopardising their longer-term strategic access? On the other hand, would failure to act court condemnation from island administrations seeking desperately to reassert their authority? How far, if at all, would island governments, under threat from internal unrest, be prepared to distinguish between their own wish to remain in power and the broader and longer-term interests of the state and society which they administered? Was it not the case, indeed, that several island governments were routinely inclined to see their own interests and those of their respective state as indivisible? Would particular governments seek to lean on Australian or New Zealand support, rather than accepting the need to adapt to legitimate pressures for change and reform?

The lack of preparedness of the Australian and New Zealand governments to deal with these and related issues was graphically illustrated by their responses to the Fiji coup. A few days after the Bavadra government was deposed by Colonel Rabuka and the Royal Fijian Military Force, the New Zealand Government ordered Special Air Service troops to intervene. Their task was to deal with the hijacker of an Air New Zealand aircraft at Nadi airport and then to travel to Suva, on the opposite side of the main island of Viti Levu, to protect New Zealand citizens. But within a few hours the mission was cancelled. This was in part because a member of the Air New Zealand crew, using a full whisky bottle as a club, had overpowered the hijacker. In addition, however, senior military officers had opposed the plan. They argued that the New Zealand high command lacked the necessary intelligence with which to mount an operation of this kind. They also considered that it was very dangerous to presume, as Lange and his colleagues apparently had, that the well-trained and well-equipped Fijian army would not oppose the proposed intervention.[3]

For its part, Australia was apparently well-placed to intervene. Four of the Royal Australian Navy's major surface vessels were fortuitously in the vicinity of Fiji on routine deployments, with two of these alongside in Suva and Lautoka at the time of the coup. To begin with any thoughts of direct military intervention to support the deposed government, or of transferring Fijian forces from Middle East peacekeeping duties to counter the coup, were abandoned. Yet within a week growing signs of civil disorder saw the Australian government step back from its initial indications of non-involvement. It put the Operational Deployment Force's lead company on immediate notice to move for possible evacuation tasks in Fiji, and deployed it a few days later to warships cruising near Fiji.[4]

Operationally, the deployment revealed some major shortcomings, including the absence of landing and loading facilities at Norfolk Island, deficiencies in equipment selection, and major problems with the suitability and reliability of embarked helicopters. Emergency modifications furnished the training ship HMAS *Jervis Bay* with a helicopter deck. The Australian High Commission in Fiji developed plans for the evacuation of Australian citizens should the situation deteriorate.[5]

No action eventuated, and the Australian and New Zealand governments consistently argued that the planning and deployments were only to ensure the safety of their own (and possibly allied) nationals. Nevertheless, the extreme sensitivity of any potential interference by these two powers in the internal affairs of their much smaller island neighbours was quickly revealed. Most of the island governments thought that Australia and New Zealand had over-reacted. In May 1987 Papua New Guinea prime minister Paias Wingti summoned the New Zealand High Commissioner from Port Moresby to Rabaul to explain suggestions by Prime Minister Lange that Australia and New Zealand support the return of Royal Fijian Military Force units from peacekeeping duties in the Middle East to oppose the coup.[6] In December 1991 Fiji's Prime Minister Ratu Sir Kamisese Mara asserted that Australia and New Zealand would have invaded Fiji if they had not been dissuaded by the island governments.[7]

About a year after the May 1987 coup in Fiji the question of intervention arose again because of events in Vanuatu. In May 1988 the Lini government was faced with tensions that threatened to run out of control and strain the policing capabilities of Vanuatu's 250 strong paramilitary security force. The unrest began with a demonstration over land issues in the capital, Port Vila, but was connected to the bitter struggle for power between Prime Minister Lini and his rival Barak Sope. After a day of demonstrations and disturbances, during which one rioter was killed, Lini called for assistance from Australia and New Zealand to restore order in Vila. Neither the rioters nor the police had used firearms, but rumours were circulating that some of Sope's supporters had a hidden supply of firearms. There were also rumours of possible Libyan involvement.[8]

At short notice Australia and New Zealand supplied the government of Vanuatu with riot control equipment to assist in restoring order. Australia also placed elements of its Operational Deployment Force on stand-by, in case more substantial assistance was required. Exactly what this force might have done remains, however, unclear. The most likely scenario requiring possible intervention was that of continued disturbances, exceeding the government's capability to contain them and posing a threat to Australian residents and tourists.

Fortunately, the situation in Vanuatu was resolved quickly. The stand-by order appears to have been primarily precautionary. Options as to just what Australia might do were apparently not thought through. One senior military officer asked, with serious intent, whether the prospective adversary would have armoured vehicles, thus making it necessary for the Australian troops to be equipped with anti-tank weapons. One can understand the officer's concern that his men be suitably equipped. But anyone familiar with the small scale of Vanuatu would regard the question as amusing. This question about armoured vehicles, and the possibility that a detachment of well-armed, highly-trained and strongly-motivated troops might be sent to the small town of Port Vila, highlight the contradiction present in some of the more likely scenarios between policy ends and the means available to pursue them.

Intervention again became at issue in 1989-90 in relation to the revolt in the North Solomons (Bougainville) province of Papua New Guinea. It was most likely during the early stages of the revolt, when several hundred Australian citizens were potentially at risk. The Australian government put a batallion of the Overseas Deployment Force on alert and deployed several Hercules aircraft and surface vessels, including the training ship HMAS *Jervis Bay*, to northern Queensland to enable a rapid response if required. But the Bougainville Revolutionary Army, conscious of its image, largely refrained from direct attacks on expatriates, a number of whom were sympathetic to its cause. In due course concern over the safety of these citizens evaporated because almost all of them departed the troubled island, using commercial transport.

Australian and New Zealand involvement in an intervention initiative again occurred in September/October 1994, when a multilateral force was assembled to keep order during peace talks on Bougainville. Papua New Guinea provided the impetus for the creation of the force, while Fiji, Vanuatu and Tonga supplied the personnel. Australia provided training, logistical and financial support, with the costs involved exceeding A$ 5 million. Meanwhile New Zealand contributed to the training programme. Australia supplied the overall commander, but the ground commander was Tongan. It was agreed that Australian personnel would not be stationed on Bougainville during the peacekeeping exercise, but would only visit briefly to assist in the landing of the multilateral force and its equipment. Nevertheless Australia's involvement attracted criticism from some quarters. Sam Kaouna, the military commander of the Bougainville Revolutionary Army, complained that Australia, because of its close links with Papua New Guinea, was not an acceptable neutral third party, and should not be involved.

THE DEBATE ON INTERVENTION

Against the background of the May 1987 coup in Fiji and subsequent events, military intervention contingencies have received increased attention in both Australia and New Zealand. The debate has centred on the published statement in December 1989 by Australia's Minister for Foreign Affairs and Trade, Senator Gareth Evans, on *Australia's Regional Security*. It has concentrated on the rationale for possible intervention, on the general circumstances in which it might take place, on whether it is justifiable, and on the general risks and disadvantages of intervention.[9]

The 1989 regional security statement struck a cautious note. It emphasised that direct intervention would only be initiated in the most extreme and unlikely circumstances, and set out cumulative criteria that might justify such action. These included the presence of a direct threat to a major Australian security interest; the existence of a clear, achievable objective and a finite timeframe for operations; the agreement, unless in exceptional circumstances, of the local authorities; and the existence of consultation with, and if possible the cooperation and participation of, other states in the region. An additional criterion, that of public support in Australia, was later announced.[10]

These policies were complemented by the setting up of more effective administrative and coordination structures within the bureaucracy. The Australian defence force also undertook some contingency planning with its New Zealand counterpart and developed arrangements for operational coordination should a combined response be required to a future crisis in the islands region. Meanwhile the possibility of responding to regional requests for assistance had been clearly recognised as an operational role for the Australian Defence Forces. Both the study put before the Australian government in 1989, entitled *Strategic Planning in the 1990s*, and the 1991 *Force Structure Review*, noted that Australia should have options for responding to such requests, even though they should not be a determinant of force structure as such. They argued that the emphasis should be on identifying and testing a range of response options, rather than on the development of specific capabilities.[11]

New Zealand's policy-makers were similarly aware of the sensitivities of any intervention in the islands region. The May 1990 report of the South Pacific Policy Review Group, *Towards a Pacific Island Community*, argued that 'the guiding principle should be that the New Zealand Government will not unilaterally or automatically intervene with its military forces.'[12] Dismissing suggestions of a standing regional multilateral force, it argued that regional consultation and consensus should be 'essential pre-requisites' of any action, and suggested that a consultative mechanism be established for this purpose. This report also noted the advantages of developing a mediation or conflict resolution role within the region, a principle reflected in due course in New Zealand's efforts to assist in the resolution of the Bougainville crisis.

Two major concerns for the Australian and New Zealand governments would undoubtedly be to gain the agreement, as far as possible, of island governments to any limited actions to protect national interests or to evacuate citizens; and to ensure that any assistance to island security forces is tailored in a way to play down unrealistic expectations of support and to avoid being drawn into protracted domestic law enforcement operations. The Australian and New Zealand governments would probably also seek to ensure that an island government which might seek assistance in particular circumstances had distinguished between its own wish to retain power and the broader interests of the state and society under its (real or nominal) administration.

The 1991 New Zealand Defence White Paper defined three situations which might call for a limited deployment of forces in the islands region. These were 'the need to evacuate New Zealand nationals; a terrorist threat or attack; and requests for assistance in dealing with low-level threats to law and order.'[13] The White Paper made the assessment that an evacuation of New Zealand nationals 'would most likely be shared with other forces, particularly those of Australia.' It also concluded that New Zealand's own counter-terrorist and explosives disposal capabilities were adequate to deal with a terrorist contingency. And it concluded that New Zealand should have the operational and logistical capabilities to respond to possible low-level contingencies, but commented that 'any decision to do so would always be a matter of the most careful political consideration.'

The policy guidelines developed by the Australian and New Zealand governments since the late 1980s should help to clarify thinking on possible intervention scenarios and options as these arise in the years ahead. They should also provide some safeguards and guarantees against hasty and ill-considered interventions. Unfortunately much less attention has been given to the question of what are the appropriate means for the effective implementation of a decision to intervene.

In raising the question of appropriate means for intervention I do not intend to suggest that Australian or New Zealand interventions in the Pacific islands region over the next decade or so are likely to be either frequent or large-scale. Despite some claims to the contrary,[14] there seems to be little evidence that either power wishes to assume the role of regional policeman, especially in relation to internal disputes. This assessment has been borne out with respect both to the Fiji coups and to Australia's helpful but essentially modest role during the Bougainville conflict. Nor do I believe that either power should assume an interventionist role, except with respect to the possibility of limited intervention in specific and extraordinary circumstances – notably where citizens are at risk.

Far from suggesting that interventions are likely to be frequent or substantial, the point I would stress is that, just because interventions are likely to be only occasional and on a small scale, the risk exists that the potential problems associated with their implementation will receive inadequate consideration. This in turn could create a gulf between policy aims and the means available to implement them, leading to confusion and failure. The key to progress on this question of appropriate means is a clear recognition of the close nexus which exists in the islands region between capability and political objective. Unless Australia and New Zealand are able to match capability to task in the region, their motives will always be open to misinterpretation and their operational effectiveness may be impeded.

PARAMILITARY POLICE FOR INTERVENTION CONTINGENCIES?

Experience over the last decade or so has suggested that, while they possess significant options for specific tasks and worst case scenarios, Australian and New Zealand forces lack genuine flexibility in the grey area between civil law enforcement and low-level military operations.

Military force would often not be well suited to the task required in a particular scenario. In many circumstances the size and relative capability of an Australian or New Zealand military intervention could, if not carefully managed, swamp the local authorities. In addition, an Australian or New Zealand military presence could encourage suspicions and create antagonism, in a manner which would be counter-productive to the particular intervention task. Island governments and populations are perhaps especially likely to respond negatively to the deployment of a military unit when the capability of a unit exceeds the requirements of the task. Indeed, any deployment of significant military units would be open to misinterpretation and would encourage charges of neo-colonial intervention, no matter how irrelevant the excess capabilities may be to the task at hand.

Except in the extreme case of a major protected evacuation, or where specialist assault capabilities are required to rescue hostages, many of the possible security tasks arising in the islands region are more akin to civil law enforcement than formal military operations. They might include: ensuring temporary access to port or airfield facilities; dispersing rioters; locating and protecting Australian and New Zealand citizens; and securing embassies and, at the request of the island government, key national assets such as communications centres.[15] In almost all circumstances, these tasks would be undertaken at the request of, or with the acquiescence of, local authorities.

It would be most unlikely that such tasks would be undertaken against the direct opposition of local security forces. There might be some danger from small arms, albeit in limited numbers. Intervention forces would however be more likely to face a range of makeshift weapons, especially rocks and clubs and possibly some commercial explosives. Violence would frequently be random and, in particular tactical situations, could erupt very quickly. Security forces would need to exercise care, however, that their own presence did not become a stimulus and focus for violence. Importantly, effectiveness would depend on the use of the minimum force necessary to contain a situation.

Neither the Australian nor New Zealand armies are well equipped for such tasks. Both developed extensive counter-insurgency doctrine during their deployments to Southeast Asia in the 1950s and 1960s, but that is primarily relevant to the types of commitments they would as far as possible seek to avoid in the islands region. Australian forces did undertake riot control training in connection with deployments to Malaysia but this had ceased, together with the holding of relevant equipment stocks, by the early 1980s.

Under the Westminster system, there are also strong domestic legal and political constraints on training, equipping and using the Defence Force for civil law enforcement tasks. Those constraints recognise that soldiers are trained primarily to operate as a formed unit under military command and to bring the maximum firepower to bear at the point of decision. Their training emphasises concentration of force, mobility, occupation of commanding heights and the establishment of clear fields of fire. In contrast dealing with a disorganised body of rioters may require the dispersal of forces, static defence of key facilities and advanced, minimally-supported, deployments. Soldiers are not, under current policies, equipped with riot shields, batons, stun and teargas grenades, rubber bullets and similar equipment, which permits the containment of riots and disturbances while minimising the risk of serious casualties. I have no doubt that Australia or New Zealand military detachments would endeavour to perform their assigned task in the most professional manner possible. But in their efforts to achieve optimal results they would nonetheless be handicapped by the inappropriateness of their training and equipment.

Moreover soldiers do not routinely have the individual obligations of a policeman to protect life and property. Neither, unless such authority is specially conferred, do they possess any enforcement authority beyond the common law right of self-defence. Australian or New Zealand soldiers could face hard choices if they were thrust into a politically sensitive law enforcement situation in the islands region. As the criticisms of the uses put to Australian-supplied helicopters during the Bougainville conflict have illustrated, even indirect and quite unintended Australian connections with human rights abuses can quickly generate domestic and international concern.

When personnel with inappropriate training and equipment are asked to deal with civil unrest, it is highly likely that civilians will be wounded or killed. Even minor incidents are likely to be magnified when the troops of an external (and former colonial) power are involved. Even fully briefed Australian or New Zealand defence force personnel deployed to the islands region to assist in the maintenance of law and order would run the risk of using excessive or inappropriate force, thus inflicting unintended casualties. This would have negative implications, both in the island state and back home.

This is not to suggest that under extraordinary circumstances, for example during a major breakdown of law and order, Australia and New Zealand should not be prepared to deploy a significant military force to an island state, especially to protect their citizens. Only the military have the capacity to deploy a large and flexible force at short notice for such purposes. But the sensitivities of becoming involved in the internal security of another state, and the contradictory demands of military and civil law enforcement training, would suggest that Australia and New Zealand should have options to respond at a lesser level without necessarily involving their Defence Forces. Indeed, Senator Evans has noted that: 'We should bear in mind that in many situations, it may be more appropriate to respond to a request for assistance with a civilian rather than a military capability.'[16]

A HELICOPTER SUPPORT SHIP?

Apart from the lack of a paramilitary capability, the other key weakness in the Australian and New Zealand defence inventories with respect to possible contingencies in the Pacific islands region is the tactical presence and lift capability equated with a helicopter support ship. This deficiency increases the difficulties, both operational and political, of attempting to establish and maintain a secure point of entry. The acquisition of a heli-copter support ship would certainly give the two countries much greater flexibility and control over any intervention. This capability could shorten reaction times and, by virtue of size and carrying capacity, allow a range of tactical response options to meet a developing situation. Apart from the political significance of such a presence, it could provide a secure focus for command and communications which would not be subject to the vagaries of political control that may occur in the island state itself.

The use of such a vessel would in most instances be preferable to the deployment of major combat units in the region. The image which Australia or New Zealand portrays will contribute to the handling of local sensitivities. In some extreme situations, the intimidating presence of major combat vessels may possibly deter direct action against Australian and New Zealand citizens. But in other circumstances, the more benign presence of a single helicopter support ship could be used to allay fears of interventionism and promote cooperation with the local authorities. In many scenarios it would be much less intrusive, and hence less politically difficult, to operate from a platform offshore instead of being obliged to establish an on-ground headquarters and operations centre. The likely peacetime use of a helicopter support ship for natural disaster relief and civil aid and development tasks would foster a positive image. Without that capability, Australia and New Zealand's flexibility and control over the political, even more than the operational, dimensions of a Pacific islands contingency will remain limited.

CONCLUSION

In my view, the deficiences in Australian and New Zealand preparedness for intervention contingencies in the islands region could be substantially remedied in two ways. Australia and New Zealand, separately or in coop-eration, could develop paramilitary policing capabilities to complement existing military force options. This would provide a more appropriate means with which to respond to several of the more likely scenarios, thus avoiding the risks and cost of 'using a sledge hammer to crack a nut'.

And Australia and New Zealand could acquire, preferably in coopera-tion in order to reduce costs, a helicopter-capable support ship. The pos-session of this capability would provide intervention force commanders with a wider range of options, and would permit them to minimise the nature and duration of intrusions on territory under the administration of a friendly but beleaguered government.

Ideally, the development of such capabilities by Australia and New Zealand should be combined with continued efforts to strengthen the effectiveness and professional standards of police and paramilitary police forces in the island states. This may involve increasing the size of these forces. In particular, their training should be designed to raise standards of discipline and conduct, especially with respect to the use of the minimum force necessary to contain disturbances. Meanwhile those island governments which also have military forces under their authority should be encouraged to strengthen the distinctions between the civil and military spheres of activity, and to regard the use of these forces in internal unrest contingencies as the absolute last resort.

9 Conclusion: An Uncertain Future

Over the next few years, in the virtual absence of external and intra-regional military threats, domestically-focused and primarily 'non-military' security issues are likely to preoccupy the Pacific island states. These issues include economic uncertainties, environmental degradation, law and order problems, internal unrest, and, in some instances, secessionist movements. The presence of some of these challenges to security will reflect in part the intractable problems of social and economic development which have emerged in several island states over the last decade or so. In some circumstances these various issues, though primarily domestic in focus, will have implications for regional affairs.

In part in search of assistance to help them manage these various problems, the island states have sought to widen their range of external contacts, with mixed results. A number of island leaders have also been motivated by opportunities for private advantage. In addition, a new assertiveness has become evident among island leaders. They are less inclined than their predecessors mostly were, some ten to fifteen years ago, to accept without question American, Australian or New Zealand leadership on security and other issues. These days the United States has only minimal involvement in the region, except in its territories and with respect to its associated states. For their part, both Australia and New Zealand, while conscious of their continued links with the island states, are preoccupied with domestic restructuring and wider international connections. They are reserved about assuming a dominant role in the region. Meanwhile, external powers and other external players have initiated or further developed a presence. In particular, the influence of Japan and other states from the Asian region has increased somewhat. Overall the region and its links with the wider world have become more complex and in some respects more volatile.

In this more complex environment the South Pacific Forum will continue to seek to defend the interests of its members, while avoiding as far as possible involvement in what are seen as their internal affairs. The Forum is likely to continue to respond positively to measures which encourage greater security and economic cooperation in the Asia–Pacific region. But it will, however, be wary lest island state interests are overlooked. And the island states are likely to have reservations about trade liberalisation measures which threaten to bring to an end to concessional trade arrangements.

The end of the Cold War, and the associated changes which have taken place in eastern Europe and elsewhere, have resulted in some benefits for the island states. The increased influence of the United Nations and other international organisations, despite their organisational and operational weaknesses, should bode well for the protection of the interests of the island states and of other small states. In addition, the island states no longer risk having their domestic and external affairs complicated by rivalries between two superpowers. In the Cold War period, the United States insisted on fashioning constitutional arrangements for the successor components of the Trust Territory of the Pacific Islands to suit its own security and defence requirements. One example of the new circumstances is the (then) Soviet Union's decision to refrain from employing its veto in the Security Council, as it had earlier intended, to block the termination of the United States' trusteeship over the Federated States of Micronesia, the Republic of the Marshall Islands, and the Commonwealth of the Northern Marianas. In the post-Cold War environment, moreover, the United States has been willing to accept greater independence of action by the Republic of the Marshall Islands and the Federated States of Micronesia than otherwise would have been the case. The United States has also felt able to offer the Palauans more reassurances than it was earlier prepared to do about its lack of an intention to establish military facilities in Palau, facilitating Palau's transition to free association status.

The island states are also likely to believe that they have benefited, at least in self-esteem, because the ending of the Cold War era has contributed to the substantial suspension of the policy of strategic denial. They now can seek to assert their independence and develop and diversify their external relations more freely, without being subject to the same advice and pressures hitherto brought to bear by their traditional Western partners. So far, however, the efforts of the island states to diversify their external connections have had varied and at times disappointing results. Island governments have become increasingly conscious that diplomatic diversification can involve risks and costs as well as benefits, and that the interest in the region of some of the newer players will not necessarily be either constructive or sustained. So they are likely to continue to focus much of their attention on their former colonial administrators and other associated powers.

In an increasingly complex, interdependent, and multipolar world, the island states have a greater range of potentially beneficial relationships to choose from, but also need to ensure that their interests are recognised and protected. In practical terms, this may not always be easy, given their limited resources, especially in skilled and experienced personnel, and given the tendency, because of their lack of clout, for other powers to take them for granted. Moreover, although the island states will no longer be potentially subject to rivalries between two ideologically-opposed super-powers, they may at some later stage find themselves caught up in rivalries between great powers.

And although few would wish for a return to the gridlocked stability of the Cold War era, it remains true that in some respects the Pacific island states were able to profit from East–West rivalry. Following Soviet discussions with Tonga in 1976 over a possible aid/fishing deal, Australian aid to the island states increased dramatically. In the years that followed Australia and the other Western powers provided substantial aid to the island states, in part to ensure their continued acceptance of Western diplomatic and security leadership. In the mid-1980s both Kiribati and Vanuatu received above commercial rates for their short-term fishing deals with the Soviet Union, presumably in part because the Soviets wished to reduce island government inhibitions about contacts with them. The wish to prevent the Soviet Union from developing links with the island states motivated increases in United States and Japanese attention and aid to the region in the 1980s, and prompted the United States to resolve its fisheries dispute with the island states.

But in the new, multi-polar world, some of the Pacific island states are finding it more difficult than in the past to gain attention, advice and assistance. By the early 1990s external aid had levelled off, and appeared likely to decline. In other parts of the world there are many other competing prospective recipients of aid and investment, notably in the successor states to the Soviet Union and in Africa. The island states will need to ensure that relatively scarce aid and investment funds are spent effectively, in order to encourage continued interest and assistance. For some island states the results of inadequate external support could be tragic, for they will need help to weather the waves of change.

The peoples of the Pacific islands region have often shown resilience in accommodating to changing circumstances. This resilience will be tested severely in the years ahead. My hope is that *all* of the island states will become more economically self-reliant, will enjoy improved living standards, will adapt their culture and traditions creatively to changing circumstances, will maintain more or less liberal-democratic forms of government, and will protect their natural environments. But given the tensions between these various possible future circumstances, and in view of the issues and trends considered in this book, this happy outcome must be a *hope* rather than a realistic expectation.

Over the next decade or so, depending on the implications of global warming, the continued viability of one or more of the island states may come under threat. Several island states may suffer from serious environmental degradation. Some of them may experience extensive social and political unrest fueled in part by poor economic management, or by the disruptions associated with rapid social and economic change. One or two island states may be subject to military or paramilitary intervention, on a short-term basis, by Australia and/or New Zealand. The political map of the region could in part be redrawn, if one or more of the various secessionist and nationalist movements achieves its goals.

One or more of the island states could become a 'failed state', along the lines of some countries in Africa and elsewhere. At the other end of the spectrum of possibilities, one or two states, benefiting from good luck and good management, may become 'success stories', though not without conflicts and upheavals along the way.

The future of most of the island states is likely to be somewhere in the range between these extremes; their setbacks and disappointments in some areas balanced by improvements and achievements in others. External powers, and especially Australia, will advise and assist. Ultimately, however, most of the heavy responsibility of building a better future, in a complex and fast-changing world, will reside with the political and community leaders of the island states themselves.

Notes and References

1 Introduction: Diversity but Common Interests

1. South Pacific Commission, *South Pacific Economies Statistical Summary, Number 12* (Noumea: South Pacific Commission, 1991), p. 9.
2. See John Connell, 'Island Microstates: The Mirage of Development', *Contemporary Pacific. A Journal of Island Affairs*, vol. 3, (1991), no. 2, pp. 251–87.
3. Michael Taylor (ed.), *Fiji: Future Imperfect?* (Sydney: Allen & Unwin, 1987), pp. 1–13.
4. R. Gerard Ward, 'Earth's Empty Quarter? The Pacific Islands in a Pacific Century', *Geographical Journal*, vol. 155 (July 1989), no. 2, pp. 325–46.
5. R.H. Jackson, *Quasi-States: Sovereignty, International Relations and the Third World* (Cambridge, 1990).
6. Jackson, *Quasi-States*, p. 5.
7. Jackson, *Quasi-States*, pp. 11, 21, 29.
8. *Nuclear Playground* (Sydney: Allen & Unwin; Honolulu: University of Hawaii Press, 1987), pp. 2–3.
9. This categorisation is in part a development of that in Steve Hoadley, *Security Cooperation in the South Pacific*, Peace Research Centre Paper 41 (Canberra: Australian National University, 1988), pp. 15–16.

2 Pacific in Nature as well as Name?

1. O.H.K. Spate, '"South Sea" to "Pacific Ocean." A Note on Nomenclature', *Journal of Pacific History*, vol. 12 (1977) nos 3–4, pp. 205–06.
2. See W.H. Pearson, 'European Intimidation and the Myth of Tahiti', *Journal of Pacific History*, vol. 4 (1969), pp. 199–217; and ibid., 'The reception of European voyagers on Polynesian islands, 1568–1797', *Journal de la Société des Océanistes*, vol. 26 (March 1970), pp. 121–54.
3. J.R.V. Prescott, 'Problems of International Boundaries with Particular Reference to the Boundary Between Indonesia and Papua New Guinea', in R.J. May (ed.), *Between Two Nations: The Indonesia–Papua New Guinea Border and West Papua Nationalism*, (Bathurst, Robert Brown, 1986), pp. 13–14.
4. Prescott, 'International Boundaries', p. 4.
5. Peter Hastings, 'A Historical Perspective', in R.J. May (ed.), *The Indonesia–Papua New Guinea Border: Irianese Nationalism and Small State Diplomacy*. Political and Social Change Working Paper 2 (Canberra: Australian National University, 1979), p. 7.
6. Ross Babbage, 'Australia and the Defence of Papua New Guinea', *Australian Outlook*, vol. 41 (Aug. 1987), no. 2, pp. 87–94, p. 88.
7. May, *Between Two Nations*, p. 120.

152

8. K. Nyamekye and Ralph Premdas, 'Papua New Guinea perceptions on the border; internal pressures and policies', in R.J. May (ed.) *Indonesia–Papua New Guinea Border* (1979), p. 77.

9. Beverly Blaskett and L. Wong, 'Papua New Guinea under Wingti: Accommodating Indonesia', *Australian Outlook*, vol. 43 (April 1989) no. 1, pp. 44–60, 55–6.

10. J.A.C. Mackie, 'Does Indonesia have Expansionist Designs on Papua New Guinea?' in May, *Between Two Nations*, p. 68.

11. See Edward P. Wolfers (ed.), *Beyond the Border: Indonesia and Papua New Guinea, South-East Asia and the South Pacific* (Waigani: University of Papua New Guinea; Suva: Institute of Pacific Studies, 1988).

12. Harold Crouch, 'Indonesia and the Security of Australia and Papua New Guinea', *Australian Outlook*, vol. 40 (Dec. 1986), no. 3, pp. 167–74, pp. 171–2; Babbage, 'Defence of Papua New Guinea', p. 90.

13. Babbage, 'Defence of Papua New Guinea', p. 91.

14. J.R.V. Prescott, 'Maritime Boundaries in the Southwest Pacific Region', in A.D. Couper (ed.), *Development and Social Change in the Pacific Islands* (London and New York: Routledge, 1989), pp. 4–21, pp. 18–20.

15. Prescott, 'Maritime Boundaries', p. 18.

16. Michael Eastly, 'Marshall Islands Claims Wake is Part of its Territory', *Pacific Magazine*, vol. 15 (Sept./Oct. 1990), no. 5, p. 8.

17. 'Island Annexations to Hawaii, Guam Proposed', *Pacific Magazine*, vol. 15 (July/Aug. 1990) no. 4; L.N. Nevels Jr, 'Wake (Enen-Kio)', *Pacific Magazine*, vol. 14 (Sept./Oct. 1990), no. 5, p. 7; Giff Johnson, 'Letter from Micronesia: High Chief Kabua doesn't get his way', *Islands Business*, vol. 16 (June 1990), no. 6, p. 54.

18. See *The Australian*, 13 May 1992, p. 8.

19. *The Military Balance, 1993–94* (London: Brassey's for the International Institute of Strategic Studies, 1993).

20. G.E. Fry, *Regional Peacekeeping in the South Pacific: Some Considerations for Prior Consideration'*, Department of International Relations Working Paper (Canberra: Australian National University, 1990); Martin Tiffany, 'Who's looking after you?' *Pacific Islands Monthly*, vol. 62 (March 1992), no. 3, pp. 6–7.

3 Beyond 'Whose Sail . . . on the Horizon': Island State Security Perspectives

1. Henry Naisali, 'Regional Security: In Harmony if not in Unison', in David Hegarty and Peter Polomka (eds), *The Security of Oceania in the 1990s. Volume 1: Views from the Region*, Canberra Papers on Strategy and Defence No. 60 (Canberra: Australian National University, 1989), pp. 38–43 (38).

2. *Ibid.*

3. Taufa Vakatale, 'Military Security in Oceania', in Hegarty and Polomka, *Security of Oceania*, pp. 31–7 (31).

4. See J. Mohan Malik, *The Gulf War: Australia's Role and Asian–Pacific Responses*, Canberra Paper on Strategy and Defence No. 90 (Canberra: Australian National University, 1992), pp. 98–9.

5. Jioji Kotobalavu, 'Trends in Perceptions of Security', in Hegarty and Polomka, *Security of Oceania*, pp. 25–30 (30).

6. Margaret Taylor, in Ramesh Thakur (ed.), *The South Pacific: Problems, Issues and Prospects* (New York: St Martin's Press, 1991), pp. 200–01.

7. Vakatale, 'Military Security', pp. 31–2.

8. Tony Siaguru, 'Small 's' Security for Small Island States', in Hegarty and Polomka, *Security of Oceania*, pp. 19–24 (20).

9. See Peter Jennings, 'Political and Constitutional Change', in Peter Polomka (ed.), *The Security of Oceania in the 1990s. Volume 2: Managing Change*, Canberra Papers on Strategy and Defence No. 68, (Canberra: Australian National University, 1992).

10. George Kejoa, 'Australia's proper role in the South Pacific – A Personal Perspective', in Grant McCall (ed.), *Sydney Talk: Australia in the South Pacific* (Sydney: University of New South Wales, 1990), pp. 1–5 (1–2).

11. Stewart Firth, 'Sovereignty and Independence in the Contemporary Pacific', *Contemporary Pacific*, vol. 1 (1989) nos 1 and 2, pp. 75–96 (82).

12. Calculated from Joint Committee on Foreign Affairs, Defence and Trade, *Australia's Relations with Papua New Guinea* (Canberra: Parliament of the Commonwealth of Australia, 1991), p. 132.

13. See Norman MacQueen, 'New Directions for Papua New Guinea's Foreign Policy', *Pacific Review*, vol. 4 (1991) no. 2, pp. 162–73 (162–3).

14. South Pacific Commission, *Report of the Special Session of the South Pacific Conference: Noumea, New Caledonia, 23–25 March 1992*, (Noumea: South Pacific Commission, 1992), p. 10.

15. Joint Committee, *Relations with Papua New Guinea*, p. 210.

16. Father Lini, interviewed in *News Drum*, 18 Jan. 1980.

17. See Bill Standish, *Melanesian Neighbours: The Politics of Papua New Guinea, the Solomon Islands, and the Republic of Vanuatu* (Canberra: Parliamentary Library Research Service, 1984).

18. *The Age*, 9 Oct. 1987, p. 6.

19. *Les Nouvelles Calédoniennes*, 17 March 1990.

20. Solomon Islands Ministry of Foreign Affairs, *Foreign Policy of Solomon Islands* (Honiara: Solomon Islands Government, 1985), pp. 1–6.

21. *New Zealand Herald*, 23 Jan. 1988; *Letter from the Minister for the South Pacific* (newsletter produced on behalf of Gaston Flosse, the (then) French Secretary of State for South Pacific Affairs), Nov. 1987, p. 5; Robert Keith-Reid, 'Regional blocs grows', *Islands Business*, vol. 14 (Feb. 1988), no. 2, pp. 8–11, 38.

22. Radio New Zealand interview reported in *Letter from the Minister for the South Pacific*, Nov. 1987.

23. Steve Hoadley, *The South Pacific Foreign Affairs Handbook* (Sydney: Allen & Unwin, 1990), p. 224.

24 See Iaveta Short, 'Autonomy, Self-government and Independence', paper presented to the Auckland Conference on Pacific Studies, 22 Aug. 1985 (Pacific Collection, University of South Pacific library.)

25. See Gary Smith, *Micronesia: Decolonisation and US Military Interests in the Trust Territory of the Pacific Islands* Peace Research Centre Monograph 10 (Canberra: Australian National University, 1991).

26. *Pacific Report*, 4 Aug. 1988, p. 6.

27. *Pacific Report*, 11 July 1991, p. 3.
28. *Pacific Report*, 17 Oct. 1991, p. 6.
29. *Islands Business*, March 1991, p. 15; Sept. 1991, p. 12.
30. *Islands Business*, July 1987, p. 9.
31. William Dihm, 'Global Change and the South Pacific Forum States', in Hegarty and Polomka, *Security of Oceania*, pp. 10–18 (18).

4 Decolonisation, Indigenous Rights and Internal Conflicts

1. See R.J. May (ed.), *Micronationalist Movements in Papua New Guinea* (Canberra: Australian National University, 1982).
2. See, for example, Albert Wendt, 'Western Samoa 25 Years After: Celebrating What?' *Pacific Islands Monthly*, vol. 58 (June 1987), pp. 14–15.
3. See various publications by Stephen Henningham: *France and the South Pacific. A Contemporary History* (Sydney: Allen & Unwin; Honolulu: University of Hawaii Press, 1992); '"The Dialogue of the Deaf": Issues and Attitudes in New Caledonian Politics', *Pacific Affairs*, vol. 61 (1988–9), no. 4, pp. 633–52; 'The Uneasy Peace: New Caledonia's Matignon Accords at Mid-Term', *Pacific Affairs*, vol. 66, (1993–4) no. 4, pp. 519–37.
4. See Steven Bates, *The South Pacific Countries and France: A Study in Inter-State Relations*, Canberra Studies in World Affairs no. 26 (Canberra: Australian National University, 1990), pp. 56–62.
5. See Henningham, 'The Uneasy Peace'.
6. G. Smith, *Micronesia: Decolonisation and US Military Interests in the Trust Territory of the Pacific Islands*, Peace Research Centre Monograph 10 (Canberra: Australian National University, 1991), p. 36.
7. See Firth, 'Sovereignty and Independence', and R.H. Smith and Michael Pugh, 'Micronesian Trust Territories – Imperialism Continues?' *Pacific Review*, vol. 4 (1991) no. 1, pp. 36–44.
8. Ian Williams, 'Freedom at last!' *Pacific Islands Monthly* (Feb. 1991), pp. 10–12.
9. See Ellen Wood, 'Prelude to an Anti-War Constitution', *Journal of Pacific History*, vol. 28, (June, 1993), no. 1, pp. 53–67.
10. Ian Williams, 'Palau Pushed Gently toward Change', *Pacific Islands Monthly* (June 1991), pp. 50–51; 'U.S. Falters on Islands' Fallback Arc', *Pacific Magazine*, vol. 14, (June 1989) no. 3, p. 56.
11. *Sydney Morning Herald*, 3 June 1992, p. 14.
12. See Jon M. van Dyke, 'The Evolving Legal Relationships between the United States and Its Affiliated U.S.–Flag Islands', in George Broughton and Paul Leary (eds), *A Time of Change: Relations between the United States and American Samoa, Guam, the Northern Marianas, Puerto Rico, and the United States Virgin Islands* (University of Guam and University of the Virgin Islands, 1994), pp. 237–90 (287). This article appeared earlier in the *University of Hawaii Law Review*, vol. 14.
13. See *Our Quest For Commonwealth* (Fall-Winter 1991).
14. Edward J. Michal, 'American Samoa or Eastern Samoa? The Potential for American Samoa to become Freely Associated with the United States', *Contemporary Pacific*, vol. 4, no. 1, 1992, pp. 137–60.

15. See Stephanie Lawson, *The Politics of Authenticity: Ethnonationalist Conflict and the State*, Peace Research Centre Working Paper 125 (Canberra, Australian National University, 1992).
16. R.J. May, 'Papua New Guinea's Bougainville Crisis', *Pacific Review*, vol. 3 (1990) no. 2, pp. 174–7.
17. *Ibid.*, p. 175.
18. Rowan Callick, 'Papua New Guinea: War that May Outlast WWII', *Australian Financial Review*, 25 Aug. 1994, as quoted in Reuters News Service.
19. 'The Federated States of Micronesia's 1990 Constitutional Convention: Calm before the Storm?' *Contemporary Pacific* vol. 6 (Fall 1994) no. 2, pp. 337–69, pp. 366–7.
20. Peter King, 'Redefining South Pacific Security: Greening and Domestication', in Ramesh Thakur (ed.), *South Pacific*, pp. 45–64; David Robie, 'Diplomacy, or turning a "blind eye"?' *Pacific Islands Monthly* vol. 62 (March 1992), no. 3, pp. 9–10.

5 Environmental, Resource and Nuclear Issues

1. Alan Thorne and Robert Raymond, *Man on the Rim: The Peopling of the Pacific* (North Ryde: Angus & Robertson, 1989), pp. 257, 260, 262–5.
2. See Edward P. Wolfers, 'Politics, Development and Resources: Reflections on Constructs, Conflict, and Consultants', in Stephen Henningham and R.J. May, with Lulu Turner (eds), *Resources, Development and Politics in the Pacific Islands* (Bathurst: Crawford House Press, 1992), pp. 238–57, 249–50.
3. Harold Brookfield, 'Global Change and the Pacific: Problems for the Coming Half-Century', *Contemporary Pacific*, vol. 1 (1990) nos 1 and 2, pp. 1–19; Muriel Brookfield and R. Gerard Ward, *New Directions in the South Pacific. A Message for Australia* (Canberra: Australian National University, 1988), p. 68.
4. 'Tuvalu: Tuvalu Prime Minister Criticizes Australia over Greenhouse Gas Emissions', Radio Australia 5 Aug. 1994, BBC Monitoring Summary, as quoted in the Reuters News Service.
5. *Environment, Aid, and Regionalism in the South Pacific* (Canberra: Australian National University, 1989), p. 1.
6. See Jeremy Carew-Reid, *Environment, Aid, and Regionalism*; Neva Wendt, 'Environmental Problems in the South Pacific: the Regional Environmental Programme Perspective', in Henningham and May, *Resources, Development and Politics*, pp. 185–94.
7. Russell Howorth, 'Mineral Resources Potential of Southwest Pacific Island Nations', in Grant McCall (ed.), *Sydney Talk, Australia in the South Pacific* (Sydney: University of New South Wales, 1990), pp. 67–73.
8. Cameron Stewart, 'Harsh Words Could Help Pacific Stay Afloat', *The Australian*, 3 Aug. 1994.
9. Mary Louise O'Callaghan, 'Australia: Pacific Islands Confronted on Logging', *The Age*, 30 July 1994, as quoted in the Reuters News Service.
10. Stewart, 'Harsh Words Could Help Pacific...'

11. See Henningham and May, *Resources, Development and Politics*.
12. Francis Billy Hilly, quoted in Michael Perry, 'Bribery, Corruption Destroying Pacific Environment', 31 July 1994, Reuters News Service.
13. 'The Local Politics of Resource Development in the South Pacific: Towards a General Framework of Analysis', in Henningham and May, *Resources, Development and Politics*, pp. 258–89 (279).
14. *Ibid.*, pp. 279–80.
15. Forum Communiqué, Twenty-Fifth South Pacific Forum, 31 July–2 Aug. 1994, para. 6.
16. See Firth, *Nuclear Playground*.
17. See Stephen Henningham, 'Coping with the post-Cold War World: Trends and Issues in French Defence and Security Thinking', *New Zealand International Review*, Oct. 1993.
18. New Zealand Ministry of Foreign Affairs, *Report of a New Zealand, Australian, Papua New Guinea Scientific Mission to Mururoa Atoll* (Wellington, 1984).
19. *Solomon Islands News Drum*, 12 Dec. 1980, p. 1.
20. *Solomon Star*, 13 July 1984, p. 7; *Papua New Guinea Post-Courier*, 12 July 1984, p. 2.
21. Interview with David Robie, *Vanuatu Weekly*, 25 Aug. 1984, pp. 15–16.
22. *Cook Islands News*, 9 Nov. 1983, p. 1.
23. *Fiji Times*, 17 Oct. 1988.
24. Sécretariat General de la Défense, *French Nuclear Tests* (Paris: 1987), pp. 17–22.
25. See *Pacific Islands Monthly* (Oct. 1990), pp. 11–12, 14–16; and *Pacific Report*, vol. 2, no. 19, 12 Oct. 1989, p. 1.
26. John F. May, 'French Polynesia', *Population Today*, vol. 16 (July/Aug. 1988) nos 7/8, p. 12; Emmanuel Vigneron *et al.* 'Aspects de la santé en Polynésie Française: Essai d'approche chrono-spatiale', in Centre de Récherche d'Etude et de Documentation en Economie de la Santé, Géographie et Socio-Economie de la Santé, (conference proceedings) (Paris: 1989); as well as the accompanying papers by Emmanuel Vigneron on 'Relations between Health Levels, Services and Demand in French Polynesia' and 'The Epidemiological Transition in an Overseas Territory: Disease Mapping in French Polynesia'.
27. See Tilman Ruff, *Fish Poisoning in the Pacific: A Link with Military Activities*, Peace Research Centre Working Paper 63, (Canberra: Australian National University, 1989), pp. 1–4.
28. M.P. Hochstein and M.J.O'Sullivan, 'Geothermal Systems Created by Underground Nuclear Testing: Implications for Long-term, Direct Effects of Underground Testing'. Paper presented to an International Scientific Symposium on a Nuclear Test Ban, Las Vegas, Jan. 1988; interview of Dr O'Sullivan on SBS Dateline Program, 27 Oct. 1990.
29. Norm Buske, *Cesium-134 at Moruroa – Review of the Calypso Water Samples* (Davenport: Search Technical Services, 1990); Radio Australia International Report, 7 Dec. 1990; *Canberra Times*, 8 Dec. 1990, p. 16; Stephanie Mills, 'What Greenpeace Thinks', *Bulletin*, 28 May 1991, p. 40.
30. See New Zealand Ministry of Foreign Affairs, *Report of a . . . Scientific Mission* (The Atkinson Report), Chapter 4.

31. *French Nuclear Tests*, pp. 21–2.
32. Cousteau Foundation, *Mission Scientifique de la Calypso sur le site d'experimentations nucleaires de Mururoa* (Paris: 1988), pp. 45–6, 51–2.
33. 'Smile and Charm Over the Rainbow', *Sydney Morning Herald*, 1 May 1991, p. 10.
34. For example, a letter published in the *Sydney Morning Herald* on 13 June 1991 (p. 10) fancifully suggested a connection between recent French underground tests and volcanic activity in the Pacific basin several weeks later. (The letter also mistakenly suggested that the United States underground tests take place in New Mexico, not Nevada; and that Mauritius is a French territory, located in the South Pacific). In fact seismic effects of underground tests are localised to a radius of some 50 km, and occur immediately or at most within a few days. Hundreds of earthquakes, large and small, occur every year; no correlation has been established between them and underground nuclear tests.
35. See *Pacific Research*, vol. 4 (May 1991) no. 2, p. 25.
36. See Gary Gray, 'Forum Has Many Solid Achievements', *Insight*, vol. 18 (July 1994), p. 5.
37. *The South Pacific Nuclear Free Zone Treaty: A Critical Assessment* (Canberra: Australian National University, 1990).
38. *Ibid.*, pp. 149–50.
39. *Ibid.*, p. 98.
40. D.W. Hegarty and P. Polomka (eds), *The Security of Oceania in the 1990s, Vol. I: Views from the Region*, Canberra Papers on Strategy and Defence no. 60 (Canberra: Australian National University, 1989), p. 2.
41. John C. Dorrance, *The United States and the Pacific Islands*, (Westport, Conn. and London: Praeger, 1992), pp. 48–9.
42. See Trevor Findlay, 'Green vs Peace? The Johnston Atoll Controversy,' *Pacific Research*, vol. 3 (May 1990) no. 2, pp. 3–7.
43. Quoted in Findlay, 'Green vs Peace,' p. 4.
44. Forum Communiqué, Twenty-Fifth South Pacific Forum, 31 July–2 Aug. 1994, para. 36.

6   External Actors: The Trend to Diversification

1. John C. Dorrance, *The United States and the Pacific Islands*, (Westport, Conn. and London: Praeger, 1992), pp. 60–68.
2. Richard Herr, 'Regionalism, Strategic Denial, and South Pacific Security', *Journal of Pacific History*, vol. 21 (1986) nos. 3–4 pp. 170–82; and his 'Diplomacy and Security in the South Pacific: Coping with Sovereignty', *Current Affairs Bulletin*, vol. 63 (Jan. 1987) no. 8.
3. *Pacific Magazine*, Sept./Oct. 1993, p. 13.
4. *Pacific Magazine*, March/April 1993, p. 8; *Pacific Report*, 25 Oct. 1993, p. 1; *Pacific Islands Monthly*, Dec. 1993, pp. 16–17; Jan. 1994, p. 13.
5. David Hegarty, 'The External Powers in the South Pacific', in Stephen Henningham and Desmond Ball (eds), *South Pacific Security: Issues and Perspectives* (Canberra: Australian National University, 1991), pp. 95–6.

6. David Hegarty, 'The Soviet Union in the South Pacific in the 1990s', in Ross Babbage (ed.), *The Soviets in the Pacific* (Sydney: Brassey's, 1989), pp. 113–27; Richard Herr, 'The Soviet Union in the South Pacific', in Ramesh Thakur and Carlyle Thayer (eds), *The Soviet Union as an Asian–Pacific Power: Implications of Gorbachev's 1986 Vladivostok Initiative* (Boulder and London: Westview Press; Melbourne: Macmillan, 1987).

7. See Ken Ross, *Regional Security in the South Pacific. The Quarter-century, 1970–95* Canberra Papers on Strategy and Defence No. 100 (Canberra: Australian National University, 1993) pp. 75–6.

8. I.J. Fairbairn, C.E. Morrison, R.W. Baker and S.A. Groves, *The Pacific Islands. Politics, Economics, and International Relations* (Honolulu: East-West Center, 1991), p. 95.

9. Dorrance, *Pacific Islands*, pp. 124–5.

10. *Ibid.*, p. 124.

11. Steven Bates, *The South Pacific island countries and France: a study in inter-state relations* (Canberra: Department of International Relations, Australian National University, 1990). S. Henningham, *France and the South Pacific: A Contemporary History* (Sydney: Allen & Unwin; Honolulu, University of Hawaii press, 1992), pp. 192–229; Georges Martin, 'France as a South Pacific Actor', in R. Thakur (ed.), *The South Pacific: Problems, Issues and Prospects* (New York, St Martin's Press, 1991).

12. Robert Aldrich and John Connell, *France's Overseas Frontier. Les Départments et Territoires d'Outre-Mer* (Cambridge University Press, 1992).

13. See Henningham, *France and the South Pacific*, pp. 209–19.

14. Statement by Mr Dominique Perben, Minister for French Overseas Departments and Territories, on French Policy in the South Pacific, to the Foreign Press Correspondents' Association, Sydney, 20 Sept. 1994, p. 5. Mr Perben may however have somewhat exaggerated the amount of French aid spent outside the French territories, because the territories also benefit from some multilateral European Union programmes.

15. Hegarty, *'External Powers'*, p. 103.

16. S. Hoadley, *The South Pacific Foreign Affairs Handbook* (Sydney: Allen & Unwin, 1992), p. 44.

17. Y. Noguchi, 'Statement by the representative of Japan', in South Pacific Commission, *Report of the Thirtieth South Pacific Conference*, pp. 249–50, 249.

18. Hoadley, *South Pacific Handbook*, p. 46.

19. Hoadley, *South Pacific Handbook*, p. 46; Dorrance, *Pacific Islands*, p. 118.

20. Thomas V. Biddick, 'Diplomatic Rivalry in the South Pacific: the PRC and Taiwan', *Asian Survey*, vol. xxix (Aug. 1989) no. 8, pp. 800–815 (812).

21. See the *Papua New Guinea Post-Courier*, 12 June 1991.

22. Jim Sanday, 'Vibrant Entities, Not Stepping Stones', *Asia–Pacific Defence Reporter*, June 1991, pp. 35 and 37 (35).

23. Dorrance, *Pacific Islands*, p. 125.

24. Hoadley, *South Pacific Handbook*, p. 100.

25. David Robie, *Blood on their Banner: Nationalist Struggles in the South Pacific* (London: Zed Books and Leichhardt: Pluto press, 1989), pp. 146–8; Stewart Firth, *Nuclear Playground* (Sydney: Allen & Unwin, 1987) pp. 133–7.

26. See Robie, *Blood on their Banner*, p. 283.
27. Dorrance, *Pacific Islands*, pp. 137–8.
28. Robie, *Blood on their Banner*, pp. 191–2.
29. Robie, *Blood on their Banner*, pp. 178–82.
30. See Brij Lal, 'Plus ça change: Resources, Politics, and Development in the South Pacific', in Henningham and May, *Resources, Development and Politics*, pp. 230–37, 231–2.
31. See Karl G.W. Claxton, 'The Nature and Impact of Crime as a Security Threat in the South Pacific, and Regional Attempts to Respond to This Challenge. Research essay, Australian National University Master of Arts Program in Strategic Studies (1994), pp. 14, 20.
32. See Ross, *Regional Security*, pp. 161–2.
33. See *Pacific Report*, 9 Aug. 1993, pp. 1–2; *Pacific Islands Monthly*, Oct. 1993, p. 13; Nov. 1993, p. 20.
34. *Islands Business*, July 1994, p. 15.
35. Radio Australia external service, 16 Sept. 1994, as quoted in Reuters News Service.
36. 'PNG Miners Bear the Brunt of Indigenous Muscleflexing', *Sydney Morning Herald*, 1 Sept. 1993, p. 17.
37. Mark Davis, 'Papua New Guinea: Asia Courtship Brings Little in Cold Cash', *Business Review Weekly*, 19 Sept. 1994, as quoted in the Reuters News Service.
38. Margaret ('Meg') Taylor, interviewed on the Background Briefing programme, Radio National, Australian Broadcasting Commission, 13 Sept. 1994.

7 The Limits on Power: Australia and New Zealand and the Region

1. 'New Zealand in the South Pacific', in R. Alley (ed.), *New Zealand and the Pacific* (Boulder: Westview Press, 1984), pp. 135–54, (143).
2. *Ibid.*
3. Mary Boyd, 'Australia, New Zealand and the Pacific', in R. Hayburn (ed.), *Australia and New Zealand Relations* (Dunedin: University of Otago, 1978), p. 34.
4. 'Security Cooperation in the South Pacific', Peace Research Centre Working Paper 41 (Canberra: Australian National University, 1988), p. 10.
5. G.E. Fry (ed.), *Australia's Regional Security* (Sydney: Allen & Unwin, 1991), pp. 126–30.
6. John C. Dorrance, *United States and the Pacific Islands* (Westport, Conn. and London: Praeger, 1992), p. 111.
7. South Pacific Commission, *South Pacific Economies Statistical Summary Number 12* (Noumea: 1991), p. 19.
8. Australian International Development Assistance Bureau, *AID 93–94. Budget Summary* (Canberra: AIDAB, 1993), p. 4.
9. See Stephen Merchant, 'Australia's Defence Cooperation Program and Regional Security', in D.W. Hegarty and P. Polomka, *The Security of Oceania, in the 1990s* (Canberra: Australian National University, 1989), vol. 1, pp. 71–8.

10. Ministry of External Relations and Trade (New Zealand), *The South Pacific Forum. 21 Years of Regional Cooperation* (Wellington: Ministry ERT, 1991), pp. 21–2.
11. Ross Babbage, *A Coast Too Long: Defending Australia beyond the 1990s* (Sydney: Allen & Unwin, 1990).
12. Quoted in Denis Mclean, 'Perspectives from New Zealand. Interests, Objectives, Means, and Prospects', in Henry S. Albinski *et al.*, *The South Pacific: Political, Economic and Military Trends* (Washington: Brassey's, 1989), pp. 85–6.
13. See Ross Babbage, 'Australian Interests in the South Pacific', in Albinski *et al. The South Pacific*, p. 64.
14. Rory McLeod, 'New Zealand's Economic Links with Pacific Island Countries', *Pacific Economic Bulletin*, vol. 6 (June 1991) no. 1, pp. 18–22 (19–20).
15. 'Australia's relations with the South Pacific – Challenge and Change', address delivered to the Foreign Correspondents' Association, Sydney, 15 June 1994.
16. *Australia's Relations With Papua New Guinea, Report of the Joint Committee on Foreign Affairs, Defence and Trade, December 1991* (Canberra, 1991), pp. 193–6.
17. *Islands Business*, November 1992, p. 23.
18. David Lange, 'The Hawke Memoirs: Streetfighter with a Poison Pen', *The Bulletin*, vol. 116 (23 Aug., 1994) no. 5934, pp. 24–9 (29).
19. See G.E. Fry, 'Australia and the South Pacific', in P. Boyce and J. Angel (eds), *Diplomacy in the Marketplace: Australia in World Affairs, 1981–90* (South Melbourne: Longman Cheshire, 1991).

8 Intervention Contingencies: A Gap between Ends and Means?

1. This chapter draws heavily on Stephen Henningham and Stewart Woodman, 'An Achilles Heel? Australian and New Zealand Capabilities for Pacific Islands Contingencies', *Pacific Review*, vol. 6, (1993) no. 2, pp. 127–43. My thanks go to Dr Woodman for permission to use a revised version of some of this material here: as noted in the acknowledgements he should be regarded as the co-author of this chapter.
2. Norman MacQueen, 'Beyond Tok Win: The Papua New Guinea Intervention in Vanuatu, 1980', *Pacific Affairs*, vol. 61 (1988) no. 2, pp. 235–52 (241, 247).
3. *The Australian*, 19 May 1992, p. 8; *Sydney Morning Herald*, 23 May 1992, p. 20; *Asia-Pacific Defence Reporter*, Aug.–Sept. 1992, p. 18: *The Dominion* (New Zealand), 18–21 May 1992, contained a series of articles detailing New Zealand's confused and apparently ill-conceived response.
4. Colonel Adrian D'Hage, 'Operation Morrisdance', *Defence Force Journal*, no. 80 (Jan./Feb. 1990), pp. 4–13.
5. For an analysis of some of the operational deficiencies experienced during Operation Morrisdance, see Mathew Gubb, *The Australian Military Response to the Fiji Coup: An Assessment*, Strategic and Defence Studies

Centre, Working Paper 171 (Canberra: Australian National University, 1988).

6. *The Australian*, 22 May 1987, p. 4.

7. *West Australian*, 5 Dec. 1991, p. 18; *Canberra Times*, 6 Dec. 1991, p. 5.

8. See Stephen Henningham, 'Pluralism and Party Politics in a South Pacific State: Vanuatu's Ruling Vanua'aku Pati and its Rivals', *Conflict*, vol. 9 (1989) no. 2, pp. 171–95.

9. See Commonwealth of Australia, *Australia's Regional Security. Ministerial Statement by Senator the Hon. Gareth Evans, QC, Minister for Foreign Affairs and Trade* (Canberra, 1989); and Greg Fry (ed.), *Australia's Regional Security* (Sydney, Allen & Unwin, 1991).

10. *Australia's Regional Security. Ministerial Statement*, p. 22; Gareth Evans, 'Ministerial Response' in Greg Fry (ed.), *Australia's Regional Security*, pp. 141–52 (149).

11. Department of Defence, *Force Structure Review 1991* (Canberra: Australian Government Publishing Service, 1991), p. 28; Department of Defence, *Australia's Strategic Planning in the 1990s*, [completed Nov. 1989], Canberra, 1992, p. 36.

12. *Towards A Pacific Island Community: Report of the South Pacific Policy Review Group, May 1990* (Wellington: New Zealand Government Printer, 1990), p. 213.

13. *The Defence of New Zealand 1991: A Policy Paper* (Wellington: New Zealand Government Printer, 1991), p. 65.

14. See, for example, some of the views expressed in Graeme Cheeseman and St John Kettle (eds), *The New Australian Militarism: Undermining Our Future Security* (Leichhardt, Pluto Press, 1990).

15. See S. Woodman and D. Horner, 'Land Forces in the Defence of Australia', in D. Horner (ed.), *Reshaping the Australian Army: Challenges for the 1990s*, Canberra Papers on Strategy and Defence 77. (Canberra: Australian National University, 1991), pp. 100–08.

16. *Australia's Regional Security, Ministerial Statement*, p. 21.

Select Bibliography

The literature on or relating to the security, defence and sovereignty of the Pacific island states is extensive. In this bibliography I have listed those works which I found particularly useful in preparing this study. The Notes and References to each chapter give further details on sources on particular topics. I have also drawn on the Reuters News Service and associated services, and on a range of journals and periodicals, especially *The Contemporary Pacific: A Journal of Island Affairs* (Honolulu), *Islands Business Pacific* (Suva), *The Journal of Pacific History* (Canberra), *Pacific Islands Monthly* (Suva), *Pacific Magazine* (Honolulu), and *Pacific Report* (Canberra). And, as noted in the acknowledgements, I have learnt much from discussions with a broad range of interlocutors.

Albinski, H.S., R. Herr, R.C. Kiste, R. Babbage and D. McLean., *The South Pacific: Political, Economic and Military Trends* (Washington: Brassey's, 1989).

Alley, R. (ed.) *New Zealand and the Pacific* (Boulder: Westview Press, 1984).

Babbage, R. 'Australia and the Defence of Papua New Guinea', *Australian Outlook*, vol. 41, (Aug. 1987) no. 2, pp. 87–94.

Babbage, R. (ed.), *The Soviets in the Pacific in the 1990s* (Sydney: Brassey's Australia, 1989).

Babbage, R. *A Coast Too Long: Defending Australia beyond the 1990s* (Sydney: Allen & Unwin, 1990).

Bates S. *The South Pacific island countries and France: a study in inter-state relations*, Canberra: Department of International Relations, Australian National University, 1990.

Blaskett, B. and Wong, L. 'Papua New Guinea under Wingti: Accommodating Indonesia', *Australian Outlook*, vol. 43 (April, 1989) no. 1, pp. 44–60.

Boyd, M. (ed.), *Pacific Horizons. A Regional Role for New Zealand* (Wellington: Price Milburn/New Zealand Institute of International Affairs, 1972).

Boyd, M. 'Australia, New Zealand and the Pacific', in R. Hayburn (ed.), *Australia and New Zealand Relations* (Dunedin: University of Otago, 1978).

Brookfield, H., 'Global Change and the Pacific: Problems for the Coming Half-Century', *Contemporary Pacific*, vol. 1, (1990) nos 1 and 2, pp. 1–19.

Brookfield, M. and R.G. Ward, *New Directions in the South Pacific: A Message for Australia* (Canberra: Australian National University, 1988).

Cheeseman, G. and St J. Kettle, *The New Australian Militarism* (Leichhardt: Pluto Press, 1990).

Cole, R.V., *Pacific 2010: Challenging the Future* (Canberra: National Centre for Development Studies, 1993).

Commonwealth of Australia, *Australia's Relations with the South Pacific* (Canberra: Commonwealth Parliament, 1989).

Commonwealth of Australia, *Australia's Regional Security. Ministerial Statement by Senator the Hon. Gareth Evans, QC* (Canberra: Commonwealth Parliament, 1989).

Connell, J., 'Island Microstates: The Mirage of Development', *Contemporary Pacific: A Journal of Island Affairs*, vol. 3 (1991) no. 2, pp. 251–87.

Crouch, H., 'Indonesia and the Security of Australia and Papua New Guinea,' *Australian Outlook*, vol. 40 (December, 1986) no, 3, pp. 167–74.

Dibb, P., *Review of Australia's Defence Capabilities: Report to the Minister of Defence* (Canberra: Australian Government Publishing Service, 1986).

Dibb, P., *The Regional Security Outlook: An Australian Viewpoint*, Strategic and Defence Studies Centre Working Paper no. 262 (Canberra: Australian National University, 1992).

Dorrance, J.C., R. Thakur, J. Wanandi, L.R.Vasey and R.F. Pfaltzgraff, *The South Pacific: Emerging Security Issues and US Policy* (Washington: Brassey's, 1990).

Dorrance, J.C., *The United States and the Pacific Islands* (Westport, Conn. and London: Praeger, 1992).

Fairbairn, T.I.J, C.E. Morrison, R.W. Baker and S.A. Groves, *The Pacific Islands: Politics, Economics, and International Relations* (Honolulu: East-West Center, 1991).

Firth, S., *Nuclear Playground*, Sydney: Allen & Unwin, 1987.

Firth, S., 'Sovereignty and Independence in the Contemporary Pacific', *Contemporary Pacific*, vol. 1 (1989) nos 1 and 2, pp. 75–96.

Firth, S., 'Australia and the South Pacific', in Paul Keal (ed.), *Ethics and Foreign Policy* (Sydney: Allen & Unwin Australian National University, 1992) pp. 221–41.

Fry, G.E., *Regional 'Peacekeeping' in the South Pacific: Some Considerations for Prior Consideration*, Working Paper, Department of International Relations (Canberra: Australian National University, 1990).

Fry, G.E., 'Australia and the South Pacific', in P. Boyce and J. Angel (eds), *Diplomacy in the Marketplace: Australia in World Affairs, 1981–90* (Melbourne: Longman Cheshire, 1991).

Fry, G.E., 'At the Margin: the South Pacific and the Changing World Order', in J.L. Richardson and R. Leaver (eds), *The Post-Cold War Order: Diagnoses and Prognoses* (St Leonards: Allen & Unwin/Australian National University, 1993).

Fry, G.E. (ed.), *Australia's Regional Security* (Sydney: Allen & Unwin, 1991)

Grynberg, R., 'The honeymoon is over', *Pacific Islands Monthly* (Sept. 1992), p. 20.

Hamel-Green, M., *The South Pacific Nuclear Free Zone Treaty: A Critical Assessment* (Canberra: Australian National University, 1990).

Hayburn, R. (ed.) *Australia and New Zealand Relations* (Dunedin: University of Otago, 1978).

Hegarty, D.W., *Small State Security in the South Pacific*, Strategic and Defence Studies Centre Working Paper 126 (Canberra: Australian National University, 1988).

Hegarty, D.W., *Libya and the South Pacific*, Strategic and Defence Studies Centre, Working Paper 127 (Canberra: Australian National University, 1988).

Hegarty, D.W., *South Pacific Security Issues: An Australian Perspective*, Strategic and Defence Studies Working Paper 147 (Canberra: Australian National University, 1988).

Hegarty, D.W., 'The Soviet Union in the South Pacific in the 1990's', in R. Babbage (ed.), *The Soviets in the Pacific in the 1990s* (Sydney, Brassey's

Australia, 1989), pp. 113–27.

Hegarty, D.W. and P. Polomka (eds), *The Security of Oceania in the 1990s Vol. 1: Views from the Region*, Canberra Papers on Strategy and Defence no. 60 (Canberra: Australian National University, 1989).

Henningham, S., 'A Dialogue of the Deaf: Attitudes and Issues in New Caledonian Politics', *Pacific Affairs*, vol. 61 (1988–9) no. 4, pp. 633–52.

Henningham, S., 'Pluralism and Party Politics in a South Pacific State: Vanuatu's Ruling *Vanua'aku Pati* and its Rivals', *Conflict*, vol. 9 (1989) pp. 171–95.

Henningham, S., 'New Caledonia and French Polynesia: Towards Independence-in-Association?', *Meanjin*, vol. 49 (1990) no. 4, pp. 652.

Henningham, S., *France and the South Pacific: A Contemporary History*, (Sydney: Allen & Unwin; Honolulu: University of Hawaii Press, 1992)

Henningham, S., 'France's Defence and Security Policies in the post-Cold War era', *New Zealand International Review*, vol. xviii (1993) no. 5 (Sept.–Oct., 1993), pp. 8–13.

Henningham, S., 'The Uneasy Peace: The New Caledonian Matignon Accords at mid-term', *Pacific Affairs*, vol. 66 (1993–4), no. 4, pp. 519–37.

Henningham, S. and D. Ball (eds), *South Pacific Security. Issues and Perspectives*, Strategic and Defence Studies Centre, Papers on Defence and Security no. 72 (Canberra: Australian National University, 1991).

Henningham, S. and R.J. May, with L. Turner (eds), *Resources, Development and Politics in the Pacific Islands* (Bathurst: Crawford House Press, 1992).

Henningham, S. and S. Woodman, 'An Achilles Heel? Australian and New Zealand Capabilities for South Pacific Intervention Contingencies', *The Pacific Review*, vol. 6 (1993) no. 2, pp. 127–43.

Herr, R., 'Regionalism, Strategic Denial and South Pacific Security', *Journal of Pacific History*, vol. 21 (1986) nos 3–4, pp. 170–82.

Herr, R., 'Diplomacy and Security in the South Pacific: Coping with Sovereignty,' *Current Affairs Bulletin*, vol. 63 (1987) no. 8, pp. 16–22.

Herr, R., 'The Soviet Union in the South Pacific', in Ramesh Thakur and Carlyle Thayer (eds), *The Soviet Union as an Asian Pacific Power* (Boulder, Colo. and London, Westview Press; Melbourne, Macmillan), pp. 135–151.

Herr, R., 'The Region in Review: International Issues and Events, 1989', *Contemporary Pacific*, vol. 2 (1990) no. 2, pp. 350–57.

Hoadley, S., *Security Cooperation in the South Pacific*, Peace Research Centre Working Paper 41 (Canberra: Australian National University, 1988).

Hoadley, S., *The South Pacific Foreign Affairs Handbook* (Sydney: Allen & Unwin, 1992).

Jackson, R. H., *Quasi-States: Sovereignty, International Relations and the Third World* (Cambridge University Press, 1990).

Jennings, P., 'Political and Constitutional Change', in P. Polomka (ed.) *The Security of Oceania in the 1990s, Vol. 2: Managing Change*, Canberra Papers on Strategy and Defence no. 68 (Canberra: Australian National University, 1990).

Joint Committee on Foreign Affairs, Defence and Trade, *Australia's Relations with Papua New Guinea* (Canberra: Parliament of the Commonwealth of Australia, 1991).

Kejoa, G., 'Australia's Proper Role in the South Pacific: A Personal perspective', in G. McCall (ed.), *Sydney Talk: Australia in the South Pacific* (Sydney: University of NSW, 1990).

Kennaway, R., *New Zealand Foreign Policy, 1951–1971* (Wellington: Hicks Smith; London: Methuen, 1972).

King, P., 'Redefining South Pacific Security: Greening and Domestication', in R. Thakur (ed.), *The South Pacific: Problems, Issues and Prospects* (New York: St Martin's Press, 1991), pp. 45–64.

Lawson, S., *The Politics of Authenticity: Ethnonationalist Conflict and the State*, Peace Research Centre Working Paper 125 (Canberra: Australian National University, 1992).

McCall, G. (ed.), *Sydney Talk. Australia in the South Pacific* (Sydney: University of New South Wales, 1990).

Mackie, J.A.C., 'Does Indonesia have Expansionist Designs on Papua New Guinea?' in R.J. May (ed.), *Between Two Nations:The Indonesia–Papua New Guinea Border and West Papua Nationalism* (Bathurst: Robert Brown, 1986).

May, R.J. (ed.), *The Indonesia–Papua New Guinea Border: Irianese Nationalism and Small State Diplomacy*, Political and Social Change Working Paper 2 (Canberra: Australian National University, 1979).

May, R.J., 'Political Style in Modern Melanesia,' in R.J. May and H. Nelson (eds), *Melanesia: Beyond Diversity*, vol. 1, (Canberra: Australian National University, 1982).

May, R.J. (ed.), *Micronationalist Movements in Papua New Guinea* (Canberra: Australian National University, 1982).

May, R.J. (ed.), *Between Two Nations. The Indonesia–Papua New Guinea Border and West Papua Nationalism* (Bathurst: Robert Brown, 1986).

May, R.J., 'East of the Border: Irian Jaya and the Border in Papua New Guinea's Domestic and Foreign Policies', in R.J. May (ed.), *Between Two Nations* (Bathurst, Robert Brown, 1986).

May, R.J., 'Papua New Guinea's Bougainville Crisis', *Pacific Review* vol. 3 (1990) no. 2, pp. 174–7.

Mediansky, F.A. 'Australia and the Southwest Pacific', in F.A. Mediansky and A.C. Palfreeman (eds), *In Pursuit of National Interests: Australian Foreign Policy in the 1990s* (Sydney: Pergamon Press, 1988).

New Zealand Ministry of External Relations and Trade, *The South Pacific Forum: 21 Years of Regional Cooperation*, Information Bulletin no. 38 (Wellington, 1991).

New Zealand Ministry of Foreign Affairs, *Report of a New Zealand, Australian, Papua New Guinea Scientific Mission to Mururoa Atoll* (Wellington, 1984).

Polomka, P. (ed.), *The Security of Oceania in the 1990s, Vol. 2: Managing Change*, Canberra Papers on Strategy and Defence no. 68 (Canberra: Australian National University, 1990).

Prescott, J.R.V., 'Problems of International Boundaries with Particular Reference to the Boundary Between Indonesia and Papua New Guinea', in R. J. May (ed.), *Between Two Nations* (Bathurst, Robert Brown, 1986), pp. 1–17.

Prescott, J.R.V., *The Maritime Political Boundaries of the World* (London and New York: Methuen, 1985).

Prescott, J.R.V., 'Maritime Boundaries in the Southwest Pacific Region', in A.D. Couper (ed.), *Development and Social Change in the Pacific Islands* (London and New York: Routledge, 1989), pp. 4–21.

Robie, D., *Blood on their Banner: Nationalist Struggles in the South Pacific* (London and Leichhardt: Zed Books Pluto Press, 1989).

Ross, K., *Regional Security in the South Pacific. The Quarter–Century, 1970–95*, Canberra Papers on Strategy and Defence no. 100 (Canberra: Australian National University, 1993).

Sanday, J., 'Vibrant Entities, Not Stepping Stones', *Asia–Pacific Defence Reporter*, June 1991, pp. 35, 37.

Short, I., 'Autonomy, Self-government and Independence', paper given at Auckland Conference on Pacific Studies, 19–22 Aug., 1985.

Smith, G., *Micronesia. Decolonisation and US Military Interests in the Trust Territory of the Pacific Islands*, Peace Research Centre, Monograph 10 (Canberra: Australian National University, 1991).

Smith, R.H. and M.C Pugh, 'Micronesian Trust Territories – Imperialism Continues?' *Pacific Review*, vol. 4 (1991) no. 1, pp. 36–44.

Standish, B., *Melanesian Neighbours: The Politics of Papua New Guinea, the Solomon Islands and the Republic of Vanuatu* (Canberra: Parliamentary Library Legislative Research Service, 1984).

Sutton, P. and A. Payne (eds), *Size and Survival: The Politics of Security in the Caribbean and the Pacific* (London: Frank Cass, 1993).

Taylor, M. (ed.), *Fiji: Future Imperfect?* (Sydney: Allen & Unwin, 1987).

Thakur, R. and C. Thayer (eds), *The Soviet Union as an Asian Pacific Power: Implications of Gorbachev's 1986 Vladivostok Initiative* (Boulder, Colo. and London: Westview Press; Melbourne: Macmillan, 1987).

Thakur, R. (ed.), *The South Pacific: Problems, Issues and Prospects* (New York: St Martin's Press, 1991).

Tiffany, M., 'Who's Looking After You?' *Pacific Islands Monthly*, vol. 62 (March, 1992), no. 3, pp. 6–7.

Turner, M., *Papua New Guinea: The Challenge of Independence* (Ringwood: Penguin, 1990).

Walker, R. and W. Sutherland (eds), *The Pacific: Peace, Security and the Nuclear Issue* (London: Zed Books; Tokyo: United Nations University, 1988).

Ward, R.G., 'Earth's Empty Quarter? The Pacific Islands in a Pacific Century', *Geographical Journal*, vol. 155 (July 1989) no. 2, pp. 325–46.

Wendt, A., 'Western Samoa 25 Years After: Celebrating What?', *Pacific Islands Monthly*, vol. 58 (June 1987), pp. 14–15.

Index

aid
  Australian 5, 35, 115–16, 122,
    129, 150
  dependence, island states 8, 46, 47
  French 39–40, 99
  Israel 106
  Japanese 101, 102
  Malaysian 38
  New Zealand 115, 116
Algeria 98
Alliance of Small Island States 72
American Micronesia xiii, 11–12, 34,
    92, 97, 101, 102, 103, 111
  decolonisation 54, 58–62
  military threats 21–2
  security issues 48–50
American Samoa xiv, 6, 13, 16, 44,
    45, 46, 55, 60, 61–2, 92
Amnesty International 66
Antarctic Treaty 84
ANZUS Treaty ix, 30, 85, 93, 108,
    118–20
Apia Convention 73
ASEAN 21, 38, 103, 104–5
Asia see Northeast Asia; Southeast
    Asia
Asia-Pacific Economic Community
    51
Asian Development Bank 109
Atkinson mission 77–8, 79–80
Australia ix, xii, 2, 7, 13, 14, 15, 16,
    56, 58, 63, 72–3, 97, 98, 108, 111,
    114–15
  armed forces 26, 115, 130–1
  chemical weapons destruction 88
  concern over nuclear testing 78–9
  decolonisation 4, 9, 91, 121
  economic links 124–6
  economic strength 115
  links with island states 29, 95–6,
    101, 115, 116–29, 148
  military intervention 22, 137–47,
    151
  neo-colonial attitudes 29–30
  Papua New Guinea relations 5, 35,
    53, 65, 115–16, 121, 122–3,
    125, 130–2
  role in Pacific region xi, xv, 20
  strategic concerns 125–7
  Treaty of Rarotonga 84, 85
  uranium exports 85, 86
Australian Conservation Foundation
    88

Bais, Tony 79
Balos, Henchi 48
Bangladesh 72
Bavadra, Timothy (Timoci) 43, 109,
    138
Belau see Palau
Bikini 10
Billy Hilly, Francis 25, 26, 75
Bilney, Gordon 128, 129, 134
Bougainville 22, 52, 64
  revolt ix, xi, xiv, 24–6, 27, 37, 42,
    52, 53, 64–6, 67, 130–2, 137,
    140, 142, 143
Bougainville Copper Limited 75
Bougainville Revolutionary Army
    25–6, 65, 131, 140
Bugotu, Francis 79
Bush, George 48, 88–9, 94, 119

Carlot Korman, Maxime 24, 37, 41,
    132
Chad 96
Chamorros, Guam 61
Chan, Sir Julius 27, 65, 109
chemical weapons, destruction 50,
    87–9, 94, 109
China 103–4
  Treaty of Rarotonga 84
Chinese community, Papua New
    Guinea 63
Christian churches, role in South
    Pacific 107

ciguatera, poisoning 81
Clark Air Base 59
Clinton, Bill 84, 94, 120
Closer Economic Relations
    arrangements 124
Cold War ix, x, xiv, 17, 21, 28, 30,
    32, 49, 59, 77, 83, 84, 106, 111,
    119, 127, 149, 150
colonialism, Pacific islands 1–2, 38
Commonwealth 13, 42, 46, 107
Commonwealth Micronesia xiii, 11,
    12–14, 115
    security issues 47
Commonwealth Secretariat 66
Cook Islands 4, 5, 13, 44, 45, 57, 79,
    84, 110, 116
    security policy 46
copper, mining 75
Cousteau mission 82
criminal groupings, international
    110–11
Cuba 39

Davis, Sir Thomas 79
decolonisation 53–62
    New Hebrides 4, 23, 38, 55, 100,
        133
    Pacific islands 3–4, 9, 19, 20
defence
    aid, Malaysian, Papua New Guinea
        38
    aid, Israel 106
Diro, Ted 20
drift-net fishing 31, 50, 74, 102
Dutch East Indies 9

East New Britain 52
East Timor 20
Easter Island xii, 71
economies, Pacific islands 7–9
Efi, Tupuola 45
environmental impact
    mining and forestry xiv, 75–7, 110
    nuclear testing xiv, 77–80, 82–3
Espiritu Santo 27, 38, 52, 54, 110,
    132, 137
ethnicity, Pacific islands 6–7
European Union 5, 103, 106, 124
Evans, Gareth 128, 132, 141

exclusive economic zones 8–9, 23,
    31, 116

Fangataufa 10, 77, 81, 82
Federated States of Micronesia xiv, 4
Fiji xiii, 1, 4, 6, 11, 12, 32, 33, 36,
    37, 42, 52, 56, 88, 94, 100, 103,
    104, 107, 109, 115, 117, 133
    armed forces 26, 27, 115, 140
    concern over nuclear testing 78,
        79–80
    economic prospects 8
    ethnic diversity 7
    Israeli defence aid 106
    military coups ix, x, xi, 30, 43, 52,
        63, 68, 99, 101, 105, 108,
        129–30, 137–9, 141, 143
    Minerva Reefs dispute 23
    relations with Australia 30, 43–4,
        63, 99, 106
    relations with Malaysia 104–5
    relations with New Zealand 30,
        43–4, 63, 99, 106
    security policy 42–4
    Treaty of Rarotonga 84
Fiji Labour Party 43, 109
fish, poisoning, ciguatera 81
fisheries
    agreements 31, 39, 47, 74, 95–6,
        102, 150
    island states 8–9, 31
    resource management xiv, 74
fishing fleets, foreign 9, 31, 39, 47,
    93, 95–6, 110
Flosse, Gaston 45
food chain, radioactive materials
    take-up 82
forestry
    exploitation 74–5, 104, 110
    management xiv, 38
Forum Fisheries Agency 74
France ix, 15, 36, 44
    decolonisation 54, 55–7, 91, 106
    Matthew and Hunter Islands dispute
        23–4
    nuclear testing xi, xiii, xiv, 4, 10,
        34, 45, 46, 57, 77–83, 87,
        89–90, 98, 109, 127
    overseas possessions 98–9

France – *continued*
  Pacific territories   xiv, 3, 5–6, 9,
    34, 45, 46, 52, 97–9, 109
  relations with Vanuatu   23–4, 38–40
  Treaty of Rarotonga   84
Free Papua Movement   xiii, xv,
    18–20, 35, 37–8, 66, 96, 104
French Indo-China   9
French Polynesia   xiii, xiv, 5, 7, 13,
    44, 45, 55, 96
  independence   56–7
  nuclear testing   xi, xiii, xiv, 4, 10,
    34, 45, 46, 57, 77–83, 87, 98
*Front de Libération Nationale, Kanak
  et Socialiste*   55–6
Front Indépendantist, New Caledonia
  ↘ 55

Germany   87, 88
  Pacific presence   3, 16, 117
global warming   xiv, 71–3, 90
Gorbachev, Mikhail   96, 97
Great Britain   *see* United Kingdom
Greenpeace   ix, 78, 82, 83, 108–9
Guam   xiv, 1, 3, 6, 11, 12, 16, 59, 60,
    61, 62, 91, 92
  naval and air bases   21
Gulf War   29

Hagelgam, John   49
Hao   81
Hawaii   xii, 59, 91, 92
Hawke, Bob   88, 134–5
health, effects of changing lifestyles
    80–1
helicopter support ships   145–6
Honiara   25
Hu Yaobang   104
Hunter Island   23–4

Iangalio, Masket   65
independence, transition to   14
India   9, 30, 103, 105
Indian community, Fiji   6, 7, 8, 43,
    63, 100, 105
Indonesia   5, 6, 15, 17, 91, 103, 107,
    112
  Papua New Guinea border   xiii, xv,
    18–21, 37–8, 104, 126

intercontinental ballistic missiles,
    testing   12, 21
International Confederation of Free
  Trade Unions   108
International Court of Justice   78–9,
    134
International Monetary Fund   109
investment, Japanese, South Pacific
    101–2
Irian Jaya   xiv, 5, 6, 7, 15, 18–19, 20,
    22, 52, 53, 91, 107
Israel   103, 105–6

Japan   ix, xv, 3, 16, 74, 87, 111, 117,
    125, 150
  involvement in South Pacific
    101–3
Johnston Atoll   50, 87, 88, 89, 94, 109

Kabua, Amata   87
Kanak nationalism   ix, 4, 23, 33, 34,
    38, 39, 40, 52, 55–6, 63, 98, 99,
    101
Kaouna, Sam   140
Keating, Paul   128
Kijiner, Tom   48
Kiribati   xii, xiii, 4, 13, 16, 49, 72, 84
  fishing agreements with Soviet
    Union   95–6
  independence   54
  security policy   47
Korea   *see* North Korea; South Korea
Kotobalavu, Jioji   133
Kuranari, Tadashi   101
Kwajalein atoll   12, 50

land, island states   68
Lange, David   118, 124, 134, 139
law enforcement, civil, intervention
    143–5
Libya   ix, 39, 66, 93, 96, 97, 101,
    106, 111, 127
Lini, Walter   19, 29, 41, 79, 107, 135,
    139
Lomé Convention   5, 8, 43, 106

Malaysia   20, 38, 103, 104–5, 112
Maldive Islands   30, 105
Mamaloni, Solomon   25, 41, 79

Mangareva 81
Maoris xii, 64, 124
Mara, Ratu Sir Kamisese 37, 43, 88, 139
Marianas trench 87
Marshall Islands xiv, 4, 5, 11, 48–50, 54, 58, 61, 72, 84, 122, 149
   missile testing 12, 21, 50, 92
   nuclear tests 77, 92, 93
   nuclear waste dumping 87
Matignon Accords 33, 36, 56, 99
Matthew Island 23–4
Melanesia xiii, 7, 11, 12, 16, 42, 43, 57, 115
   common identity 32–5
Melanesian Spearhead Group 33, 37, 41, 44–5, 56, 79
Melanesians xii, 6–7, 19, 64, 107
   New Caledonia xiv, 4
Micronesia xii, 3, 4, 7, 9, 10, 11–13, 16, 17, 33, 56, 92
   Federated States xiv, 5, 11, 48–50, 54, 58, 61, 66–7, 84, 122, 149
Micronesians 6–7, 107
military aid, Israel 106
military aid, Malaysia 38
military intervention
   in politics 68
   island states xi, xv, 22, 137–47, 151
military operations, low-level 143–5
military threats
   intra-regional 22–7
   Pacific Islands xiii, 17–22
mineral resources, seabed 9, 74, 95
Minerva Reefs 23
mining, environmental effects 75–6
Mino, Sir Charles 110
missile testing 12, 21, 86
Mitterrand, François 77, 89
Moruroa 10, 77, 81, 82, 83
multinational companies 109–10
Murdani, General Benny 20

Namaliu, Rabbie 37, 109
National Federation Party, Fiji 43
nationalism
   indigenous, island states 62–7
   Kanak ix, 4, 23, 33, 34, 38, 39, 40, 52, 55–6, 63

Nauru xiii, 4, 8, 16, 49, 84, 85–6, 110, 115, 117, 135
   phosphates 13–14, 47, 76, 133–4
   negative sovereignty 10
neo-colonialism 38
Neo-Melanesian 33
Netherlands 15, 91
   decolonisation 16–17
   Pacific presence 3
New Caledonia 3, 5, 7, 12, 36, 46, 98, 104, 106
   Kanak nationalism ix, 4, 23, 33, 34, 38, 39, 40, 50, 52, 55–6, 63, 66, 96, 98, 99, 101, 127
   Melanesian community xiv, 4
New Hebrides
   Anglo-French condominion 16, 100, 117
   decolonisation 4, 23, 38, 55, 100, 133
   see also Vanuatu
New Zealand xii, 2, 7, 13, 14, 15, 16, 56, 63, 72–3, 88, 97, 98, 108, 114–15
   armed forces 26, 115
   ban on nuclear ships 30, 46, 118–19
   concern over nuclear testing 78–9, 93
   decolonisation 4, 9, 91, 121
   economic links 124–6
   economic strength 115
   links with island states 29, 95, 101, 116–29, 131, 148
   military intervention 22, 137–47, 151
   neo-colonial attitudes 29–30
   role in Pacific region xi, xv, 5
   strategic concerns 125–7
   Treaty of Rarotonga 84
Niue 1, 4, 5, 13, 67, 84, 117
   security policy 46
Non-Aligned Movement 39
Norfolk Island 138
North Korea 97
North Solomons province, Papua New Guinea ix, xiv, 22
Northeast Asia 123
   economic trends ix, x

Northern Mariana Islands xiv, 4, 6,
54, 55, 57, 58, 60–1, 87, 149
Nuclear Free and Independent Pacific
movement 86,108
nuclear tests 10, 17, 42, 50, 76–83,
108
France xi, xiii, xiv, 4, 10, 34, 45,
46, 57, 77–83, 87, 89–90, 98
powers 83–4
underground 79–80, 89–90
nuclear waste
disposal xiv, 42
dumping 86–7, 90, 102, 108

Olter, Bailey 48
Ona, Francis 65
Organisasi Papua Merdeka (OPM)
xiii, xv, 18–20, 35, 37–8, 66, 96,
104, 126

Pacific Conference of Churches 88
Pacific islands
alignment with Western states
30–2
colonial heritage 1–4
decolonisation 3–4, 9, 19, 20, 23,
38, 53–62, 100, 133
economic vulnerability 7–9
environmental issues 71–6
exclusive economic zones 8–9
indigenous nationalism 62–7
internal tensions 67–9
internal threats 52–3
intra-regional threats 23–7
military capabilities 26–7
military threats xiii, 17–22
Pacific Way 15
security x–xi, xiii–xiv, 11–14,
29–32, 148–51
sovereignty 120–1
sub-regions xiii, 11–14
traditional values 6
Western expansion 16–17
Palau xiv, 4, 5, 11, 48–50, 54, 58–9,
60, 69, 84, 122, 149
Papua 52
Papua New Guinea 1, 4, 6, 12, 16,
30, 31, 39, 41, 42, 44, 71, 94, 103,
109, 110

armed forces 26, 27, 55, 68, 115,
130–2, 137, 140
Australian aid 5, 35, 115, 122
Bougainville revolt ix, xi, xiv,
24–6, 35, 37, 38, 42, 53, 64–6,
67, 130–2, 137, 140, 142, 143
common Melanesian identity 32–3
concern over nuclear testing 78, 79
economic prospects 8
foreign policy 35–8
Indonesian border xiii, 18–21,
37–8
internal tensions 68, 69
links with Australia 5, 35, 53, 65,
115–16, 117, 121, 122–3, 125
links with Israel 106
Malaysian links 38, 104
OPM xiii, xv, 18–20, 35, 37–8, 66,
96, 104, 126
reaction to Fiji coups 63
relations with Asian countries 112
relations with Soviet Union 97
secessionism 52
Treaty of Rarotonga 84, 85
paramilitary intervention xi, xv,
143–5
Peacock, Andrew 121
Pearson, James 132, 133, 134
Perben, Dominique 99
Philippines 59
phosphates, mining 13–14, 47, 76
pidgin English 33
Pitcairn xiii, 100
police, paramilitary 143–5
political independence, Pacific islands
4–5
Polynesia xiii, 11, 12–14, 16, 33,
42–3, 56, 115, 117
security issues 44–7
Polynesians xii, xiii, 6–7, 64, 107,
124
population increase 68
positive sovereignty 10

Rabuka, Sitiveni 43, 44, 63, 107,
129–30, 138
radioactive materials, leaching 78, 82
radionuclides 82
Rainbow Warrior ix, 78, 82, 108–9

Rapa 7
Rarotonga, Treaty of xiv, 34, 45,
    83–6, 135
Reagan, Ronald 119
resources, exploitation 73–6
Rocard, Michel 56,82
Rongelap Island 108
Rotuma 52
Russia 97

Samoa *see* American Samoa;
    Western Samoa
sea levels, rising 71–3
Second World War 10
Siaguru, Sir Anthony 31
Singapore 60
Sokamanu, George A. 132–3
Solomon Islands 1, 4, 12, 22, 33, 35,
    37, 53, 65–6, 87, 94, 100, 103,
    104
    common Melanesian identity 32–3
    concern over nuclear testing 79
    logging 75, 104
    paramilitary police 27
    security policy 41–2
    Treaty of Rarotonga 84, 85
    Western Province 52, 67
Somare, Sir Michael 25, 37
SOPAC 95
Sope, Barak 41, 96, 133, 139
South Korea 74, 112
South Pacific Applied Geoscience
    Commission 74
South Pacific Commission 6, 15,
    36–7, 44, 100, 102–3, 132–3
South Pacific Forum xiv, xv, 5, 15,
    21, 33, 37, 42, 43, 44, 46, 47, 48,
    49, 101, 121, 124
    chemical weapons destruction
        87–8, 109
    global warming 72
    Kanak delegation 55–6
    member states 2
    nuclear testing 45
    regional peacekeeping force 27
    resources management 74, 75
    security and economic cooperation
        50–1
    UN observer status 128–9

South Pacific Nuclear Free Zone xiv,
    34, 45, 83–6, 135
South Pacific Organisations
    Coordination Committee 36
South Pacific Regional Environment
    Program 73
South Pacific Trade Union Forum
    108
Southeast Asia 123
    economic trends ix, x
sovereignty
    island states 9–10
    Pacific islands 4–5
Soviet Union ix, xiv, 12, 21, 32, 49,
    58, 66, 93, 94–6, 101, 111, 120,
    127, 149
    fisheries 39, 47, 95–6
    Papua New Guinea embassy 97
    Treaty of Rarotonga 84
Spain 1, 3, 16
Sri Lanka 30, 105
Stephens, Jimmy 54
strategic denial 17, 96–7
Subic Naval Base 59
subsistence sector, island economies 7

Tahiti 3, 98
Taiwan 74, 103
Tanna 52
Taufa'ahau Tupou IV, King of Tonga
    45
tax havens 110
Taylor, Margaret 30
Tlatelolco, Treaty of 84
Tokelau 13, 45, 67, 72, 116, 117, 121
Tonga 1, 4, 13, 43, 45, 57, 95, 100,
    150
    armed forces 26, 27, 115, 140
    Minerva Reefs dispute 23
    monarchy 6
    security policy 45
Torres Strait Islands xii
toxic waste, dumping 86–8, 90, 102
trade unions 108
tuna fishing, US 31, 47, 74, 93, 110
Tupouto'a, Crown Prince 45
Tuvalu 4, 45, 67, 72, 73, 84, 110
    independence 54
    Trust Fund 46–7

Union of Moderate Parties, Vanuatu
24, 39, 41, 132
United Kingdom x, 14, 15, 123, 124
decolonisation 4, 9, 54, 91, 99–100
nuclear tests 10, 76–7
Pacific involvement 2, 4, 99–100
Treaty of Rarotonga 84, 86, 100
United Nations 9, 42, 46, 72, 74, 102,
106–7, 149
Convention on the Law of the Sea
23, 93, 137
General Assembly 79
Security Council 4, 49, 58
United States x, 14, 15, 20, 44, 97, 123
bases 59–60
chemical weapons destruction 50,
87–9, 94, 109
decolonisation 54, 57–62
links with island states 29, 30, 150
multilateral fisheries agreement
31, 39, 47, 74, 94
nuclear tests 10, 76–7
Pacific interests xiv, 3, 5, 6, 9,
11–12, 17, 48–50, 91–4, 95,
108, 122, 149
relations with New Zealand 30, 46,
118–20
spent nuclear fuel storage 86
Treaty of Rarotonga 84–5, 86
urbanisation 68
USSR *see* Soviet Union

Vakatale, Taufa 30
Vanua'aku Pati 38, 39–41, 54, 55,
66, 96, 104
Vanuatu 4, 7, 12, 14, 19, 29, 30, 35,
37, 42, 44, 84, 107, 117, 121,
132–3, 134

common Melanesian identity 32–3
concern over nuclear testing 79
Espiritu Santo attempted secession
27, 38, 52, 54, 55, 110, 132,
137
fishing agreements with Soviet
Union 95–6
foreign policy 38–41
French aid 39–40
Matthew and Hunter Islands dispute
23–4
paramilitary police 26–7
relations with France 23–4, 38–40
Treaty of Rarotonga 84, 85
unrest 68–9, 139–40
see also New Hebrides
Vietnam 39

Wallis and Futuna xiv, 5–6, 13, 57,
98
waste, dumping 42, 86–8, 90, 102
West New Guinea 3, 17
Western Province, Solomon Islands
24–5, 52
Western Samoa 13, 16, 44, 57, 84,
94, 103
elected oligarchy 6
independence 4, 116, 117, 121
security policy 45–6
Whitlam, Gough 121
Wingti, Paias 19, 35, 37, 63, 65, 109,
139
World Bank 109
World Federation of Trade Unions
108
World War II 10, 93, 117

Yakusa gangs 111